Immigrants and Minorities, Politics and Policy

For further volumes:
http://www.springer.com/series/8832

Lisa Magaña · Erik Lee
Editors

Latino Politics and Arizona's Immigration Law SB 1070

Springer

Editors
Lisa Magaña
Arizona State University
Tempe, AZ
USA

Erik Lee
North American Center for Transborder Studies
Tempe, AZ
USA

ISBN 978-1-4614-0295-4 ISBN 978-1-4614-0296-1 (eBook)
DOI 10.1007/978-1-4614-0296-1
Springer New York Heidelberg Dordrecht London

Library of Congress Control Number: 2013932456

Printed on acid-free paper

Springer is part of Springer Science+Business Media (www.springer.com)

Preface

Arizona is one of the fastest growing Latino immigrant destinations in the United States. Within the last five years, a series of responses by Arizonans intending to make life for unauthorized immigrants increasingly impossible have been implemented at the state and local level. The number of vigilante organizations along the border, anti-immigrant policies and targeting for deportation activities by local police have increasingly risen. In 2010, then Arizona state senator Russell Pearce maintained that the federal government had been hampering the immigration enforcement actions of police. Therefore, he introduced the "Support Our Law Enforcement and Safe Neighborhoods Act." Better known as SB 1070, the policy allows police officers in Arizona to arrest unauthorized immigrants under the state's trespassing law. The law also gives officers the latitude to question and detain those that may appear suspicious. For many, this means those that look Latino. Under the State's statute, immigrants can also be criminalized for their mere presence in Arizona, the law makes it a crime for an unauthorized immigrant to seek or engage in work. Furthermore, the policy also allows officers to arrest someone without warrant if there is probable cause. And it makes it a state crime if a legal immigrant does not carry identification.

On April 23, 2010, the governor signed SB 1070 into law, generating a number of immensely complex issues at the state, national, and international levels. The measure has affected an already problematic U.S.–Mexico, bi-national relationship at a time of increased security cooperation between the two countries. Furthermore, the President of Mexico criticized the law, issuing a travel advisory. Trade between Arizona and Mexico has been reduced. Elected officials across the country called for a variety of economic boycotts and campaigns that would discourage the full implementation of the law. Over 15 major cities have ended business contracts with Arizona. And the state tourism industry lost almost one-billion dollars in less than 6 months as a result of this policy.

SB 1070 sparked a remarkable variety of legal activity, including several lawsuits filed by individuals, organizations, and cities (most notably Tucson and Flagstaff) and amicus briefs filed by several Latin American nations, including Mexico. The U.S. Department of Justice filed suit against Arizona in 2010. *The United States of America v. Arizona* resulted in a preliminary injunction against parts of the law by U.S. District Judge Susan Bolton on July 28, 2010, the initial injunction was later upheld by the federal Ninth Circuit Court in April 2011. Arizona subsequently appealed the decision to the U.S. Supreme Court, which heard arguments by the state and the Obama Administration on April 25, 2012.

In June 2012, the U.S. Supreme Court handed down a final decision on SB1070 that caused both sides of the battle to proclaim victory. Essentially, the Supreme Court overturned most parts of the bill except for Section 2B. This provision requires police officers to make a reasonable attempt when determining the immigration status of a person stopped, detained, or arrested. There must be reasonable suspicion that the person is in the country illegally. The court held out the possibility of reconsidering its decision if civil rights violations took place.

September 2012, the American Civil Liberties Union, the National Immigration Law Center, and the Mexican American Legal Defense and Educational Fund requested that a new injunction be placed on the law. These organizations maintained that the law would encourage lengthy detentions of people with a Latino phenotype and that the law violated the Equal Protection Clause of the 14th Amendment. Judge Susan Bolton declined to issue a new injunction against Section 2b.

At the international level, the law had a number of short- and medium-term consequences. As many analysts expected, the Government of Mexico reacted strongly to the law, issuing a travel advisory for Mexicans visiting Arizona (mirroring U.S. State Department advice against traveling to certain regions of Mexico). Mexico is an active signatory of numerous international accords on human rights, and Mexico's legal thinking on migration happens within this human rights framework. As most Americans habitually think in terms of civil rights and overall rule of law, consequently there is a fundamental disconnect in our two countries' thinking on immigration. And as a practical matter, Mexico did not relish the logistical challenge of having to deal with numerous individual states' immigration laws through its extensive consular network in the United States. There were additional international consequences. As a practical matter, many U.S. state governments need to conduct international business and essentially international relations through a variety of regional mechanisms. The U.S.–Mexico Border Governors Conference has functioned as the most visible of these mechanisms for Arizona, California, New Mexico, and Texas for the past three decades. Arizona was scheduled to host the 2010 Border Governors Conference, though Governor Brewer was forced to cancel the conference when the six Mexican border state governors refused to participate. New Mexico Governor Bill Richardson then stepped in and convened an interim meeting of the Border Governors Conference in Santa Fe with the state of Arizona declining to attend (the North American Center for Transborder Studies at Arizona State University did attend, however).

This edited manuscript examines a variety of issues and consequences of SB 1070 at the local, national, and international level. In Chap. 1: Eileen Diaz McConnell provides an informed discussion and evaluation of Latino politics, immigration, and transborder relations in Arizona in the SB 1070 era. This chapter provides a demographic profile of Arizona and its three most populous counties with a focus on Latinos. Data about Latinos are contextualized through consideration of relevant national patterns and other racial/ethnic groups in Arizona. The profile draws from the 2009 American Community Survey, released in September 2010, and describes the racial/ethnic composition of the state and Maricopa, Pima, and Pinal counties. Other characteristics covered in the chapter include age, nativity, year of arrival and citizenship status of the foreign-born, household size, and household type.

In Chap. 2 the author shows how Arizona, particularly the Maricopa County has become such an important immigration destination. As Chap. 1 illustrates, the 2000 census showed that the population in Arizona grew more than three times as fast as the rest of the nation. Reasons for the increased population in the state include, but are not limited to: international immigration continues to influence demographic growth; the state of Arizona is one of the fastest growing in the country; recent economic development and job opportunities encourages migration, individuals, both citizen and natives, are coming from other states for new opportunities; and, Arizona is no longer a gateway state, meaning Texas and California were primary destinations for immigrants, however, border enforcement policies since the mid-1990s have redirected immigration to Arizona. This chapter examines how anti-immigrant policies are passed and supported in Arizona. It appears that popular and emotional reactions to undocumented immigration develop at the local level. When these sentiments eventually reach politicians, they respond with new policies in order to appease their constituents. Not surprisingly, a majority of Latino immigrants are non-citizens and cannot vote. Furthermore, when these immigration policies are hastily assigned to policy players, like police or social workers, without adequate explanation or supervision it results in poor policy implementation.

In Chap. 3, Rodolfo Espino examines politics. Latino voters have long been termed the "sleeping giant" of American politics with the potential to alter the American political landscape. For the most part, however, Latinos have been the objects of political campaigns rather than the agents of political change. Dr. Espino presents results from a survey of Latino voters in Arizona that give voice to this growing segment of the electorate and shed light on how partisanship and immigration politicking influence the turnout calculus of Latino voters.

In Chap. 4, Robert Donnelly examines state-level immigration-related legislation. In the face of perceived federal ineffectiveness on immigration, states are more aggressively considering immigration-related legislation. The number of bill introductions involving immigrants rose from 570 in 2006 to 1,169 in 2007, then to more than 1,400 for the first half of 2009 and 1,374 for the first half of 2010. A large percentage of the bills remain in committee or never make it to a floor vote, but their presence and debate in legislatures across the country still suggests a widespread dissatisfaction with federal policy. Many of the bills also appear motivated by so-called nativist fears of immigrants stealing jobs, exploiting social services, and unsettling long-standing socio-cultural paradigms. Not surprisingly, the growth in legislative debate also has tracked the strong increase in this decade of Latino settlement in so-called "non-traditional" regions, such as the South, the Midwest, and the metropolitan suburbs, although the border state Arizona, with a historically large Latino population, was its most prominent exponent in 2010. In fact, for first-half of 2010 immigration-related bill introductions were distributed in all of the 46 assemblies then in session, with 44 legislatures actually approving legislation. (It should be noted that not all immigration-related legislation should be termed "anti-immigrant," with some legislation funding, for example, municipal integration initiatives or citizenship drives for eligible immigrants).

The issue of state-level immigration-related legislation is an important one. As the Arizona case shows, such legislation can cause disruptive constitutional conflicts with the federal government; create new policy and enforcement challenges, especially for local police; and makes entities more vulnerable to the threat of civil litigation. At the same time, it is unclear if the risks of such legislation outweigh the benefits, if the fiscal improvements claimed by sponsors are actually perceived, or if the driving concerns about immigration policy are, in the end, adequately addressed.

This chapter will analyze state-level immigration-related legislation in the United States. It will examine the legislation by subject-matter and by geographical provenance, seeking to establish trends and draw conclusions. The chapter will also look at the promotion and motivation of such legislation from sources both internal and external to the states in question. It will close by discussing immigration-related political discourses and their saliency and impact ahead of the 2012 general elections.

In Chap. 5, McDowell and Provine illustrate how journalists and other observers often portray Arizona's SB 1070 as a product of the state's "frustration" with federal inaction in controlling the flow of unauthorized immigrants into the state. This characterization suggests that Arizona had assiduously pursued every avenue available to make its concerns known to federal authorities before finally adopting SB 1070. This study tests the "frustration" hypothesis. We look at Arizona's participation in a highly accessible avenue for communication between states and the federal government: Congressional hearings called to hear state and local perspectives on the impact of unauthorized immigration. We examine Arizona's voice in these hearings over the two decades prior to the adoption of SB 1070. This study shows that Arizona had relatively little to say about unauthorized immigration over these two decades, and that it gave no warning that it was contemplating a comprehensive enforcement-only law of its own. SB 1070 emerges, not as a product of frustrated conversation with the federal government, but rather as a pre-emptive strike designed to advance local political careers and to move the national immigration debate in an enforcement-only direction.

In Chap. 6, Santos, Menjivar, and Godfrey examine the effects of SB 1070 on children's wellbeing. Specifically, it focuses on the relationship between children's awareness of SB 1070 and how they identify ethnically, their perceptions of discrimination, and ultimately how all this affects their wellbeing. Empirically, the chapter is based on data collected from 726 middle school children in the Phoenix metro area. Importantly, this examination allows us to see the reach of this law (and the effects of simply having passed), as the majority of these children are U.S. citizens and are at a crucial stage of development when identities are formed and a sense of the self is developed.

In Chap. 7, Plascencia, examines the conceptual and juridical genealogy of the core policy formalized by the enactment of Arizona's SB 1070 on April 23, 2010: attrition through enforcement. This Chapter provides a brief historical and contemporary context for the multiple efforts by states and municipalities to regulate migration and migrants through various ordinances. The majority of such efforts are aimed at Latino migrants in general, and Mexican migrants more specifically. The essay traces the importance of the Department of Justice, Office of Legal Counsel's April 3, 2002 Memo in promoting the idea that states and local governments have an "inherent arrest authority" to stop and arrest persons suspected of violating federal immigration laws. It is argued that the broad support for the concept of attrition through enforcement and local efforts to enforce federal immigration law can be interpreted as part of ongoing states of despair and anguish about the nation, about membership and belonging. In other words, the despair appears to be part of socio-political anxieties about the circle of membership in the present and future of the nation. Three core elements are examined: a fear of a loss of a presumed mono-cultural nation, a fear about the future racial/ethnic composition of the United States, and the prominence and political status of the increasing Latino population. The essay suggests that the strategy of attrition through enforcement represents an approach that effectively integrates, depends on, and fosters such anxieties.

In Chap. 8, Lara-Valencia and Fisher explore the pattern of spatial distribution of informal day labor activity in the Greater Phoenix area focusing particularly on the social composition of the surrounding neighborhoods to draw several conclusions. First, day labor activity is an informal employment modality performed mainly by undocumented immigrant workers. Second, day labor activity tends to concentrate within or near neighborhoods with a high density of foreign-born population. Third, the geography of day labor activity reflects the sheltered nature of ethnic spaces that reduce the vulnerability of the most exposed class of immigrant workers. The analysis rests on data collected through mixed research methods and applies spatial statistics to develop a typology of day labor hiring sites based on socio-spatial elements. This typology is used to comment on recent state and local policies toward immigrants in Greater Phoenix.

In Chap. 9, Aguila and Lee, illustrate how the Mexican government has aggressively sought to solidify its relationship with its expatriate community in the United States. The primacy of this objective has resulted from many historical legacies that have intensified in recent years, especially the size of the expatriate population and Mexican public opinion that no longer views emigrants as vende patrias, but as victims of an imbalanced bi-national economic system and failed public policy. This relationship dates back to the 1848 signing of the Treaty of Guadalupe Hidalgo, when Mexican authorities commissioned various agents in the ceded territories to implement repatriation projects for Mexican citizens wishing to return home to their native land.

Contents

Chapter 1
Latinos in Arizona: Demographic Context in the SB 1070 Era

Eileen Diaz McConnell

An informed discussion and evaluation of Arizona's Latino politics, immigration, transborder, and binational relations after the passage of SB1070 requires recent demographic information about the state.[1] An accurate depiction of the demographics of Arizona and Arizona's Latinos are important for additional reasons. Nationally, there are misperceptions about the racial/ethnic composition of the country. For example, groups such as U.S.-born Non-Hispanic Whites overestimate the size of Latinos and other minorities (e.g., Nadeau et al. 1993; Alba et al. 2005; Ortman and Kluegel 2005).[2] Moreover, studies have documented connections between (mis)perceptions of demographics and policy positions. For instance, persons who overestimate the present size and growth rates of Latinos are more likely to support policies that restrict Latin American migration (Ortman and Kluegel 2005). Research further shows that although the majority of Latinos are born in the United States (Pew Hispanic Center 2006a); U.S.-born Latinos, Mexican-origin populations, and others have been racialized as illegal immigrants (e.g., De Genova 2004; Chavez 2008; Cobas et al. 2009; Massey 2009). In the case of Arizona, demographic change in the state, misperceptions about those changes, a general conflation of Mexican-origin populations (including natives) with unauthorized immigrants, and concerns about unauthorized immigration may help explain both the passage of SB 1070 in the Arizona legislature and public support for the legislation.

---

1 The terms Latino and Hispanic are used interchangeably in this paper to refer to this group. The federal government considers Latinos to be an ethnic group that can be of any race.

2 See McConnell (2011) for an analysis of media representations of Latino population growth in another context.

E. D. McConnell (✉)
School of Transborder Studies, Arizona State University, 873502,
Tempe, AZ 85287-3502, USA
e-mail: Eileen.Diaz.McConnell@asu.edu

L. Magaña and E. Lee (eds.), *Latino Politics and Arizona's Immigration Law SB 1070*,
Immigrants and Minorities, Politics and Policy, DOI: 10.1007/978-1-4614-0296-1_1,

For these reasons, this chapter provides a demographic profile of Arizona and its three most populous counties, focusing specifically on Latinos. It begins with a brief overview of demographic trends in the United States in recent decades before moving on to the demographics of Arizona. Data about Latinos are contexualized through consideration of relevant national patterns and contrasts with other groups in Arizona. The next section focuses on Arizona and county-level population counts between 1980 and 2000, highlighting changes in the total population and specifically for Latinos, Whites, Blacks, and American Indians and Alaska Natives.[3] This 20-year overview documents the dynamism of Arizona's population generally. The heart of the chapter uses the 2009 American Community Survey, released in September 2010, to describe Latinos and in Arizona in the year before SB1070 was passed.[4] The text and accompanying figures describe important characteristics for Arizona's Latinos in 2009, such as the distribution of Latinos by specific group, by age, nativity, year of arrival for those born in Latin America, citizenship status, and recent births to mothers by race/ethnicity. Where appropriate and available, characteristics of Latinos are compared to Whites, African Americans, American Indians, and in some cases, contrasts those born in Latin America and Asia.[5]

The great majority of Latinos in the state, both historically and today, are of Mexican origin or descent. Although this profile emphasizes recent patterns, the Mexican-origin population in Arizona has lived, worked, and contributed to Arizona for many generations (e.g., Benton-Cohen 2009; Meeks 2007; Officer 1987;

---

[3] This section draws from decennial census data, other sections of the chapter rely on 2000 or 2009 American Community Survey data released by the U.S. Census Bureau. The Appendix provides additional technical information about the data sources and materials consulted for this chapter. Whites, Blacks/African Americans, Asians, American Indian, and Alaska Natives discussed here refer to those who are not Hispanic. Further, the figures used here for Non-Hispanic Whites, Blacks, American Indian, and Alaska Natives, and Asians refer to those identified as one race and do not include those who identified with two or more races. In Census parlance, then, the figures refer to those are "White alone", "Black or African American alone", "Asian alone", and "American Indian and Alaska Native alone" who are not Hispanic or Latino. Although the ACS reports data on a combined American Indian and Alaska Native group, the majority of those in this category in Arizona are American Indian of a specific tribe. To streamline the table and figures and reduce reader burden, most Latino demographic characteristics are compared with the largest racial/ethnic groups in the state. For demographic profiles that focus on African Americans in Arizona and Asians in Arizona, see http://www.asu.edu/vppa/asuforaz/projects.html.

[4] Other profiles of Latinos in Arizona use 2006 ACS data (Pew Hispanic Center 2008) and 2007 ACS data (McConnell and Skeen 2009).

[5] The American Community Survey, like other data collected by the U.S. Census Bureau, defines the foreign-born population as those who were not U.S. citizens at birth or whose parents were not U.S. citizens. This definition is different from the common usage of the term, "immigrants". For example, some might consider Puerto Ricans as immigrants/migrants, but as they are U.S. citizens at birth, they are not classified as foreign-born in the ACS. Thus, when referring to descriptions of ACS data, I use the term "foreign born" when applicable (e.g., the universe of Latin American-born respondents excludes Puerto Ricans and other U.S. citizens) and Latin American (or Latin American-born) to refer to the foreign-born and those who are U.S. citizens at birth but who were born in Latin America (Puerto Ricans). The term immigrant is not used when discussing 2009 ACS data.

Ríos-Bustamante 1998; Rosales and Marín 2009). In discussing the more recent growth of Latinos, especially Mexicans, in Arizona, it is important to note that Mexican-origin populations have comprised a significant proportion of the state for more than a century. For example, historical census data indicates that Mexicans accounted for 24.0 % of the population of Arizona in 1910, 26.5 % in 1920, and 26.2 % in 1930 (Gibson and Jung 2002).[6] This historical concentration of Mexicans in Arizona is unsurprising: the state was part of Sonora, Mexico before the Mexican–American War, and since that time, there have been rich social, economic, and political connections between peoples living in the border-region.[7] As such, although this chapter employs aggregated data that is often only available for a larger panethnic category such as Latino, the people within this broader category might prefer more specific terms like Chicano, Mexican, Mexicano, and/or Mexican–American.[8]

National Trends

In discussing the demographics of Latinos in the state of Arizona, it is important to provide national and temporal context. According to the U.S. Census Bureau, there were approximately 14.6 million Latinos in the United States in 1980, 22.3 million in 1990, and 35.3 million in 2000. These figures indicate that the Latino population increased by 53.0 % during the 1980s and 57.9 % during the 1990s. The Latino growth rate in the United States in recent decades has exceeded the growth of the total U.S. population. For example, between 1990 and 2000, the U.S. population increased by 13.2 %; Latinos accounted for approximately 39.6 % of the entire net increase of the country's population growth over the decade.

The numeric increase of U.S. Latinos since 2000 continues to be significant, rising from 35.3 million to an estimated 48.4 million by 2009, a growth of about 37 % in 9 years. During this period, Latinos accounted for a little more than half, 51.0 %, of the total population growth of the United States. Thus, by 2009, Latinos comprise 15.7 % of the U.S. population. The Census Bureau estimates that by 2050, nearly one-quarter, 24.4 % of the US population are expected to be Latino (U.S. Census Bureau 2004). Given the current size of Latinos, growth rates since 1980, and projections about future increases, the characteristics and demographic trends involving this group have implications for the entire United States.

---

[6] Comparing U.S. census data for Latinos across time periods is complicated by significant differences in how this information was collected since the first census of 1790. See Rodriguez (2000) for a detailed review of changes in federal data collections.

[7] See *State of Latino Arizona*, 2009 for a concise report of the role of Latinos/Mexican Origin Populations in Arizona's history and their characteristics vis-à-vis politics, education, the economy, and other domains.

[8] Much of the data used in this chapter are based on one-year estimates with fairly small sample sizes; data for many characteristics used here are not released for specific origin/ancestry Latino groups.

The U.S. Latino population is dynamic and heterogeneous, which reflects the unique and varied economic and political relationships between Latin America and the United States. As such, the Latino population in the United States is diverse in terms of heritage/national origin, nativity, geographic location in the United States, and in other ways. For example, although the majority of U.S. Latinos in 2009, 65.5 %, reported being of Mexican heritage, significant proportions report that they are Puerto Rican (9.1 %), Cuban (3.1 %), or other groups (21.8 %). Latinos are also heterogeneous in their nativity. In 2000, approximately 60 % of all Latinos in the U.S. were native-born.[9] Latino immigrants are predominantly from Mexico; however, the increase of "other" Latinos in recent years noted above is partially due to increasing numbers of immigrants from the Dominican Republic, El Salvador, Guatemala, Honduras, and elsewhere.

Latinos have become more geographically dispersed throughout the United States in recent years. During the 1990s, the Latino population increased significantly in every region of the country, some with growth rates that were higher than the national average. Indeed, between 1990 and 2000, Latinos increased by 81.0 % in the Midwest, 71.2 % in the South, 51.8 % in the West, and 39.9 % in the Northeast. The Latino population more than doubled in states such as Minnesota (166.1 %) and tripled in states such as Georgia (299.6 %) and North Carolina (393.9 %) between 1990 and 2000. Arizona also experienced significant growth vis-à-vis Latinos over the decade, increasing by 88.2 %. 2009 ACS data confirms that this geographic dispersion of Latinos across the country has continued since 2000.

Additional characteristics of the total U.S. Latino population should be considered in understanding Latino demographics in Arizona. For example, Latinos in the U.S. are a young population. In 2000, the median age of the U.S. Latino population was 25.8, compared with 35.3 for the total U.S. population. In 2000, the average Latino household size was 3.62, compared with 2.59 for the total U.S. population. The majority of Latino households are headed by a married couple, 53.9 %, with much smaller proportions of households headed by males (8.2 %), females (17.8 %), or nonfamily households comprised of unrelated people or one person living alone (20.0 %). More recent data at the national level suggest similar patterns, with the primary difference that slightly less than half of households headed by Latinos in 2009 are composed of married couples, 49.4 %.

Arizona

The Dynamics of Population Growth and Change in Arizona

The total population of Arizona has grown dramatically since 1980, with simultaneous increases of multiple racial/ethnic groups.[10] Table 1.1 presents the size and

---

[9] Again, as Puerto Ricans are U.S. citizens at birth, they are classified as U.S.-born.

[10] For an overview of changes in census questions about race and Hispanic origin between the 1990 and 2000 censuses see Grieco and Cassidy (2001).

Table 1.1 Change in Arizona and by county for the total, Latino, White, Black, and American Indian/Alaska Native populations, 1980–2000

	Total			Latino			Non-Hispanic White			Non-Hispanic Black			Non-Hispanic American Indian and Alaska Native		
	1980	2000	% Change	1980	2000	% Change	1980	2000	% Change	1980	2000	% Change	1980	2000	% Change
Arizona	2,718,215	5,130,632	88.8	444,102	1,295,617	191.7	2,260,288	3,274,258	44.9	74,159	149,941	102.2	152,342	233,370	53.2
Apache	52,108	69,423	33.2	1,983	3,119	57.3	10,827	12,281	13.4	269	163	−39.4	38,964	53,036	36.1
Cochise	85,686	117,755	37.4	22,846	36,134	58.2	57,323	70,754	23.4	3,095	5,062	63.6	496	978	97.2
Coconino	75,008	116,320	55.1	7,315	12,727	74.0	45,045	66,969	48.7	1,246	1,150	−7.7	20,913	32,557	55.7
Gila	37,080	51,335	38.4	7,723	8,546	10.7	24,083	35,391	47.0	88	174	97.7	5,085	6,412	26.1
Graham	22,862	33,489	46.5	5,457	9,054	65.9	14,068	18,488	31.4	456	602	32.0	2,744	4,819	75.6
Greenlee	11,406	8,547	−25.1	5,446	3,681	−32.4	5,664	4,604	−18.7	14	34	142.9	235	117	−50.2
La Paz	–	19,715	42.4	–	4,420	40.8	–	12,573	48.0	–	149	44.7	–	2,155	7.5
Maricopa	1,509,052	3,072,149	103.6	199,003	763,341	283.6	1,224,494	2,034,530	66.2	47,177	108,521	130.0	22,903	45,703	99.6
Mohave	55,865	155,032	177.5	2,148	17,182	699.9	51,918	130,283	150.9	92	787	755.4	1,469	3,238	120.4
Navajo	67,629	97,470	44.1	4,538	8,011	76.5	30,226	41,196	36.3	589	794	34.8	32,129	45,846	42.7
Pima	531,443	843,746	58.8	111,418	247,578	122.2	384,932	518,720	34.8	14,666	24,047	64.0	14,928	21,821	46.2
Pinal	90,918	179,727	97.7	26,752	53,671	100.6	52,720	105,641	100.4	2,974	4,658	56.6	8,167	12,419	52.1
Santa Cruz	20,459	38,381	87.6	15,229	31,005	103.6	5,024	6,835	36.0	47	75	59.6	57	95	66.7
Yavapai	68,145	167,517	145.8	4,205	16,376	289.4	62,492	145,037	132.1	189	589	211.6	1,005	2,355	134.3
Yuma	90,554	160,026	76.7	26,638	80,772	203.2	57,446	70,956	23.5	2,343	3,136	33.8	3,247	1,819	−44.0

Source U.S. Census Bureau: 1990, 2000 Census data; Social Science Data Analysis Network (SSDAN): 1980 Census data
Note 1980 census data was not available for La Paz County; percent change for La Paz County is between 1990 and 2000

percent change of the total, Latino, Non-Hispanic White, African American, and American Indian and Alaska Native populations in Arizona and by county, 1980–2000. Arizona's population grew by 88 % between 1980 and 2000, an absolute size increase of 2,412,417 persons. This is a *much* larger increase than the 24.2 % growth rate of the entire United States that occurred during the same 20-year period. The total population of Maricopa County more than doubled, increasing by 103.6 % over the 20-year period. Other counties in the state, such as Mohave, Pinal, and Yavapai counties had percent increases that exceeded the state growth rate as a whole, as well. These strong population increases since 1980 helped Arizona transition from the 29th largest state in 1980 to the 14th largest state in the country by 2008 (Saenz 2010). Reasons commonly given for Arizona's population growth in recent decades include increases in job opportunities, an affordable cost of living, and migration from other states due to relatively inexpensive housing compared to California and elsewhere.

Table 1.1 also documents the substantial changes in the four largest racial/ethnic groups occurring in the state and by county between 1980 and 2000. A comparison of the percent change columns in Table 1.1 indicates that most counties in Arizona experienced substantial percentage increases in Latinos, Whites, African Americans, and American Indians and Alaska Natives over the time period. Maricopa County was by far the most populous county in the state, more than doubling between 1980 and 2000 (103.6 % growth), with percent increases of 283.6 % of Latinos, 66.2 % of Whites, 130.0 % of African Americans, and 99.6 % of American Indians and Alaska Natives. Greenlee County, a less populous county, was one of the few areas that experienced declines in overall population and for nearly all racial/ethnic groups.

Between 1980 and 2000, Non-Hispanic Whites in Arizona increased by 44.9 % compared with 53.2 % for American Indians and Alaska Natives, 102.2 % for African Americans, and 191.7 % for Latinos. Non-Hispanic Whites had the largest absolute size growth of any group in the 20-year period, with about 1.0 million Whites added to Arizona's population. Therefore, although the percent change of Whites is smaller than groups such as Latinos, the absolute increase of Whites is *larger* than other groups.[11] The absolute size increase of Latinos in Arizona between 1980 and 2000 was a little more than 850,000 people.

The population of Arizona has experienced continued growth between 2000 and 2009. Figure 1.1 shows the substantial increase in the total population of the state and the four largest racial/ethnic groups. The Latino population in the state grew by 56.8 % over the time period, Whites increased by 15.1 %, and the

[11] Although the percent change statistic is useful in discussing changes in a population, it can also be misleading. The size of the percent change depends on the population base (denominator) at the beginning of the time period of interest; therefore, a group with an initially large population base, such as Non-Hispanic Whites, may have what appears to be a fairly low percent change over time but also have a larger absolute size increase than other groups. For example, a 66.2 % change of Whites in Maricopa County between 1980 and 2000 means that about 810,000 Whites were added to the county over the two decades. In contrast, a 283.6 % increase of Latinos corresponds to about 565,000 Latinos added to the population over the same time period.

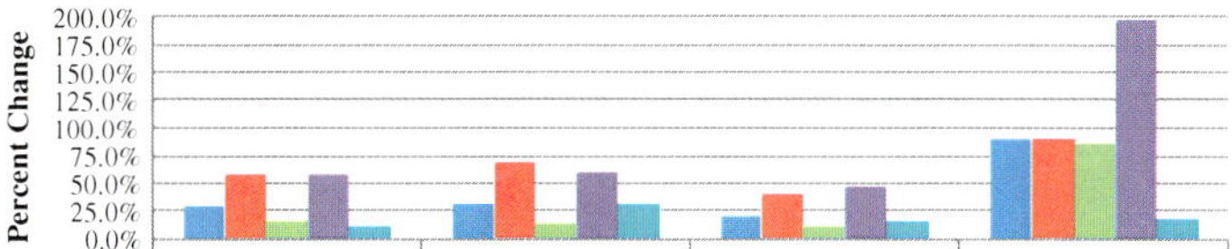

	Arizona	Maricopa County	Pima County	Pinal County
Total	28.6%	31.0%	20.9%	89.7%
Latino	56.8%	67.8%	38.9%	89.6%
White	15.1%	13.3%	10.5%	86.0%
Black	58.2%	59.8%	45.6%	197.8%
American Indian	11.8%	31.8%	16.7%	17.7%

Fig. 1.1 Racial/ethnic population change, 2000–2009. *Source* Author's calculations of 2000 Census data and 2009 American Community Survey data for Arizona. *Note* See the Appendix for more details about the data. The "American Indian" population in Fig. 1.1 includes those who identify as Alaska Natives

numerically smaller African American and American Indian and Alaska Native populations increased by more than 58.2 and 11.8 % between 2000 and 2009, respectively.[12] The three most populous counties of Arizona display similar patterns of strong growth. Maricopa County, the most populous county in the state, had the largest numerical increase of any U.S. county between 2000 and 2006 (U.S. Census Bureau 2007). Maricopa County has had the largest numeric growth of non-Hispanic Whites of any U.S. county, as well (Census Bureau 2009). Pinal County, with the smallest population counts of the three counties, has experienced the largest percent changes over the 9-year period, with increases of 86 % or more for the total population and for Latinos, Whites, and Blacks.

Racial and Ethnic Composition

Figure 1.2 presents the racial/ethnic composition of the state in 2009. Approximately 31 % of the state's population in 2009 are Latino, 57 % are Non-Hispanic White, 4 % are Non-Hispanic Black or African American, 4 % are American Indian and Alaska Native, nearly 3 % are Asian and the remainder are of other races or race combinations.[13] The racial/ethnic compositions are similar for

---

[12] In 2009, ACS data suggest that 94% of those within the American Indian and Alaska Native category provided a specific American Indian tribe. The most commonly reported American Indian tribe in Arizona in 2009 is Navajo; about 48.5 % of all those in the AIAN category in AZ identified as Navajo.

[13] In this figure, the "Other races" category aggregates multiple groups: Native Hawaiian and Other Pacific Islander alone (Not Hispanic), Some Other race alone (Not Hispanic), and Two or more races.

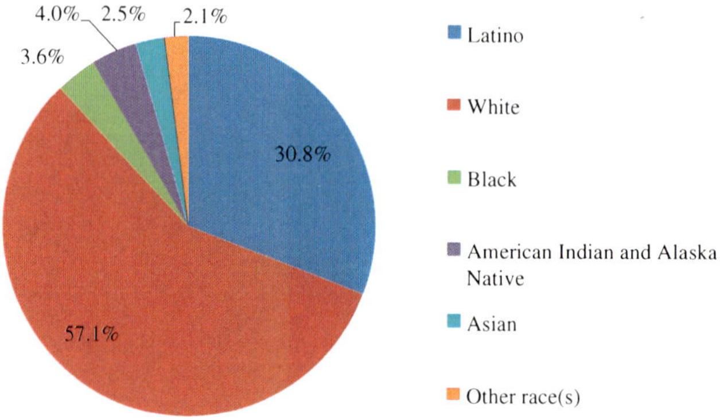

Fig. 1.2 Race/Ethnicity of Arizona, 2009. *Source* Author's calculations of 2009 American Community Survey data for Arizona

most counties for which 2009 data are available, such as Maricopa, Pima, and Pinal.[14]

The proportion of Arizona that identifies as Latino in 2009 may appear "high" compared to other states and the country as a whole. However, historical census data provided at the beginning of the chapter indicates that in years from 1910 to 1930, between 24.0 and 26.5 % of the state were Mexican. Clearly, recent trends are in line with those at the beginning of the twentieth century.

Specific Latino Group

As noted earlier, due to Arizona's geographic location and the long-standing and dense connections throughout the region, a great majority of the state's Latinos are of Mexican heritage. In 2009, approximately 91.6 % of Latinos in Arizona identify their origin or ancestry as Mexican, 1.6 % as Puerto Rican, 1.9 % identify with a specific Central American group (primarily as Salvadoran and Guatemalan), 1.1 % with a specific South American group (primarily as Colombian and Peruvian), and less than 5 % as other Latino groups.[15] Although most Latinos in the state identify

[14] ACS data about race/ethnicity are available for more counties than for other population characteristics. Compared to the state, Mohave and Yavapai Counties have fairly low proportions of Latinos and higher proportions of Non-Hispanic Whites. Coconino County has a larger proportion of individuals who are American Indian and Alaska Native than most other counties in the state.

[15] Statistics about specific Latino group do not attempt to discern nativity, that is, whether Latinos were *born* in these countries or regions but rather their origin or ancestry. The Hispanic Origin code list, showing how different responses to this question could be classified is available at: http://www.census.gov/acs/www/Downloads/data_documentation/CodeLists/2009Code_Lists.pdf.

as Mexican, recent work points to a growing number of Central Americans and other Latinos in the state as well (e.g., Menjívar 2001; Moran-Taylor and Menjívar 2005). The composition of Latinos vis-à-vis specific groups in counties such as Maricopa are nearly identical to the state-level figures.

Age

As Fig. 1.3 shows, persons between the ages of 18- and 64-years old are the largest proportion of Arizona's population for all four groups (Latinos, Non-Hispanic Whites, Blacks or African Americans, American Indian, and Alaska Natives). Indeed, 2009 estimates indicate that between 58 and 62 % of each group's population are within the 18–64-year age range. However, there are some differences in the age structure by race/ethnicity in Arizona. For example, 30 % or more of Latinos, African Americans, and American Indian and Alaska Natives are under 18 years of age, compared with 19.1 % of Non-Hispanic Whites. More specifically, 37.1 % of Latinos, 31.6 % of African Americans, and 33.4 % of American Indian and Alaska Natives are 18 years or younger. These three groups also are much less likely to be 65 years of age or over, compared with Non-Hispanic Whites.

These contrasts highlight the value of including multiple groups rather than comparing the age structures simply of Latinos and non-Hispanic Whites. In fact, comparisons for multiple groups reveals that the pattern for Whites is unusual, compared to Latinos and other racial/ethnic groups in Arizona, as well. Statistics about median age also shows this clear divide, with the median age of Whites in the state at 43.4, compared with 25.7 for Latinos, 28.6 for African Americans, and 26.7 for American Indians and Alaska Natives. The age composition of Latinos, coupled with their comprising 30.8 % of the state's population in 2009, suggests that Latinos will continue to comprise a significant proportion of the under-18 population. Although the Black and American Indian populations are much smaller in the state, their youth also have implications for the future composition of the state.

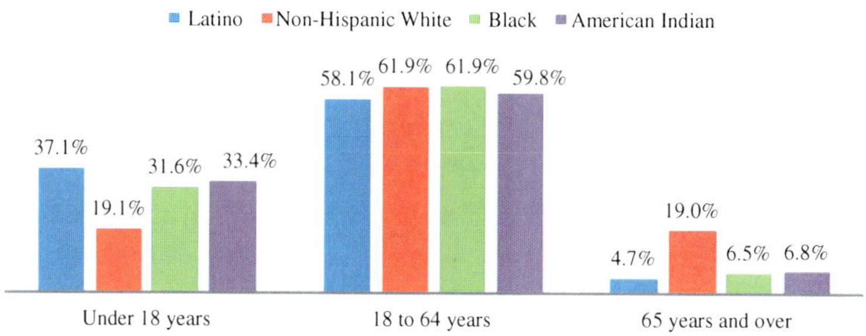

Fig. 1.3 Age distribution of largest racial/ethnic groups, Arizona: 2009. *Source* Author's calculations of 2009 American community survey data for Arizona

Nativity of Latinos

ACS data indicate that the majority of Arizona's Latinos in 2009, 69.0 %, were born in the United States (Fig. 1.4). Approximately 75.2 % of Latinos in Pinal County are U.S.-born, compared with an estimated 66.8 % of Maricopa County's Latinos, and 73.3 % of Latinos in Maricopa County.

Country/Region of Origin for Foreign-Born

A topic that is of much interest in Arizona concerns the foreign-born population of the state. According to ACS estimates, nearly a million foreign-born individuals, 925,376 reside in Arizona in 2009. Figure 1.5 provides the region of origin of the foreign-born in the state and in Maricopa, Pima, and Pinal counties. The majority of foreign-born in the state, 69.4 %, are from Latin America. Those from Asia and Europe comprise 15.0 and 8.9 %, respectively, of Arizona's foreign-born population, while those from other regions account for 6.7 %. Data on country of origin indicate that most foreign-born individuals in the state, about 63 % and numbering about 582,000, are from Mexico. After Mexico, foreign-born persons are most likely to be from Canada, India, the Philippines, and China.

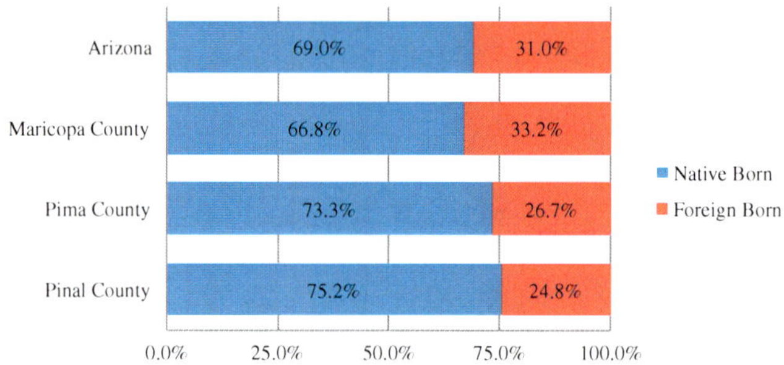

Fig. 1.4 Latinos by Nativity, 2009. *Source* Author's calculations of 2009 American community survey data for Arizona

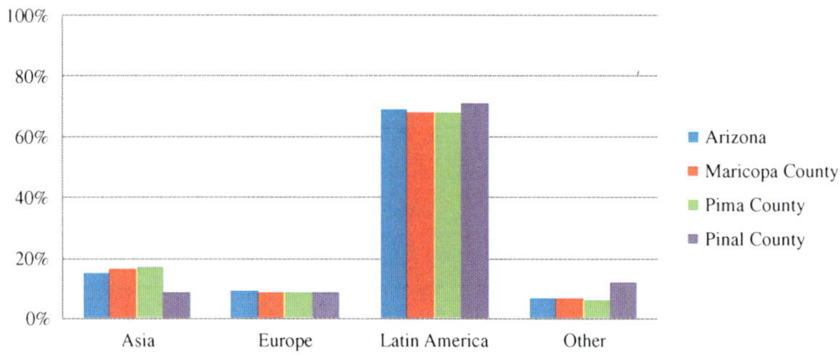

Fig. 1.5 Region of origin of foreign-born population 2009. *Source* Author's calculations of 2009 American Community Survey data for Arizona

Period of Entry

Figure 1.6 presents information pertaining to the period of entry for those born in Asia and Latin America, in order to provide some context for period of entry patterns for the Latin American-born.[16] Period of entry refers to when the person came to live in the United States.[17] Most Latin American-born individuals in Arizona arrived in the United States before 2000: 15.9 % before 1980 (15.9 %), 20.7 % between 1980 and 1999 (20.7 %), 32.0 % between 1990 and 1999. About 31.4 % arrived in the U.S. 2000 or later. Asian-born individuals in Arizona have similar trends to the Latin American-born with respect to when they came to live in the United States, although larger proportions are estimated to have entered the U.S. since 2000.

The next figure focuses specifically on period of entry for those born in Latin America and living in Maricopa, Pima, and Pinal counties in 2009.[18] As Fig. 1.7 shows, most Latin Americans in the three counties came to live in the United States before 2000. For example, in 2009, 12.2 % of Latin Americans in Maricopa County arrived before 1980, 19.8 % between 1980 and 1989, 34.6 % between 1990 and 1999, and 33.3 % came to live in the U.S. in 2000 or more recently. Estimates for Pima and Pinal Counties have similar trends, but suggest that perhaps larger proportions of Latin Americans arriving to the U.S. before 1980 relative to Maricopa County.[19] These trends are in line with the nation as a whole (Pew Hispanic Center 2008).

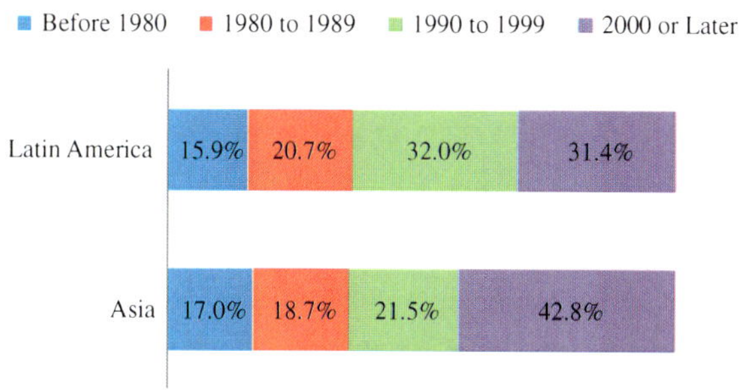

Fig. 1.6 Individuals born in Latin America and Asia by period of entry, Arizona 2009. *Source* Author's calculation of 2000 census data and 2009 American community survey data for Arizona

[16] The ACS asked all respondents who were not born in the United States in what year they came to live in the country, including those born in Puerto Rico. Therefore, these data are not limited simply to the foreign-born population but include those born in Latin America. This has a small impact on the denominator for period of entry: 2009 ACS estimates suggest that there are 641,832 Latin Americans in the state, of which 629,781 are foreign-born, or not U.S. citizens at birth, the remainder are Puerto Rican or from other territories.

[17] Publicly available ACS data does not provide the year of entry, but rather the following year ranges: before 1980, 1980–1989, 1990–1990, and 1999 or later.

[18] The ACS includes those who are U.S. citizens at birth (e.g., Puerto Ricans) in this question, therefore, it is technically inaccurate to use the term foreign-born in this context.

[19] See the Appendix for information about sampling error in the American Community Survey.

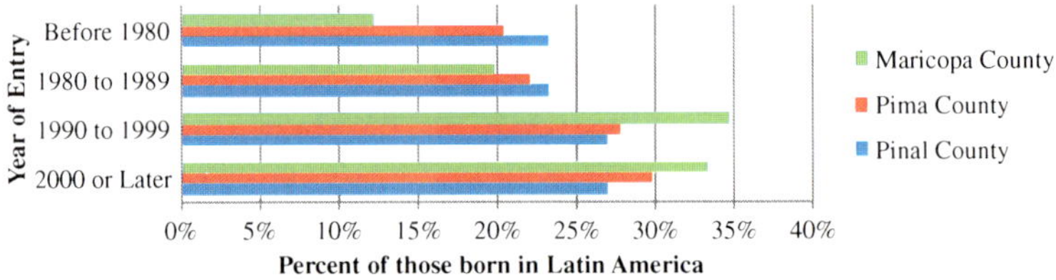

Fig. 1.7 Latin American-born by year of entry, 2009. *Source* Author's calculations of 2009 American community survey data for Arizona

Citizenship Status of the Foreign-Born Population

Recent estimates suggest that there are approximately 375,000 unauthorized immigrants in Arizona in 2009, a decline from the numbers of unauthorized immigrants estimated for 2008 (Passel and Cohn 2010).[20] Discussions about the unauthorized immigrant population, in both Arizona and nationally, tend to focus on those who *entered* the country without authorization. However, between one-third and one-half of unauthorized immigrants in the U.S. are estimated to be visa "overstayers", or persons who entered the country legally with visas through a port of entry or used a temporary Border Crossing Card (Pew Hispanic Center 2006b).[21] These individuals became unauthorized when they remained in the country after the visas expired. The remainder entered the country without authorization. Recent estimates by Passel and Cohn (2010) suggest that about 80 % of unauthorized immigrants in the U.S. are from Latin America, mainly from Mexico.[22] Of the remaining 20 %, about 11 % are from South and East Asia, 4 % are from Europe and Canada and 4 % from Africa and other places (Passel and Cohn 2010).

The 2009 ACS data provides estimates of the citizenship status of the foreign-born population by region of origin and period of entry. Citizenship status refers to whether persons who were not U.S. citizens at birth are naturalized U.S. citizens or non-citizens. Non-citizens can include persons who are Lawful Permanent Residents, temporary migrants with visas, refugees, and other humanitarian migrants, as well as persons without legal permission to live or work in the United States. Therefore, ACS data does not specifically identify whether non-citizens have legal permission to reside and work in the United States.

The detailed tables of 2009 ACS data used here report whether the foreign-born arriving before 2000 are naturalized U.S. citizens or non-citizens, but does not report the citizenship status of those coming to the U.S. to live since 2000. This

[20] The U.S. Department of Homeland Security (2008) defines unauthorized residents as "foreign-born persons who entered the United States without inspection or were admitted temporarily and stayed past the date they were required to leave".

[21] See Pew Hispanic Center (2006b) for more information.

[22] None of these studies provide estimates of the numbers of Latin American immigrants in Arizona that are unauthorized.

is because for most categories of migrants, the process of naturalization requires continuous residence in the U.S. for five years after admission as a lawful permanent resident. Consequently, the large proportions of Latin American foreign-born who have arrived since 2000 who may be otherwise eligible for naturalization have not yet met the continuous residence requirement to become naturalized.

In 2009, most Latin American foreign-born in Arizona and in Maricopa, Pima, and Pinal counties are not naturalized U.S. citizens. For example, in the state of Arizona, 77.0 % of the Latin American foreign-born are not naturalized citizens; in Maricopa, Pima, and Pinal counties the figures are 81.3, 69.2, and 73.6 %, respectively. Among other reasons, the recency of arrival to the country for many Latin American foreign-born individuals (Fig. 1.6) could help explain these patterns. For instance, some of these persons could be legal permanent residents who are not yet eligible to become naturalized citizens. Still others could have temporary visas, be refugees, or lack legal authorization. These trends should not be interpreted as referring to the citizenship of *Latinos* in Arizona, only Latino foreign-born. As noted earlier in the chapter, the majority of Latinos in the state and all three counties in 2009 are native born. Further, nativity and citizenship data for the foreign-born indicates that more than three quarters of all Latinos in Arizona in 2009, 76.3 %, are either U.S.-born or are naturalized U.S. citizens. Between 73.1 and 81.8 % of Latinos in Maricopa, Pima, and Pinal counties are natives or are naturalized U.S. citizens.

Statistics on citizenship by age are also informative. Calculation of 2009 ACS data, not shown, suggest that for the entire state of Arizona, 64.3 % of Latino men and 68.6 % of Latinas over 18 years of age are either native born or naturalized citizens. The remainder of Latino adults, about 23.7 %, are not U.S. citizens; which includes permanent residents, temporary migrants, refugees, those with Temporary Protected Status (some Hondurans, Nicaraguans and Salvadorans), and those who are unauthorized. This pattern directly addresses the commonly held misperception that Latino children in Arizona might be authorized, but their parents are not. Most Latino adults in the state also are citizens.

Estimates of the Unauthorized Population

As the ACS data does not provide additional information about citizenship other than whether the foreign-born are naturalized U.S. citizens or non-citizens, it is necessary to draw from other sources to estimate what proportion of Arizona Latinos have legal permission to live and/or work in the United States and what proportion do not. Passel and Cohn (2010) estimate that there are approximately 375,000 unauthorized immigrants in Arizona.[23] Nationally, they estimate that about 80 % of the unauthorized are from Latin America (Passel and Cohn 2010). Extrapolating from this information suggests that approximately 14.8 % of Latinos in Arizona could be unauthorized and that perhaps 8.8 % of Arizona's Latinos

[23] See Passel and Cohn (2010) for detailed information about their methodology.

could be non-citizens who are legal permanent residents, temporary migrants with visas, or refugees.[24] Data presented earlier show that the remainder, the majority of Latinos in the state, were born in the U.S. or are naturalized citizens.

Births in Previous Year and Birth Rates

The 2009 ACS estimates suggest that 93,353 women between the ages of 15 and 50 gave birth in Arizona in the previous 12 months. Figure 1.8 shows that of these women with births in the previous year, 36,639, or 39.2 %, were Latinas. Another 45.2 %, or 42,223 women with births were Non-Hispanic White women. The remaining 15.6 % of women giving birth were of other racial groups, particularly American Indian and Alaska Native and African Americans.

In the state, the proportion of women giving birth in the previous year who are Latina is larger than the total proportion of women of that age group who are Latina. For instance, Latinos account for 30.8 % of the state (Fig. 1.2), but Latinas comprise 39.2 % of women between the ages of 15 and 50 giving birth in the previous 12 months. Reasons for this pattern include their youth relative to non-Hispanic Whites and a variety of other factors.

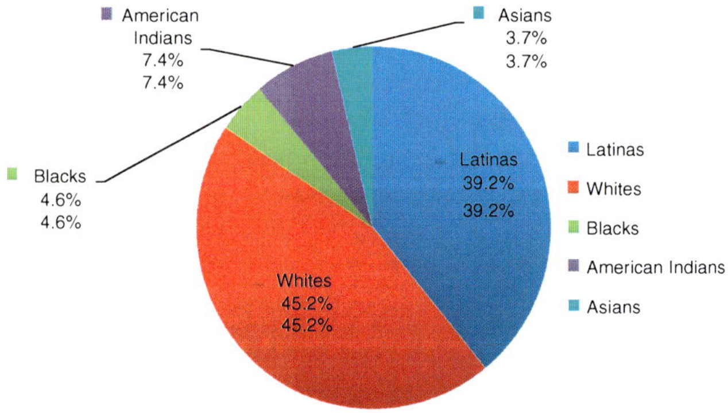

Fig. 1.8 Women with birth in previous year by race/ethnicity, Arizona 2009. *Source* Author's calculations of 2009 American Community Survey data for Arizona. *Note* Women are 15–50 years old. The "American Indian" group includes Alaska Natives. Percents may add up to more than 100 % because of rounding

[24] This figure is derived from multiplying the estimate of unauthorized immigrants in Arizona (375,000) by the proportion estimated to be Latin American (80 % or 0.80) to calculate an estimated number of unauthorized immigrants in Arizona who are from Latin America: 300,000. Dividing 300,000 by the number of Latinos in the state in 2009 (2,031,651) produces the 14.8 % figure. Using a more generous estimate, such as considering that 90 % of all unauthorized immigrants in Arizona could be Latin American, suggests that 16.6 % of all Latinos in the state could be unauthorized. The 8.8 % figure of legal immigrants/non-immigrants is derived from subtracting 14.8 % from 23.6 %, the percent of Latinos in the state who are non-citizens.

The Arizona Department of Health Services (2010) reports that there were 103,172 pregnancies in Arizona in 2009, with 92,616 live births. The remainder resulted in abortions or fetal deaths. The total birth rate per 1,000 females aged 15–44 in Arizona in 2009 is 68.9. Birth rates per 1,000 females by race/ethnicity differ: 92.4 for Latinas, 53.3 for Non-Hispanic White women, and between 73.8 and 79.3 for women of other races. Comparing these figures requires caution, as the total birth rate does not account for the fact that Latinas tend to be at the lower end of this age range and non-Hispanic women tend to be at the higher end of the range. The number of pregnancies and live births in Arizona in 2009 are at their lowest levels in at least 10 years. Latinas had the largest annual drop in the number of births of all groups, a decline of 16.1 % between 2007 and 2009. The number of births among the state's Non-Hispanics decreased by 4.7 % in the 2-year period, symbolizing a "recession effect" (Arizona Department of Health Services 2010, p. 3).

Future Projections

As noted earlier, both Arizona and the country as a whole have experienced strong population increases in recent decades. Population projections released by the Arizona Department of Economic Security (2006) indicate that Arizona's population might be as large as 10.9 million in 2034, suggesting a 72 % increase in population over the 2007 estimate of approximately 6.3 million. Additional projections suggest that there may be as many as 12.8 million Arizonans by the year 2050, with more than 7.6 million residing in Maricopa County alone. Similarly, Latino population increases in the state (and nationally) in recent years have been larger than past projections would indicate. For example, a 1996 Census Bureau Report suggested that Latinos would likely represent 32.2 % of Arizona in 2025. Given that Latinos represent about 30 % of Arizona in 2009, Latinos may comprise more than one-third of the state's population well before 2025. There are additional factors suggesting that Latinos and other non-White groups may represent an increasingly important component of Arizona's population in the coming decades, including strong growth rates between 1980 and 2009, their relative youth, higher birth rates, and migration from Latin American and Asia in the last 30 years. However, in light of recent changes in the national and state-level economy, legislation such as SB 1070, the significant and sustained downturn in the state's housing market, and other factors, it is difficult to accurately predict how the state's population size and racial/ethnic/nativity composition will change in the short term and in the decades to come.

Conclusion

This chapter provides a detailed profile of Arizona and Arizona's Latinos in the years preceding SB 1070. The goal is to provide recent demographic information that covers a broad array of topics with public policy implications, such as age, figures on recent births, and with respect to migration, details about nativity, year of arrival, and citizenship. As outlined in the chapter, understanding and interpreting this information requires sensitivity to larger national trends, historical and current population changes in Arizona, and variation by racial/ethnic group and by county. Beginning with this contextualized and nuanced perspective generates a more considered discussion and evaluation of Arizona's Latino politics, immigration, transborder, and binational relations in the post-SB1070 era.

Appendix

Decennial census data used in the profile come from Summary Tape File 1 (STF1) of the 1990 Census of the Population and Summary Files 1 and 3 (SF1 and SF3) of the 2000 Census. These data are accessible via http://factfinder.census.gov/. Census data for 1980 were accessed using the CensusScope project developed by the Social Science Data Analysis Network (SSDAN) at http://www.censusscope.org/. Data on pregnancies and birth rates for the state were derived from the Arizona Department of Health Services (2010) report. National-level projections through 2050 are based on the U.S. Census Bureau (2004), and state-level projections are based on the Arizona Department of Economic Security (2006). Data derived from STF1 (1990) and SF1 (2000) of the decennial census are based on 100 % of the U.S. population, not samples, therefore there is no sampling error associated with these figures and any differences across population subgroups or geographic areas are considered to be statistically significant.

The American Community Survey (ACS) is a national continuous survey that provides annual demographic, economic, housing, social, and economic data. Its primary purpose is to measure the social and economic characteristics of the U.S. population, released the year after the data are collected. The questionnaire and instruction guide for completing the ACS Form is available in English and Spanish.[25] Each year the ACS samples approximately 3 million addresses each year and conducts nearly two million interviews. The U.S. Census of the Population taken every 10 years is available at every geographic level, from the nation to street blocks. The ACS is not available at all of these geographies; as it is not based on a complete enumeration of the U.S. population and has a fairly small sample, the ACS aggregates data from multiple years to produce reliable numbers for small counties and smaller geographic units. Moreover, ACS data disseminated to the public are much more limited than the decennial census. One-year estimates, in this case from 2009, are available for areas with populations larger than 65,000. One-year estimates from ACS for 2009 are available for Arizona and most consistently available for Maricopa, Pima, and Pinal counties, and are the

[25] Content from the 2009 ACS in English is available at: http://www.census.gov/acs/www/Downloads/questionnaires/2010/Quest10.pdf and in Spanish at: http://www.census.gov/acs/www/Downloads/questionnaires/2010/Quest10SP.pdf.

counties discussed in this profile. In order to provide a consistent demographic profile, this chapter uses only 2009 one-year estimates, rather than three-year estimates (2006–2008) available for areas with 20,000 or more in population (U.S. Census Bureau 2010).

ACS data are based on a sample of the population; therefore, the data produced are estimates subject to sampling error. ACS figures include a published margin of error at the 0.90 level of significance, which allows for calculations of confidence intervals. This calculation is necessary to identify whether differences in ACS estimates across racial/ethnic groups and/or geographic areas are statistically significant. This demographic profile focuses on providing a descriptive profile of Arizona and counties where data are most consistently available (Maricopa, Pima, Pinal counties), and does not focus on identifying county or group-level differences in the estimates. Information about sampling error, confidence intervals, and other technical ACS information are available at: http://www.census.gov/acs/www/Downloads/ACSGeneralHandbook.pdf.

References

Alba R, Rumbaut R, Marotz K (2005) A distorted nation: perceptions of racial/ethnic group sizes and attitudes toward immigrants and other minorities. Soc Forces 84:901–920

Arizona Department of Economic Security (2006) Arizona Population Projections 2006–2055. Research Administration, Population Statistics Unit. Phoenix, AZ. http://www.azcommerce.com/econinfo/demographics/Population%20Projections.html

Arizona Department of Health Services (2010) Arizona Health Status and Vital Statistics 2009. Bureau of Health Statistics. Table 1A-1, Table 1A-6. http://www.azdhs.gov/plan/report/ahs/ahs2009/toc09.htm

Benton-Cohen K (2009) Borderline Americans: racial division and labor war in the Arizona borderlands. Harvard University Press, Cambridge

Chavez L (2008) The Latino threat: constructing immigrants, citizens, and the nation. Stanford University Press, Palo Alto

Cobas JA, Duany J et al (eds) (2009) How the United States racializes Latinos. Paradigm, Boulder

De Genova N (2004) The legal production of Mexican/migrant "illegality". Latino Studies 2(2):160–185

Gibson C, Jung K (2002) Historical census statistics on population totals by race, 1790 to 1990, and by Hispanic origin, 1970 to 1990, for the United States, regions, divisions, and states. Working Paper Series No. 56. Population Division. U. S. Census Bureau. Washington. http://www.census.gov/population/www/documentation/twps0056/twps0056.html#sou

Grieco EM, Cassidy RC (2001) Overview of race and Hispanic origin, 2000. U.S. Department of Commerce Economics and Statistics Administration, US Census Bureau. Washington. http://www.census.gov/prod/2001pubs/cenbr01-1.pdf

Massey DS (2009) Racial formation in theory and practice: the case of Mexicans in the United States. Race Soc Probl 1:12–26

McConnell ED (2011) An 'incredible number of Latinos and Asians': media representations of racial and ethnic population change in Atlanta, Georgia. Latino Studies 9(2–3):177–197

McConnell ED, Amanda Skeen (2009) Demographics: Contemporary Characteristics of a Dynamic Population. In: Looking ahead (Viendo Adelante): the past, present and future of Hispanic populations in the State of Arizona, 2009–2034. Arizona State University and the

Arizona Latino Research Enterprise, Tempe. http://www.asu.edu/vppa/asuforaz/downloads/state_of_latino_arizona_report.pdf

Meeks EV (2007) Border citizens: the making of Indians, Mexicans, and Anglos in Arizona. University of Texas Press, Austin

Menjívar C (2001) Latino immigrants and their perceptions of religious institutions: Cubans, Salvadorans, and Guatemalans in Phoenix, AZ. Migraciones Internacionales 1(1):65–88

Moran-Taylor M, Menjívar C (2005) Unpacking notions of return: Guatemalan and Salvadoran migrants in Phoenix. Int Migr 43(4):91–131

Nadeau R, Niemi RG, Levine J (1993) Innumeracy about minority populations. Publ Opin Q 57:332–347

Officer JE (1987) Hispanic Arizona, 1536–1858. University of Arizona Press, Tucson

Ortman J, Kluegel J (2005) Public opinion and the 'Hispanic challenge'. In: Paper presented at the American Sociological Association, Philadelphia

Passel JS, D'Vera Cohn (2010) U.S. unauthorized immigration flows are down sharply since mid-decade, Pew Hispanic Center, Washington. Sept 1. http://pewhispanic.org/files/reports/126.pdf

Pew Hispanic Center (2006a) A statistical portrait of Hispanics at mid-decade. Pew Hispanic Center, Washington

Pew Hispanic Center (2006b) Modes of entry for the unauthorized migrant population. Washington. May 22. http://pewhispanic.org/files/factsheets/19.pdf

Pew Hispanic Center (2008) Arizona: population and labor force characteristics, 2000–2006. Washington. Jan 23. http://pewhispanic.org/files/factsheets/37.pdf

Rodriguez C (2000) Changing race: Latinos, the census, and the history of ethnicity in the United States. New York University Press, New York

Ríos-Bustamante A (1998) As *Guilty as Hell*: Mexican copper miners and their communities in Arizona, 1920–1950. In: Hart JM (ed) Border crossings: Mexican and Mexican American workers. Scholarly Resources, Wilmington

Rosales FA, Marín C (2009) Histories of Mexican-origin populations in Arizona. In: State of Latino Arizona. The Arizona Latino Research Enterprise, ASU Department of Transborder Chicana/o Latina/o Studies and ASU Office of Public Affairs. Arizona Board of Regents

Saenz R (2010) Latinos, whites, and the shifting demography of Arizona. Population Reference Bureau, Washington. Sept. http://www.prb.org/Articles/2010/usarizonalatinos.aspx

Social Science Data Analysis Network (SSDAN). CensusScope. University of Michigan, Ann Arbor, MI. http://www.censusscope.org/

U.S. Census Bureau (1996) State population rankings summary, Arizona's population projections: 1995 to 2025. Population Paper Listing #47, "Population Projections for States, by Age, Sex, Race and Hispanic Origin: 1995 to 2025." U.S. Bureau of the Census, Population Division, Washington. http://www.census.gov/population/projections/state/9525rank/azprsrel.txt

U.S. Census Bureau (2004) U.S. interim projections by age, sex, race, and Hispanic origin. Table 1a. Projected Population of the United States, by Race and Hispanic Origin: 2000 to 2050. http://www.census.gov/ipc/www/usinterimproj/

U.S. Census Bureau (2007) Arizona's maricopa leads counties in population growth since census 2000. U.S. Census Bureau, Washington. News release, 22 Mar 2007. http://www.census.gov/newsroom/releases/archives/population/cb07-42.html

U.S. Census Bureau (2009) Census bureau releases state and county data depicting nation's population ahead of 2010 census. U.S. Census Bureau, Washington. News release, Thursday, 14 May 2009. http://www.census.gov/newsroom/releases/archives/population/cb09-76.html

U.S. Census Bureau (2010) 2009 American community survey, 1 Year survey estimates summary file. Washington. http://factfinder.census.gov/

U.S. Department of Homeland Security (2008) Estimates of the unauthorized immigrant population residing in the United States: January 2007. Hoefer M, Rytina N, Baker BC. Office of Immigration Statistics. Washington. Sept. http://www.dhs.gov/xlibrary/assets/statistics/publications/ois_ill_pe_2007.pdf

Chapter 2
Arizona's Immigration Policies and SB 1070

Lisa Magaña

Enforcement directives are politically popular in Arizona, galvanizing support for elected and public officials. Some of the rhetoric regarding immigration has been largely symbolic and unfairly scapegoats immigrants. Starting in the mid-1990s, there have been a variety of policies passed in Arizona that target unauthorized immigrants. In 2010, one of the most controversial immigration policies in the United States, SB 1070, was passed in the state setting off debates nationally and internationally. As the unauthorized immigrant population increased, so did the number of laws targeting their presence. Immigration policy reform or more enforcement directives becomes politically popular in Arizona, galvanizing support for those elected officials that oppose illegal immigration. This chapter is a review of some of the laws, policies, and bills that led to the passage of SB 1070.

Arizona as an Immigrant Destination

When Operation Gatekeeper 1994 and Operation Hold-the Line 1993 were implemented, they redirected unauthorized immigration from California and Texas into Arizona. By enhancing the number of border patrol agents in California and Texas, unauthorized immigrants were subsequently entering regions in less-monitored Arizona. It is during the 1990s, when Arizona becomes a major destination point for unauthorized immigrants.

L. Magaña (✉)
School for Transborder Studies, Arizona State University,
S Myrtle Ave 975 Tempe, Phoenix 85287, Arizona, USA
e-mail: lisa.magana@asu.edu

L. Magaña and E. Lee (eds.), *Latino Politics and Arizona's Immigration Law SB 1070*,
Immigrants and Minorities, Politics and Policy, DOI: 10.1007/978-1-4614-0296-1_2,

In 1996, Congress passed the illegal immigration reform and responsibility act (IIRA). This Act established restrictions on legal immigrants from receiving social services, denying some from using food stamps and social security. Since unauthorized immigrants were already barred from most forms of welfare, the IIRA broadened restrictions for unauthorized immigrants from federal, state, and local benefits. Congress also increased criminal penalties for immigration-related offenses as well as hired more enforcement personnel. Another provision of the IIRA was a little-known policy called 287(g). The Act authorizes local law enforcement agencies after they are formally trained to implement immigration policies. This policy will set the stage for a major immigration debate in 2010 (Magaña 2011).

In 1997, the city of Chandler, a growing suburb just outside of Phoenix, implemented a policy known as Operation Restoration. For almost five days, the Chandler Police detained individuals that appeared to be Hispanic and asked them for proof of U.S. citizenship. If proper documentation was not provided, individuals were apprehended and subject to deportation. Over 400 individuals were detained as part of this process. U.S. citizens that appeared to be Hispanic were detained and denied certain civil and procedural rights until proof of citizenship could be provided. The city was sued, eventually paying more than $500,000 in out-of-court settlements (Johnson 2007).

On September 11, 2001 attacks on the World Trade Center and the Pentagon resulted in new immigration policy mandates. Immediately after the attacks, the Border Patrol was charged with sealing off the nation's southern borders and deploying agents to airports. Because several of the terrorists had entered the U.S. "legally" with visas, public sentiment shifted its focus to visa over-stayers. A new system for reporting the status of foreign and exchange students was eventually implemented.

Congress also disbanded the immigration and naturalization service (I.N.S.). The agency's two functions, enforcement and service, were separated and placed under the supervision of the department of homeland security department (DHS). The Border Patrol was placed in the Bureau of Customs and Border Protection while the previous service functions of the I.N.S. are now in the Bureau of Citizenship and Immigration Services.

In Arizona, growing fear and concern over terrorism and immigration was heightened when it turned out that several of the 9/11 terrorists lived in metropolitan Phoenix. Some scholars even felt that metropolitan Phoenix had been home to a "sleeper cell" of Osama bin Laden (Wagner and Zoellner 2010). Lotfi Raissi lived in North Phoenix and provided flight training to four of the terrorists in Arizona. Hani Hanjoor was one of the terrorists that crashed into the Pentagon and lived in Phoenix and took flight-training courses in Scottsdale. Nawaf Al-Hazmi, also on the Pentagon flight, took training courses in Phoenix. Furthermore, reports that terrorists were going to infiltrate through the southern border continued to fuel fear in Arizonians (Wagner and Zoellner 2010).

Around 2002, the prominence of immigrant vigilante groups grows, most notably the Civil Homeland Defense and the Minute Man Project. Volunteers from all over the country come to the state in order to participate in patrolling the borders, using surveillance technology and reporting the presence of unauthorized immigrants to the Border Patrol. Minute Man members officially cannot have any physical contact with immigrants (Doty 2009).

In 2004, a citizen's group called protect arizona now (PAN), placed an initiative on the ballot that would require: (1) proof of citizenship when registering to vote; (2) an identification card at polling places; (3) proof of immigration status when applying for state public welfare benefits; and (4) government workers were to report suspected unauthorized immigrants seeking benefits (Avalos et al. 2010). PAN received substantial financial support from the federation for American immigration reform (FAIR). The goals of FAIR are strengthened militarized borders, significant decreases in the rate of illegal immigration, greater deportations of unauthorized immigrants, and opposition to any amnesty proposals. Fifty-six percent of Arizona's voters supported the proposition (Avalos et al. 2010).

In 2006, more state initiatives were passed illustrating the growing anti-immigrant sentiment in Arizona. First, voters passed an English-only proposition that requires all governmental materials be provided in English. Teachers can be penalized for teaching in Spanish. Citizens also approved Proposition 100 that denies bail for immigrants unlawfully in the country. Proposition 102 denies an unauthorized immigrant from bringing a lawsuit or winning any damages. For instance, if an immigrant is hurt at a worksite because of employer negligence, he or she cannot claim damages. Proposition 300 makes anyone without legal status ineligible for in-state tuition, grants, scholarships, and financial aid. For instance, students born in Mexico but have lived in Arizona their whole life would be charged out-of-state tuition. And HB 2592 prohibits cities in Arizona from funding any day labor sites or places where immigrants and citizen laborers congregate for work.

In 2006, the Secure Fence Act was enacted. The DHS was charged with securing approximately 700 miles of the border between U.S. and Mexico. With an allocated 1.2 billion dollars, DHS was responsible for building a wall that was to be impenetrable by unauthorized entries. Monies were also provided for more cameras for surveillance, motion sensors, and strengthening of existing barriers. Since 2006, only sections of the barrier have been completed. In Arizona, there are a variety of spatial and environmental issues that hinder completion. There are areas that are mountainous, making a continuous wall difficult if not impossible to complete. Furthermore, Native Americans on the Tohono O'odham Indian Reservation complain that the barrier desecrates ancient burial sites. Environmentalists also find that the structure is damaging to the migration of endangered species (Wood 2008).

In 2007, Governor Janet Napolitano signed House Bill 2779. The law requires employers to verify that their employees are in the country legally. If an employer knowingly hires an unauthorized worker, he or she is subject to a 10-day suspension of a state business license. A second offense can result in permanent revocation of a state license. Verification of a worker's status is made at an Employment Eligibility Verification System, commonly known as E-Verify. If an employee is in the country illegally or his or her status cannot be verified, the employer receives a "Notice of Suspect Documents". Employers are then considered informed and must terminate employment as well as not rehire the employee in the future.

Arizona Gets Hotter

Maricopa County is the most populated region in Arizona and has the highest proportion of unauthorized immigrants. Joe Arpaio, the head of the maricopa county sheriff's office (MCSO), calls himself the Toughest Sheriff in America. He has been reelected six times, starting his career in 1993. Much of his popularity stems from his stance on unauthorized immigration. The MCSO has been sued over 2,300 times for various reasons, including cruel treatment to inmates, racial profiling, and illegally carrying out immigration policy. There have also been several lawsuits won by families whose loved ones have died while in MCSO jails (Finnegan 2009).

Federal policy players, not police or local enforcement agents, traditionally carry out immigration policies and the constitution stipulates states and local entities cannot carry supersede federal laws under the supremacy clause. When the IIRA passed in 1996, a small provision called 287(g) allowed local police officers to work with U.S. Immigration and Customs Enforcement (I.C.E.) if they are formally trained. Officers must receive specialized guidance from I.C.E. instructors. This coordination is to provide officers necessary resources and latitude to pursue investigations relating to violent crimes, human smuggling, gang/organized crime activity, sexual-related offenses, narcotics smuggling, and money laundering (I.C.E. 2009). The provision stipulates that you cannot stop a person simply based on appearance or if the individual is perceived to be an unauthorized immigrant.

Police agencies that participate in the training receive funding in order to subsidize immigration enforcement activities. In order to carry out 287(g) you must be a U.S. citizen, pass a background investigation, have a minimum of 2 years' experience, and no disciplinary actions pending. ICE provides 4 weeks of training at the Federal Law Enforcement Training Center in Charleston, South Carolina. (I.C.E. 2009).

The MCSO has the most deputies in the nation trained through 287(g), approximately 170. In Phoenix, the MCSO implements controversial programs under the 287(g) called "crime suppression sweeps". The MCSO sets up coordinated checkpoints around various parts of the county where immigrants are known to live. Latino immigrants have been arrested for minor traffic violations and then subsequently deported. As stipulated in 287(g), individuals are not to be targeted for minor offenses. The policy is intended to pursue investigations relating to violent crimes, human smuggling, gang/organized crime activity, sexual-related offenses, narcotics smuggling, and money laundering—not immigration enforcement. The MCSO is under investigation for the practice of crime suppression sweeps. There is growing concern that police officers enforcing immigration policies have compromised positive relations between police and immigrants. Individuals that may have called the police for help may not for fear they may be deported. As Arpaio described it, "We are quickly becoming a full-fledged anti-illegal immigration agency" (Magaña 2011).

In 2009, the government accountability office (GAO) released a report on the impact of 287(g). They found that immigration officials failed to develop key internal controls over the controversial program that trains local police to identify illegal immigrants involved in crime. They found that some departments were focusing on minor violations rather than ones that are serious, ignoring the policy objectives. For instance, some officers were arresting and processing unauthorized immigrants for deportation for minor violations like speeding (Aizenman 2009). The authors warned that confusion over the purpose of 287(g) could result in referrals of an unmanageable number of low-priority illegal immigrants to ICE as well as misuse of authority by local officials. One sheriff said that his understanding of his authority was that 287(g)-trained officers could go to people's homes and question individuals regarding their immigration status even if the individual is not suspected of criminal activity. The report also showed that the program has expanded rapidly in recent years, "receiving $60 million between 2006 and 2008, training 951 state and local law enforcement officers in 67 agencies and resulting in the arrests of at least 43,000 immigrants, almost 28,000 of whom ultimately were ordered out of the country" (Aizenman 2009).

In another study conducted by the Goldwater Institute, researchers found that the policy is highly ineffective and deters officers from pursuing more law enforcement activities. They find that before 287(g), MCSO targeted more smugglers or coyotes—those individuals who illegally bring people into the country. In 2006 and 2007, the MCSO arrested only low-level operatives, such as drivers and drop-house guards. The researchers noted that out of the eight patrol sweeps that have taken place in six communities in Phoenix not one smuggler boss has been arrested (Goldwater 2008).

The researchers also found that the policy has diverted substantial resources away from other law enforcement activities. In 2005, MCSO had a response of 5 minutes, in 2007 its median response time was over 7 minutes, and in 2008 the average response time was nearly 11 min. They illustrate that the Phoenix Police Department that does not have 287(g) directives has an average response time of 4 minutes (Goldwater 2008).

Federal officials came under increasing pressure to end 287(g) because of racial profiling. In October of 2009, I.C.E. renewed their contract with MSCO. This time, however, funding was to be used only for processing immigrants after arrest. Disappointed in the loss of 287 (g) money Joe Arpaio quips to reporters, "This just includes the jail, and deep down, I feel that I ought to take it and rip it all up. On the other hand, I feel it's very critical to have the jail... it looks like they're taking away my authority on the streets for political reasons. They don't have the guts and the courtesy to even come back and say in writing, we are not going to continue" (Hensley 2009).

Enter SB 1070

In 2010, State Senator Russell Pearce maintained that the government had been hampering the immigration enforcement actions of police agencies in Arizona. That is why he was introducing the Support Our Law Enforcement and Safe Neighborhoods Act later to be known as SB 1070. FAIR, the organization that helped fund Proposition 200 was again involved in the backing of the proposal. Under the state's trespassing statute, immigrants can be criminalized for their mere presence in Arizona. Additionally, the proposal would bar cities from enacting policies that prevent them from enforcing federal immigration laws. SB 1070 also makes it a crime to stop a vehicle on the road to hire a day laborer if it impedes traffic. Arizonians are no longer able to transport, harbor, conceal or shield an unauthorized immigrant. Finally the legislation would strengthen the states employer sanctions laws, giving prosecutors more latitude in investigations.

On April 28, 2010, Governor Jan Brewer signed SB 1070, setting off national and international controversy. Polls showed that support for the bill as well as her anti-immigrant stance boosted her popularity with many Arizonians. Not surprising, when Governor Brewer ran for reelection she maintained that immigration was out of control in Arizona and that law enforcement agencies have found bodies in the desert that have been beheaded. She has also maintained that the majority of immigrants are bringing drugs into the state. When Senator McCain ran for reelection his platform was also largely based on immigration enforcement as well as support for SB 1070.

Recent data show the proportion of unauthorized immigrants in Arizona as well their impact on crime. The overall population of Arizona is a bit higher than 6 million. The Pew Foundation found that during 2008 the unauthorized population in Arizona was around 5.5 % or 375,000 people. The authors maintain that these numbers have undoubtedly declined. Furthermore, they note that unauthorized immigrants were leaving the state before SB 1070. Out-migration was largely based on an ailing economy and not enforcement policies. Next, the FBI released crime statistics data illustrating that violent crime in Arizona fell nearly 14 % in 2009, the largest drop of any state except South Dakota. Murder and non-negligent manslaughter dropped by 22 %. Forcible rape fell by 3.8 % (Montini 2010).

SB 1070 was immediately challenged by a broad coalition of groups, including the American Civil Liberties Union, Mexican–American Legal Defense Education Fund, National Immigration Law Center the National Association for the Advancement of Colored People, ACLU of Arizona, National Day Laborer Organizing Network and the Asian Pacific American Legal Center. The lawsuits charged that the Arizona law interferes with federal power and authority over immigration, violates the supremacy clause of the U.S. Constitution, invites racial profiling and infringes on the free speech of immigrants in Arizona. Several prominent law enforcement groups, including the Arizona Association of Chiefs of Police, opposed the law because it diverts limited resources from law enforcement's responsibility and destroys police-citizen relationships that are integral when policing diverse communities. The U.S. Department of Justice also brought suit, stating that the state law superseded federal immigration law.

On July 28, 2010, Judge Susan Bolton's ruled for a temporarily injunction on four of the law's provisions. Temporarily stopped by the Judge's orders include: Officers do not have to make a reasonable attempt to determine the immigration status of a person stopped, detained or arrested if there's reasonable suspicion they are in the country illegally; it will not be a crime if you are not carrying an alien-registration papers; officers cannot make warrant less arrests of persons; and it is not a crime for illegal immigrants to solicit, apply, or perform work.

What has gone into effect and not temporarily stopped: It is a crime to pick up a day laborer in a roadway if it impedes traffic; law enforcement still must enforce federal immigration laws to the fullest extent of the law; Individuals will still be able to sue an agency if it is perceived that they are not enforcing the law. Governor Brewer remarked that the Judge's ruling "as a little bump in the road", and Maricopa County Sheriff Joe Arpaio maintained that he was not surprised by Bolton's ruling, but it will have little impact on his planned crime-suppression operations. The injunction was later upheld by the Ninth Circuit Court in April 2011. Arizona later appealed the decision to the U.S. Supreme Court, which heard arguments by the state and the Obama Administration on April 25, 2012.

June 2012, the U.S. Supreme Court overturned most parts of the bill except for the provision that requires police officers to make a reasonable attempt when determining the immigration status of a person stopped, detained or arrested. The Supreme Court also maintained that there must be reasonable suspicion that the person is in the country illegally. Most important, the stated that they would reconsider its decision if civil rights violations took place.

September 2012, the American Civil Liberties Union, the National Immigration Law Center and the Mexican–American Legal Defense and Educational Fund requested that a new injunction be placed on the law after the Supreme Court's ruling. The plaintiffs maintained that the law encourages the lengthy detention of people with a Latino phenotype and that the law violated the Equal Protection Clause of the 14th Amendment. Judge Susan Bolton declined to issue a new injunction.

Conclusion

Arizona has been implementing policies that target unauthorized immigrants for the last 15 years. Enforcement directives are politically popular in Arizona, galvanizing support for elected and public officials. Some of the rhetoric regarding immigration has been largely symbolic and unfairly scapegoats immigrants. It is important to note that even though the most controversial parts of SB 1070 have been stopped, the impact of the policy is apparent in Arizona. In many ways, the discourse around immigration has been almost as powerful as the law itself.

According to the Arizona Tourism Alliance, the controversy over SB 1070 has cost the state over 2 billion dollars and roughly 30,000 jobs. Convention business that has been canceled in protest of SB 1070 has cost the state $15 million. Although the most controversial parts of SB 1070 have been stopped, the state still is being boycotted.

References

Aizenman N (2009) Report cites problems in ICE training program. Washington Post

Avalos, Magaña ML, Pantoja AP (2010) Battleground voters in a battleground state? In: de la Garza R, Desipio L, Leal D (eds) Beyond the barrio: Latinos in the 2004 elections. Notre Dame Press, Notre Dame, pp 159–170

Doty R (2009) The law into their own hands: immigration and the politics of exceptionalism. University of Arizona Press, Tucson

Finnegan W (2009) Sheriff Joe: Sheriff Joe is tough on prisoners and unauthorized immigrants. What about crime? NY Mag

Goldwater Institute (2008) Mission unaccomplished: the misplaced priorities of the Maricopa County sheriff's office. Phoenix, AZ

Governmental Accounting Office (2009) Immigration Enforcement Better Controls over Programs Authorizing State and Local Enforcement of Federal Laws

Hensley, J. (2009, Oct. 3). Sheriff Arpaio may lose some immigrant authority. Ariz Repub

Immigration Customs and Enforcement (2009) Delegation of immigration authority section 287(g) immigration and nationality act the ICE 287(g) program: a law enforcement partnership

Johnson K (2007) Opening the floodgates: why America needs to rethink its borders and immigration laws. NYU Press, New York

Magaña L (2011) Fear of calling the police. In: Schiele J (ed) Sage Press, pp 255–279

Montini E (2010) Bad news for Gov. Jan Brewer and Sen. John McCain. Ariz Repub

Wagner D, Zoellner T (2010) Arizona was home to bin laden "sleeper cell". Ariz Repub

Wood B (2008) Where U.S.-Mexico border fence is tall, border crossings fall. Christ Sci Monit

Chapter 3
Immigration Politicking and the Perceptions of Latino Voters in Arizona

Rodolfo Espino

Latino Voters, SB1070, and Political (De)Mobilization

On April 23, 2010, Governor Jan Brewer of Arizona signed into law a bill that had been passed out of the Arizona legislature earlier that month along nearly perfect partisan lines. The Arizona House of Representatives passed the bill 3521 on April 13 and the Arizona Senate passed the bill 1711 on April 19. Only one Republican, Senator Carolyn Allen, voted against the bill. Although most observers anticipated she would sign the bill into law, Brewer took her time explaining that she needed to carefully study the law. At a highly covered press conference, she did exactly what most observers expected her to do. In the aftermath of the bill's signing, protests for and against the law broke out and lawyers for both sides scrambled to defend and challenge the law. While jurists will continue to argue over interpretations of the constitutionality of this legislation as it works its way through the judicial system, the interpretations of this legislation by voters in the public also carry important political significance. The passage of this bill and others very similar to it in other states will potentially produce reverberations on elections to come once again, highlighting the centrality of race and ethnicity in American elections (Hutchings and Valentino 2004).

While the passage of Arizona's Senate Bill 1070 garnered lots of national and international media attention, it is important to note that this was not the first time that Latinos in Arizona found themselves in political crosshairs; and it will

R. Espino (✉)
School of Politics and Global Studies, Arizona State University,
873902, Tempe, AZ 85287-3902, USA
e-mail: espino@asu.edu

L. Magaña and E. Lee (eds.), *Latino Politics and Arizona's Immigration Law SB 1070*,
Immigrants and Minorities, Politics and Policy, DOI: 10.1007/978-1-4614-0296-1_3,

undoubtedly not be the last time. In 2004, Proposition 200 was passed by Arizona voters. This proposition mandated that proof of citizenship would be required to receive government services and in order to vote in person. Proposition 200 drew comparisons to California's Proposition 187 passed a decade earlier and which had the effect of moving California's Latino voters solidly away from the Republican Party (Barreto and Woods 2005). In 2006, several other propositions were also placed on the ballot and passed by voters. Proposition 100 denies the right to bail for individuals who could not prove their citizenship, Proposition 102 denies punitive damages in civil lawsuits to individuals who could not prove their citizenship, and Proposition 103 made English the official language of Arizona.

The actions of certain elected officials have also brought decidedly intense government scrutiny upon Latinos in Arizona. Perhaps, most notable in recent years have been the "crime suppression" sweeps of Maricopa County Sheriff Joe Arpaio in which Sheriff deputies and volunteer Sheriff posse members will target high Latino density neighborhoods, stop individuals for apparent traffic infractions, and inquire about those individuals' citizenship status. This has obviously led to tensions between the Latino community and the Maricopa County Sheriff's office. Latino community leaders have accused the Sheriff's office of racial profiling, while the Sheriff's office asserts that they follow strict federal guidelines on how to avoid racial profiling.

The sweeps by the Maricopa County Sheriff's office have drawn comparisons to an incident in 1997 referred to as the "Chandler roundup" or officially by law enforcement officials as "Operation Restoration." In that incident, police officers in Chandler, a suburb of Phoenix, spent several days stopping Latinos and inquiring about their citizenship status. Following that incident and the subsequent investigations, the city of Chandler was required to settle costly civil lawsuits for violating the civil rights of many U.S. citizens.

Given increased federal scrutiny over potential civil rights violations since the 1960s, law enforcement officials and politicians sponsoring legislation such as SB1070 have been extremely cautious in avoiding direct usage of ethnic labels of target populations. Nevertheless, this has not prevented feelings of frustration and discontent from many within Arizona's Latino community, regardless of citizenship status, against such legislation and against behavior from the likes of Sheriff Arpaio. Myriad protests and demonstrations have been held to draw attention to what many in Arizona's Latino community feel are actions to explicitly target all Latinos in Arizona. This discontent has led some to speculate as to whether Latinos in Arizona would start flexing their political muscle, similar to what has happened with Latinos in California over the past decade. However, the opposite outcome could also be a potential outcome namely, Latinos in Arizona will feel so efficacious because of the passage of SB1070 and other similar legislation or ballot proposition that they will turn off from politics instead of turning out to the voting booth.

The evidence and arguments presented by those who study minority political behavior could lead one to generate equally justified hypothesis that the effect of SB1070 on Arizona voters could lead to either mobilization or demobilization. In the case of the latter, Frymer (1999) has noted that within the American two-party system, the ability for African American voters or other minorities, for that matter, to effectively exact influence is constrained because of Downsian competition for the median voter, thus leading to their effective disenfranchisement. Similarly, Hero (1992) argues that because of the demographics of the Latino population, the pluralist model (Dahl 1961) that assumes that even minority groups can achieve effective representation is misguided. The opportunity to be politically influential is set to a much higher level and this, too, leads to little responsiveness to the interests of Latinos. And recent evidence presented by Hajnal (2009) indicates that the system of majority rules elections in American politics makes African Americans perpetual "losers" and, under certain contexts, Latinos, too.

The norm in American politics is for minorities not to show up to the voting booth (Wolfinger and Rosenstone 1980). So much research has focused on explaining the conditions under which minorities will be motivated to participate in politics. Some research has focused on the effects of minority elected officials on minority voter mobilization. Once significant numbers of minorities exist in a concentrated area, the opportunity to elect minority officials presents itself; and once that is achieved minorities acquire a sense of empowerment and increased political efficacy that would sustain the continued presence of minority election officials (Bobo 1990). While such research in political science initially focused on the situation of African Americans, recent research has extended the focus to Hispanic Americans and has generally found that Latinos are also empowered by the presence of Latino candidates and willing to lend their voting support to co-ethnic candidates (Barreto 2007; Manzano and Sanchez 2010).

The mere presence of a minority candidate on the ballot, though, is sometimes not sufficient for minority voters to become mobilized. For instance, direct appeals to race/ethnicity are sometimes required, although, this, too does not always guarantee Latino voter mobilization especially in the face of the competing process of economic and ethnic assimilation (Marquez and Espino 2010). In some ways, this creates a high hurdle for the opportunity to mobilize Latino voters as a singular, ethnic voting bloc. To do so, requires strong ethnic and/or class identification. Yet as Latino voters achieve higher rates of integration, this can mitigate the ability for ethnic voter mobilization. Sometimes, the correct racial and economic aggregate conditions surrounding the individual voter are also required for Latino voters to become mobilized along ethnic lines (Branton and Jones 2005; Matsubayashi 2010).

Furthermore, not only do particular aggregate demographic or economic conditions serve to contribute to minority voter mobilization, so too, do particular political conditions that can arise out of the political campaign environment or triggered by the behavior of elected officials. With respect to Latino voter mobilization, it has already been mentioned that the impact of racially charged ballot propositions pushed forth by Republicans in California in the 1990s pushed Latinos away from the Republican Party. Interestingly, these propositions combined with the way in which high profile Republican officials framed them in terms of race not only pushed away Latino voters but also pushed away White voters making California a very solid Democratic state (Bowler et al. 2006). In addition, the effect of these racialized political conditions made Latino voters more tuned into politics and more politically knowledgeable (Pantoja and Segura 2003).

It is little wonder then that political pundits speculated as to whether such conditions were ripe for Latino voter mobilization in Arizona following the passage of SB1070, a racially charged ballot proposition arising out of a racially charged political environment. Drawing comparisons between events in California and Arizona are somewhat obvious given the similarities in political conditions and the fact that both states have had nontrivial Latino populations. Yet, drawing generalizations from one particular context, such as California, to the situation Latinos faced in Arizona may not necessarily lead to the same expected outcomes. The conditions may appear comparable at first glance; but the perception of political conditions by Latino voters in Arizona could be completely different. For this reason, we will need to turn to individual survey data of Latino voters in Arizona. This chapter begins to explore how Latino voters in Arizona felt in the wake of the passage of SB1070 with an eye toward whether the potential exists for Latino voters to become mobilized or demobilized. I will utilize a unique survey of Latino voters in Arizona conducted in the week following the passage of SB1070 when existed, perhaps, the most opportune time for potential political mobilization of the Latino electorate of Arizona.

The Unifying Effect of SB1070

Between April 30 and May 5, a survey sponsored by Arizona State University, Northern Arizona University, and National Council of La Raza (ASU/NAU/NCLR) was conducted among 402 registered Latino voters in Arizona. The primary goal of the survey was to understand the perspective of Latino voters in the wake of the passage of SB1070. Specifically, questions were asked to probe attitudes toward elected officials and political parties and understand views of Latino voters toward immigration reform.

The NAU/ASU/NCLR survey revealed overwhelming displeasure toward SB1070 by Latinos voters in Arizona. First, as an indication of how salient the debate over this legislation was for Latinos, the survey found that over 98 % of respondents reported that they heard about the passage of SB1070. Even high-profile Presidential campaigns do not garner that level of awareness in the American electorate. When asked whether they oppose or support SB1070, over 80 % of respondents expressed opposition to SB1070 with just approximately 15 % expressing support for the legislation. Specifically, 11.67 % expressed strong support, 3.82 % somewhat support, 3.24 % neither, 10.65 % somewhat opposed, and 70.62 % expressed strongly opposed. Media attention following the passage of SB1070 largely focused on poll results from conservative pollster Rasmussen and the Pew Foundation showing 70 % of Arizonans and 59 % of Americans, respectively, supported SB1070. Yet, scant attention was directed toward the overwhelming opposition by Latinos toward SB1070 and its potential implications.

Given the partisan leanings of Latinos compared to the rest of the American electorate (de la Garza et al. 1992), it is worth parsing out expressed levels of support or opposition to SB1070 by partisan identification. Those percentages are presented in Table 3.1. It may not be surprising that self-identified Latino Democrats express a higher level of opposition to SB1070 (88 % opposed). Yet, we see that the majority of Latino Independents (77 %) and majority of Latino Republicans (58 %) also express opposition to SB1070.

Given the observed differences between Latino Republicans and Democrats, it is worthwhile to examine whether the differences in average level of opposition to SB1070 are statistically significant between self-identified partisan groups. To facilitate interpretation, these difference of means (on a 5-point scale) are illustrated in Fig. 3.1. This figure shows that there are no statistically significant differences between Latino Republicans and Latino Independents or between Latino Democrats and Latino Independents. At the 95 % confidence level,

Table 3.1 Support/opposition to SB1070 by partisanship

	Democrats	Independents	Republicans
Strongly support	7.68	11.99	29.86
Somewhat support	2.55	5.52	5.79
Neither	1.98	5.25	6.34
Somewhat oppose	6.77	16.33	12.38
Strongly oppose	81.02	60.90	45.63
N	215	101	55

Note Cell entries are weighted percentages

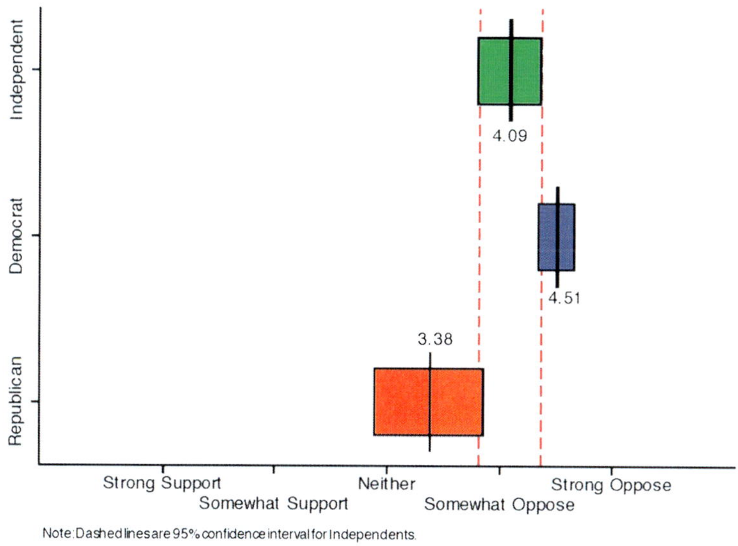

Fig. 3.1 Mean level of opposition to SB1070 by partisanship

Latino Democrats and Latino Republicans are statistically different with Latino Democrats expressing an overall higher level of opposition to SB1070.

However, while statistical significance is detected between Democrats and Republicans these differences are not substantively significant. Latino Republicans do have a higher average level of support for SB1070 than do Latino Democrats or Latino Independents. However, the important observation derived from Fig. 3.1 is that the majority of each partisanship group is opposed to SB1070. The average score on the 5-point scale for all political groupings is on the side of opposition rather than support of SB1070. So while the exact same level of opposition is not shared by Latino Democrats and Latino Republicans, both groups find themselves on the same side of the aisle in opposition to the legislation.

This is an important observation derived from these survey data because partisanship, which often serves as a polarizing gulf in the modern American electorate (Brewer 2005), does not arise as a substantively significant source of division among Latino voters with respect to attitudes toward SB1070. In other words, we must accept the proposition that Latino voters, regardless of partisan affiliation, are more alike than different in their attitudes toward the actions of certain elected officials. And despite the claims by proponents of SB1070 that the legislation was not designed to target all Latinos, the perception by the majority of Latino voters was quite the opposite. The survey data reveal that over 75 % of Latino voters felt that if the majority of immigrants in Arizona were White Europeans that SB1070 would not have passed. Thus, the hostile rhetoric surrounding this legislation appears to have unified rather than divided Latinos across party lines. In what follows, I will further explore the perceptions of Latino voters in Arizona with particular attention to the potential for political mobilization.

Tuning in but Turning Off

Given the level of opposition toward SB1070 expressed by Latino voters of all political stripes, is there evidence to suggest that the sleeping giant of American politics will wake up in Arizona? The rhetoric surrounding SB1070 seems to have provided the opportunity to mobilize Arizona's Latinos heading into the midterm elections of 2010.

Latino voters surveyed in the ASU/NAU/NCLR poll expressed a high level of awareness of SB1070 with 97 % of respondents indicating that they were aware of the legislation. In an era with extremely low levels of political awareness and knowledge (Carpini and Keeter 1997), this level of attention to politics is very remarkable. To gauge the level of enthusiasm among Latino voters heading into the 2010 elections the following was asked of respondents: "Thinking back over the last year since Obama became president and the Democrats have had control of the Congress, how enthusiastic are you about voting in the November 2010 elections?" The vast majority of Latino voters expressed high levels of enthusiasm with 45.8 % "very enthusiastic" and 33.7 % "somewhat enthusiastic." 15.1 % of respondents said they were "not too enthusiastic" and 5.5 % said they were "not at all enthusiastic." These numbers point very firmly to the potential of Latino voters in Arizona to serve as a strong voting bloc in the upcoming elections.

It is important, though, to make a distinction between general levels of enthusiasm and particular levels of enthusiasm. An individual may have high levels of political enthusiasm but no meaningful outlets to channel that enthusiasm. Understanding excitement toward specific groups or candidates can thus serve as a gauge of future political activity and also underlies the sense of efficacy voters may feel toward the political system. To assess this, I turn to another set of questions in the survey that asked respondents to reflect upon their level of excitement toward the two major political parties.

Latino voters in the survey were asked their levels of excitement toward the Republican and Democratic parties. Specifically, one question asked Latino voters about Republicans: "Thinking back over the past year since Obama became President, do you consider yourself more excited about the Republican Party and what they are doing, or less excited about the Republicans?" Similarly, Latino voters were asked about Democrats: "Thinking back over the past year since Obama became President, do you consider yourself more excited about the Democratic Party and what they are doing, or less excited about the Democrats?" The resulting responses and the differences in excitement between the two parties are displayed in Fig. 3.2.

It is, perhaps, not too surprising to see that in the wake of the passage of SB1070 and the support offered by prominent Republican elected officials in Arizona, that the vast majority of Latino voters feel less enthused about the Republican Party with over 80 % of survey respondents indicating that they feel

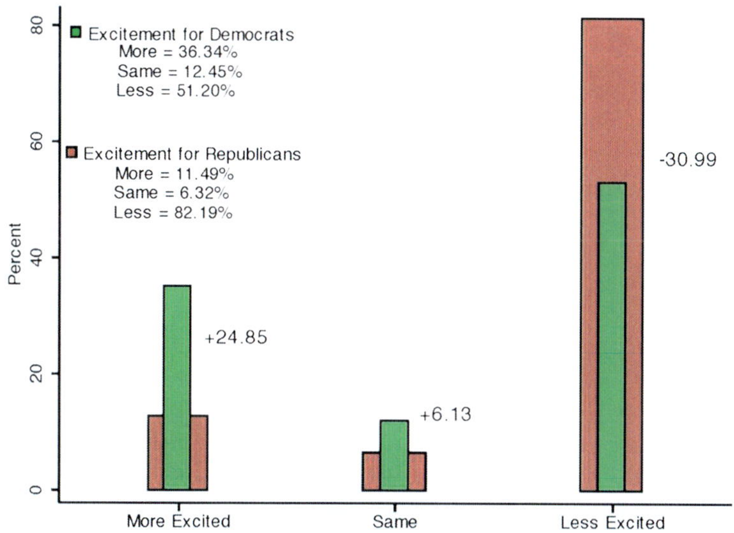

Fig. 3.2 Enthusiasm toward the two parties

less excited about Republicans. Yet, this push by Republicans against Latinos did not automatically translate into increased affinity toward the Democratic Party by Latino voters. The fact that the majority of Latino voters in Arizona (51 %) indicated that they also felt less excited about the Democratic Party suggests that while the Republicans were pushing Latinos away, Democrats were doing little to pull Latinos toward them. It serves as an indication that Latino voters may have perceived Democrats doing very little to fight back against legislation such as SB1070. This was, perhaps, best epitomized when the House minority leader, Democrat David Lujan, failed to appear to cast a vote against SB1070 on the day that it was considered on the House floor.

This is not to say that all Latino elected officials acted passively toward the passage of SB1070. Most vocal and notable in his opposition to SB1070 was Democratic Congressman Raul Grijalva who represents Arizona's 7th congressional district which spans a large portion of the Arizona Mexico border and includes Yuma and portions of Tucson two of Arizona's largest cities after Phoenix. Representative Grijalva was featured prominently in the news following the passage of SB1070 for being a strong, vocal critic of the legislation and even indicating that he would support an economic boycott of Arizona. Grijalva was villified by supporters of SB1070 and even had his home district office vandalized for his opposition to the bill.

Grijalva represents one of Arizona's two majority Latino districts and as discussed earlier the majority of Latino voters in Arizona also expressed opposition to SB1070. In fact, survey respondents in the ASU/NAU/NCLR survey were asked whether they agree or disagree with the following statement, "People should boycott Arizona based companies or stop doing business with the state to send a message that the new immigration law is wrong." The majority of Latino voters (57 %) expressed support for such an economic boycott. Specifically, 42.5 % expressed "strong support" and 15.0 % expressed "somewhat support." 10.2 % of respondents indicated they would "somewhat oppose" an economic boycott and 32.4 % said they would "strongly oppose" a boycott. So while Grijalva received lots of media attention and criticism for his position, what was overlooked was the fact that he was acting responsive and giving voice to a large segment of his constituency a critical component of the "electoral connection" noted by congressional scholars (Mayhew 1974).

Returning to the discussion of how Latino voters in Arizona felt toward particular individuals or organizations specifically and issues of immigration policy more generally, I turn to a question in the ASU/NAU/NCLR survey that provides insight into how Latino voters assign responsibility toward the passage of SB1070. This question asked: "Which political party here in Arizona do you think is responsible for this law [SB1070] being passed? The Republicans, the Democrats, or both political parties?" The majority of respondents, 63 %, assigned blame to the Republicans and 35 % assigned blame to the Democrats. Now, of course, partisanship and existing predispositions toward SB1070 may influence how an individual attributes blame for the passage of SB1070. So we would like to account for partisan identification in examining these numbers. The simple cross tabulation in

Table 3.2 Responsibility for SB1070 by partisanship

	Democrats	Independents	Republicans
Republicans	74.62	45.5	46.05
Both	23.13	51.69	48.63
Democrats	2.25	2.81	5.32
N	218	94	45

Note Cell entries are weighted percentages

Table 3.2 presents the blame Latino voters assign to the respective political parties on the passage of SB1070.

In a somewhat similar pattern as we saw in Table 3.1, Latino voters are similar across partisan categories in assigning relatively little responsibility toward the Democratic Party for the passage of SB1070. While it should not be too surprising to see that Democratic voters would assign more blame to Republicans and less blame to the Democrats, the notable result in Table 3.2 is that both Latino Republicans and Independents assign a large amount of blame to the Republican party or both political parties and very little blame to the Democratic party. Given the projected growth of Latinos as part of Arizona's electorate, this antipathy toward the Republican party by Latino voters with little or no affinity toward the Democratic party can signify the potential for electoral realignments in future elections in Arizona.

However, in a state, such as Arizona, where Republicans wield overwhelming control over most political institutions and have been rather vocal in their support of SB1070, asking voters to assign more blame to one party versus the other is akin to asking a child whether they want brussel sprouts or ice cream for dessert. A more revealing insight can be gleaned if we remove the obvious choice of blaming the Republican Party for the passage of this legislation. The survey followed up with respondents who expressed moderate or strong opposition to the passage of SB1070 with the following statement that they were asked to agree/disagree with: "The Democratic party did not do enough to block this law from being passed." This cross tabulation is presented in Table 3.3.

The percentages in Table 3.3 add more support to the previously presented survey results namely, Latinos, regardless of partisan affiliation express similar sentiments about the passage of SB1070. In this case, we see that the majority of all

Table 3.3 Democratic party responsibility for SB1070 passage

	Democrats	Independents	Republicans
Strongly agree	43.18	55.63	53.11
Somewhat agree	25.12	18.38	20.53
Somewhat disagree	15.20	11.63	9.24
Strongly disagree	16.51	14.36	17.12
N	187	69	25

Note Cell entries are weighted percentages

Latinos who expressed opposition to SB1070 believe that the Democratic party did little to prevent its passage. This leaves little doubt that not only do Latinos feel ostracized by the Republican party but also feel abandoned by the Democratic party as alluded to earlier in Fig. 3.2.

The survey also probed Latino voters for their feelings about the work of the political parties at the national level on immigration policy more generally. The responses offered by Latino voters in Arizona show consistency in the belief of Latino voters that not only are Republicans preventing meaningful reform of the nation's immigration policies but that Democrats are doing little meaningful work in advocating for the reform of such policies. Specifically, Latino voters in the survey were asked the following question about their views of Republicans and Democrats in the United States Congress: "From what you have heard, do you think Democrats/Republicans in the U.S. Congress are: ignoring or avoiding the issue of immigration reform; working on passing immigration reform; or opposing or blocking immigration reform?" The opinions and, specifically, the differences between the two parties, are illustrated in Fig. 3.3. While Latino voters are more likely to view Republicans than Democrats in Congress as blocking immigration reform 39 % versus 12 %, Latino voters are more likely to see Democrats in Congress actually ignoring immigration reform, 47 %, as opposed to working on it, 41 %. Substantively, that is little different than the 39 % of respondents who felt the Republicans were ignoring immigration reform.

If we turn our attention specifically to the most prominent figure of the Democratic Party, President Barack Obama, we find that Latinos express some ambivalence toward him. Survey respondents were asked about their approval/

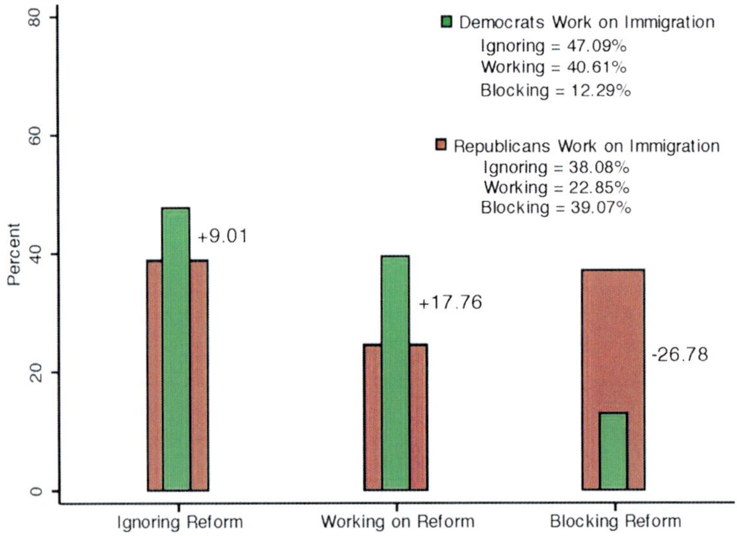

Fig. 3.3 View of political parties on immigration reform

disapproval of President Obama generally and more specifically about his handling of immigration policy. These results are displayed in Fig. 3.4. Although Latinos express generally high levels of support for President Obama in his job, approximately 73 % express approval of him in his job generally, they are a bit colder toward him in regard to his work on immigration. Close to a majority of Latino voters in the survey, approximately 48 %, expressed disapproval over the way President Obama has handled immigration since being elected to office.

As Latinos grow to become a more decisive and larger voting bloc in American elections, the need by candidates to heed the concerns of Latinos also grows more important. The fact that Latinos in Arizona were expressing retrospective disappointment with the organizations and officials presumed to be representing their interests does not, at first glance, appear to bode well for the Democratic party in elections to come. More proximate, of course, following the passage of Arizona's SB1070 were the critical 2010 midterm elections. Political scientists have long noted that the president's party typically loses congressional seats during midterm elections and that the midterm elections can serve as a referendum on the president's past performance in office (Campbell 1985; Erikson 1988). The 2010 midterm elections, though, were anticipated to be a particularly tough election battle for Democrats. Given that American voters tend to be somewhat retrospective in their voting calculations (Fiorina 1981) and, in fact, can be rather myopic in performing retrospective, economic evaluations (Bartels 2010), President Obama and Democrats were facing an uphill battle in minimizing the number of congressional seats lost. Thus, turning out the Democratic base, especially Latino voters would be extremely important. Given the evidence presented, thus far, it seems

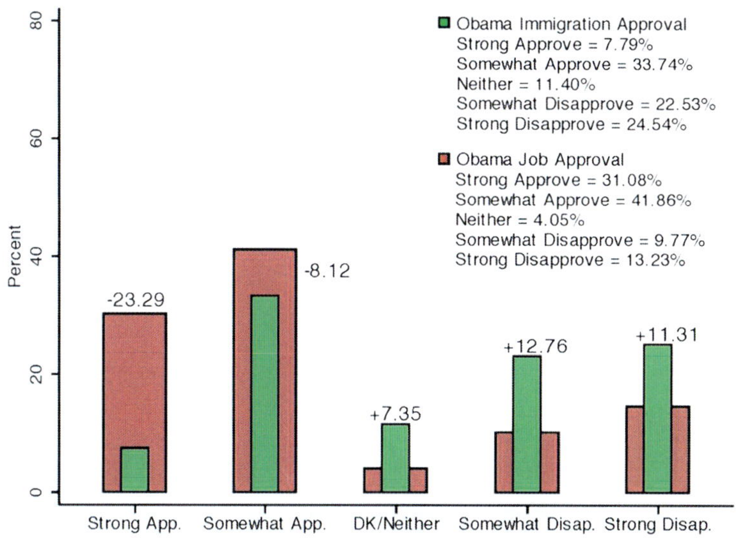

Fig. 3.4 Obama job and immigration approval

like Latino voters would need extra motivation to vote for the Democratic ticket. So would they be willing to turn out for the party that many felt abandoned them on issues critical to them?

Insight into this question can be gleaned from another question on the survey that asked Latino voters in Arizona the following: "During the 2008 election Barack Obama promised to pass immigration reform that provided a pathway to citizenship. More recently, Obama has said that immigration reform may have to wait until later. If immigration reform is not passed before the November 2010 election, would you say that is understandable given all the issues faced by the country or going back on a campaign promise?" 57.1 % of Latino voters indicated that they would feel it was going back on a campaign promise, while 42.9 % indicated that they would understand given all the issues facing the country. For those who believed it was going back on a campaign promise, a follow-up question asked whether that would change their voting decision for President Obama and the Democrats for the next election. Among those Latino voters, a plurality, 44.2 %, indicated it would cause them to vote against Obama and the Democrats. A total of 37.5 % indicated that they would still vote for Obama and the Democrats, while 18.3 % indicated that they would be uncertain about their voting decision if immigration reform is not passed.

As we now know, immigration reform was not passed out of the Democratic controlled Congress. Nor did the Obama White House make a strong, concerted effort to pressure Congress to pass immigration reform. Because of the protracted process to pass health care reform legislation over strong Republican opposition, the congressional calendar became compressed heading into the summer of 2010. Democratic leaders in Washington, D.C. were faced with the dilemma of prioritizing the remainder of their agenda. Two of those items on the agenda were immigration reform legislation and climate change legislation. Ultimately, Democratic leaders chose to pursue climate change legislation and not tackle immigration reform. For many Latino voters, immigration reform should have been prioritized over climate change legislation as evidenced by results in the ASU/NAU/NCLR survey. Respondents were asked about the comparative importance of climate change legislation versus immigration reform legislation. They were then queried about their likelihood of turning out to vote if immigration reform legislation was not passed. The percentage differences in these sets of options are illustrated in Figs. 3.5 and 3.6. These figures provide even further evidence that Latinos voters in Arizona were highly primed and motivated to participate at the voting both only if they were reached out to and made to feel that their concerns were a priority.

Fears and Future Solutions

The findings from the ASU/NAU/NCLR survey data presented here have painted a picture of opportunities presented and then lost to mobilize Latino voters in Arizona to the voting booth. Those opportunities to mobilize Latino voters to the

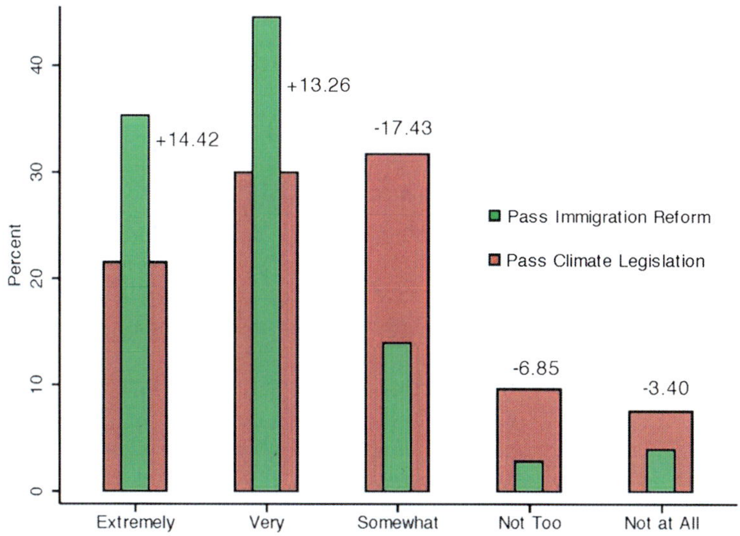

Fig. 3.5 Importance of immigration reform versus climate change

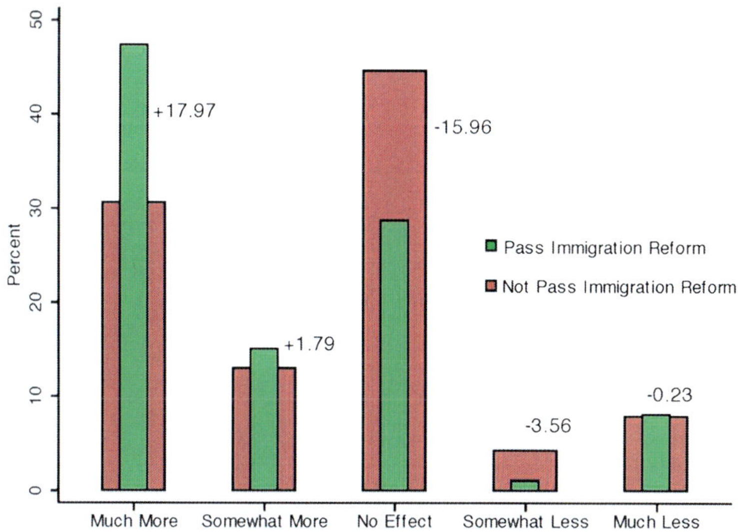

Fig. 3.6 Likelihood of turnout in response to immigration reform

polls in future elections may not be completely lost, however. Latino voters interviewed in the survey expressed strong fear of being racially targeted following the passage of SB1070 with over 85 % of respondents indicating that they were fearful that Latinos would more likely to be stopped by law enforcement officials now. This number is unlikely to significantly drop anytime in the immediate future, so Latino voters will still likely be primed for appeals to vote if candidates simply reach out to Latino voters.

Candidates for elected office seeking to mobilize Latino voters to the polls, thus, must recognize the need to place priority on those issues important to the Latino community namely, comprehensive immigration reform. In the survey, 59 % of Latino voters considered immigration to be the most important political issue. Comparatively, only 22 % of voters considered fixing the economy to be the most important issue a remarkable indication, given the state of economic conditions in 2010, of how important Latinos consider immigration reform.

Furthermore, Latino voters speak in a rather unified voice on the options for reform. Sixty percent of Latino voters interviewed in the ASU/NAU/NCLR survey indicated that offering an eventual pathway to citizenship would be their preferred policy outcome. Only 17 % supported immediate legalization and only 17 % supported a guest worker program. Thus, Latino voters are closer to the median position with respect to immigration reform making this an opportune issue for candidates to appeal to Latino voters and provide substantive representation without necessarily alienating blocs of other voters in the electorate. Yet, as candidates and officials from both sides of the political aisle continue to scapegoat or ignore Latino voters, the sleeping giant of American politics has little incentive to emerge from its lengthy slumber.

References

Barreto MA (2007) ¡S'ı Se Puede! Latino candidates and the mobilization of Latino voters. Am Polit Sci Rev 101(03):425–441

Barreto MA, Woods ND (2005) The anti Latino political context and its impact on GOP detachment and increasing Latino voter turnout in Los Angeles county. In: GM Segura and Bowler S (eds) Diversity in democracy: minority representation in the United States. University of Virginia Press, Charlottesville, VA, pp 148–169

Bartels LM (2010) Unequal democracy: the political economy of the new gilded age. Princeton University Press, Princeton

Bobo L, Gilliam FD (1990) Race, sociopolitical participation, and black empowerment. Am Polit Sci Rev 84(2):377–393

Bowler S, Nicholson SP, Segura GM (2006) Earthquakes and after shocks: race, direct democracy, and partisan change. Am J Polit Sci 50(1):146–159

Branton RP, Jones BS (2005) Reexamining racial attitudes: the conditional relationship between diversity and socioeconomic environment. Am J Polit Sci 49(2):359–372

Brewer MD (2005) The rise of partisanship and the expansion of partisan conflict within the American electorate. Polit Res Q 58(2):219

Campbell JE (1985) Explaining presidential losses in midterm congressional elections. J Polit 47(4):1140–1157

Carpini MXD, Keeter S (1997) What Americans know about politics and why it matters. Yale University Press, New Haven

Dahl Robert A (1961) Who governs?. Yale University Press, New Haven, CT

de la Garza RO, De Sipio L, Garcia FC, Garcia J, Falcon A (1992) Latino voices: Mexican, Puerto Rican, and Cuban perspectives on American politics
Erikson RS (1988) The puzzle of midterm loss. J Polit 50(4):1011–1029
Fiorina MP (1981) Retrospective voting in American national elections
Frymer P (1999) Uneasy alliances: race and party competition in America. Princeton University Press, Princeton
Hajnal ZL (2009) Who loses in American democracy? A count of votes demonstrates the limited representation of African americans. Am Polit Sci Rev 103(1):37–57
Hero RE (1992) Latinos and the US political system: two-tiered pluralism. Temple University Press, Philadelphia
Hutchings VL, Valentino NA (2004) The centrality of race in American politics. Ann Rev Polit Sci 7:383–408
Manzano S, Sanchez GR (2010) Take one for the team? Limits of shared ethnicity and candidate preferences. Polit Res Q 63(3):568
Marquez B, Espino R (2010) Mexican American support for third parties: the case of La Raza Unida. Ethn Racial Stud 33(2):290–312
Matsubayashi T (2010) Racial environment and political participation. Am Polit Res 38(3):471
Mayhew David (1974) Congress: the electoral connection. Yale University Press, New Haven
Pantoja AD, Segura GM (2003) Fear and loathing in California: contextual threat and political sophistication among Latino voters. Polit Behav 25(3):265–286
Wolfinger RE, Rosenstone SJ (1980) Who votes?. Yale University Press, New Haven, CT

Chapter 4
State-Level Immigrant-Related Legislation: What it Means for the Immigration Policy Debate

Robert Donnelly

The U.S. states are actively legislating on immigrant-related issues. Bill introductions have more than doubled in the past 5 years, rising from 570 in 2006 to 1,374 for first-half of 2010.[1] The trend is expected to continue in the near term, with Arizona SB 1070-copycat bills especially popular in the current session. Perceived federal policy failures are commonly given as reasons for the increase in legislation. For the growth in pro-enforcement legislation, the "porous" southern border and Washington's inability to control unauthorized migration are frequently cited. For the more modest number of pro-integration bills, the failure of federal immigration reform, with its pathway to citizenship provisions, is said to be a driving force. Other factors have influenced the timing of bill introductions—the emergence of the Tea Party movement, news-grabbing crimes allegedly involving unauthorized migrants, and recent demographic trends in the South and Midwest, among others. This chapter examines state-level immigrant-related legislation for first-half of 2010, assesses post-2010 state-legislative trends, and addresses the roles that "nativism" plays in the development of this legislation.

[1] The number of bill introductions involving immigrants rose from 570 in 2006 to 1,169 in 2007, then to more than 1,400 for the first-half of 2009, and 1,374 for the first-half of 2010. See National Conference of State Legislatures. NCSL News. "States Step Up to the Plate on Immigration: With no federal legislation, legislators move to enact local solutions", 28 July 2010. Also see "States Assert New Activist Immigration Role in Altered Political Landscape". Muzaffar Chishti and Claire Bergeron, 18 Jan 2011. Migration Policy Institute/Migration Information Source. "Midterm Elections Generate Rush of Immigration Measures". Muzaffar Chishti and Claire Bergeron, 15 Oct 2010. Migration Information Source/Migration Policy Institute.

R. Donnelly (✉)
Mexico Institute, Woodrow Wilson International Center for Scholars,
Ronald Reagan Building and International Trade Center, One Woodrow Wilson Plaza,
1300 Pennsylvania Avenue, Washington, NW DC 20004-3027, USA
e-mail: donnellr@live.unc.edu

L. Magaña and E. Lee (eds.), *Latino Politics and Arizona's Immigration Law SB 1070*, Immigrants and Minorities, Politics and Policy, DOI: 10.1007/978-1-4614-0296-1_4,

In the face of perceived federal inaction, the U.S. states are more aggressively debating and enacting immigrant-related legislation. Thematically, bills may be grouped in two main camps: (1) pro-enforcement legislation aimed at making life harder for unauthorized migrants through enhanced criminal sanctions and the denial of social services, and (2) pro-integration legislation intended to help legal immigrants through integration, citizenship, and education policy. As elaborated in greater detail in a following section, this research found that pro-enforcement bills were enacted at more than twice the rate of pro-integration bills. Geographically, legislation was introduced in almost every state, with the most conspicuous growth in the South; in first-half of 2010, all 46 assemblies then in session recorded immigrant-related bill introductions, with 44 legislatures approving legislation. Politically, support for immigrant-related legislation appeared bipartisan, and the most efficient combination for passage of pro-enforcement legislation appeared to be the duo of a Republican governor and a Republican legislature.[2]

The increase in immigrant-related legislation—throughout the country, mostly to enhance enforcement, and with the support of both parties—calls for a research plan to better understand its influences and effects. What does the rise in legislation tell us—if anything—about "xenophobia", "nativism", or anti-immigrant sentiment in the United States? And, what does it augur for comprehensive immigration reform at the federal level? This paper will address these and other questions through an analysis of the immigrant-related legislation passed at the state-level in first-half of 2010.

A principal objective of this research is to better understand the motivations behind the legislation. Is it, on balance, disposed against or toward immigrant families? What share of bills can be qualified as restrictive/punitive and what share as beneficial to immigrant and refugee households? Have the media overemphasized the punitive/restrictive aspects of high-profile legislation, such as Arizona's SB 1070, while other bills that might help immigrant families quietly and non-controversially receive less interest? In numbers, does legislation in support of immigrant integration, citizenship, and English-language education outweigh legislation that denies social services, enhances criminal sanctions, and creates new barriers to lawful employment? Which bills straddle the line and overlap both categories? And finally, how does immigrant-related legislation divide geographically and break down by party?

Another interest of the research is to better understand the political factors contributing to the increase of such legislation this decade. The refrain that the federal government's ineffectiveness at controlling the southern border explains the growth of state-level initiatives may be true. However, there are also other factors at play, e.g., the emergence of the Tea Party movement, the endurance of border vigilante groups in local immigration politics, etc. and these will be discussed over the succeeding pages. The paper additionally examines the impact that the

[2] For a survey of recent state-level immigrant-related legislation, see "The Next Wave: Employer Sanctions Bills in the States," State Legislative Update, Immigration Works USA, 3 Feb 2011.

state-level legislation, as well as the political circumstances shaping it, is having on the national comprehensive immigration reform debate, as well as on prospects for CIR passage in the short term. Finally, the paper examines the overlapping issues of "nativism", "xenophobia", and anti-immigrant sentiment, and discusses the role of these in shaping legislation.

State-Level Immigrant-Related Legislation: Why Now?

A frequent argument to explain the expansion in state-level legislation faults the federal government for failing to either secure the southern border or pass comprehensive immigration reform. The argument goes that these shortcomings have forced state assemblies to step into meet constituent's demands that action be taken on immigration. "The federal government's failure to enforce our border has functionally turned every state into a border state .... The states are stepping in and filling the void left by the federal government", said Randy Terrill, a Republican lawmaker in Oklahoma, one of the half-dozen or so states in 2011 pursuing SB 1070-like legislation.[3] The U.S. Congress is famously paralytic seeming on a range of policy issues and not just on immigration, but the argument has validity given the high salience that "undocumented immigration" obtains throughout the country. In fact, national and state polls show that respondents rate "undocumented immigration" as a pressing concern, even in locations far from the southern border and with small foreign-born populations.[4] This is still the case even as the unauthorized migrant population declines in many parts of the United States, and the unauthorized migrant population falls from its 2007 peak.[5] Moreover, the enhanced roles that state and local authorities are now playing in federal immigration enforcement also suggests that constituents may be expecting state officials to step forward more vigorously on immigration matters. Meanwhile in immigrant-friendly locales with large foreign-born populations, such as San José, CA, the failure of Comprehensive immigration reform (CIR) and the absence of strong federal leadership have forced local governments to compensate with their own integration, citizenship, and education efforts, in order to meet growing demand.[6] Another recent catalyst for pro-integration legislation at the state-level

---

[3] Julia Preston. The New York Times. Political Battle on Illegal Immigration Shifts to the States, 31 Dec 2010.

[4] New citation.

[5] For information on the unauthorized and legal immigrant populations in the United States, see Pew Hispanic Center. News release, 1 Feb 2011. "Unauthorized Immigrant Population: National and State Trends" and *U.S. illegal immigrant population steady* in National Institute for Latino Policy. 2 Feb 2011, Reuters newswire.

[6] For the specific case of San Jose, see *Context Matters: Latino Immigrant Civic Engagement in Nine U.S. Cities*. Series on Latino Immigrant Civic Engagement, summary on San Jose 61–63 Donnelly, Fox, Bada, and Selee. Woodrow Wilson Center, 2010.

was the U.S. Senate's inability to bring to a vote the D.R.E.A.M. (Development, Relief, and Education for Alien) Act in December 2010—considered the last best chance for such a vote in the foreseeable future. Nevertheless, what was a failure for the bill's backers has helped to fuel support for state-specific D.R.E.A.M. Acts, such as those being talked about in Massachusetts and Maryland.[7]

Anti-immigrant politics have contributed to the rapid growth in state legislative activism. In the run-up to the November 2010 midterms, candidates for assembly offices throughout the country scored points with voters by pronouncing in favor of copycat laws to Arizona's SB 1070 and by voicing support for the revision of state and federal birthright citizenship laws. Making campaigns referendums on undocumented immigration proved a smart strategy for some politicians, as the politics surrounding passage of Arizona's SB 1070 showed in April 2010. Facing a tough re-election bid, incumbent Governor Jan Brewer used her support of the bill as a shield, strongly deflecting a tough primary challenge from the Right and forcing her main rival to drop out. In the general election, Brewer easily trounced the Democratic candidate, former state Attorney General Terry Goddard, winning by 12 % points. Even though the main provisions of the controversial bill have been suspended, following a federal judge's injunction in July, the mere signing of the bill into law proved a boon for Brewer.[8, 9]

Beyond Arizona, candidates in 2010 blasted opponents with anti-immigrant rhetoric. Nevada Republican Senate candidate Sharron Angle called her opponent, Sen. Harry Reid, "the best friend an illegal alien ever had", while Louisiana Sen. David Vittier made a similar accusation against his opponent.[10] Elsewhere candidates from California, Colorado, and Kansas lined up to pick up endorsements from Maricopa County (Arizona) Sheriff Joe Arpaio, a leading proponent of "get tough" enforcement measures against unauthorized persons.[11] Media coverage also appeared to affect the timing and sequence of legislative activity. The widely publicized slaying of Cochise County rancher Robert Krentz in March 2010 fueled support for SB 1070 in the month before the bill was eventually voted—although initial suspicions of an unauthorized border-crossing killer have so far gone unproven. In Virginia, news reporting on the August 2010 death of nun Denise

---

[7] See *Md. legislation proposes in state tuition benefits for some illegal immigrants.* The Washington Post. Shankar Vedantam, 29 Dec 2010. For more on the legal grounds for in state tuition waivers, see the news release. MALDEF. MALDEF lauds California Supreme Court ruling upholding AB 540, waiver of out-of-state fees for all qualified students. Los Angeles, 15 Nov 2010.

[8] See Staff Commentary: "Even Mostly Unimplemented SB 1070 Still Having a Big Impact" 29 July 2010 Robert Donnelly. Woodrow Wilson Center Mexico Institute.

[9] http://www.realclearpolitics.com/epolls/2010/governor/az/arizona_governor_brewer_vs_goddard-1409.html

[10] Migration Information Source, States Assert New Activist Immigration Role in Altered Political Landscape. Migration Policy Institute.

[11] For a detailed analysis, see Midterm Elections Generate Rush of Immigration Measures. Muzaffar Chishti and Claire Bergeron. Migration Policy Institute, 15 Oct 2010.

Mosier, who was killed in a car crash caused by a drunken undocumented immigrant with two prior drunken-driving convictions, likely contributed to pro-enforcement public opinion.[12]

Trends hint that pro-enforcement state legislative activism will continue in the near term. The presence of border vigilante groups as a kind of semi-permanent backdrop in the media and the appeal of the politically influential Tea Party movement are two such forces, shaping local immigration politics at the border and elsewhere. In her book, *The Law into Their Own Hands*, Roxanne Lynn Doty suggests that border vigilante groups help to socially construct undocumented immigrants as dangers to the social order that require extraordinary controls. Though unsupported by the existing data, the assertion that undocumented immigrants are would be terrorists and violent criminals undeserving of social, political, and economic rights operates as a powerful rallying tool for some politicians, she says. Furthermore, constituting migrant populations as "enemies" and defining non-migrant U.S.-born populations as "friends" advances a simple yet effective dichotomy, which, in an increasingly diverse society, helps to unambiguously define American essentialism and national identity.[13] Another trend-shaping force is the politically influential Tea Party movement. At the 2010 midterms, contenders endorsed by the conservative Tea Party won several key Republican Senate primary contests, in Alaska, Delaware, Kentucky, and Colorado, and some Tea Party candidates won general elections, such as the senatorial and gubernatorial contests in Florida, among other races. Heading into the 2012 elections, the movement is expected to exert influence over the selection of Republican candidates in many different races, amplifying the importance of its member's views on immigration.[14]

Nativist and Xenophobic Impulses

What are the consequences of such legislative activism at the state-level? Do the bills being passed in the different assemblies reflect a pervasive nationwide disgust with undocumented immigrants and, possibly even, with the legal foreign-born? Could this sentiment culminate in tough enforcement laws like SB 1070 or repeal of the 14th Amendment and its birthright citizenship provisions? To what extent is such legislative activism properly classified as xenophobic or nativist? Or is this cycle's

---

[12] See Randal C. Archibold. "Ranchers Alarmed by Killing Near Border". The New York Times, 4 April 2010. Also see Jennifer Buske and Paul Duggan. Driver in fatal Va. Crash had previous DUI convictions, 3 Aug 2010. Washington Post.

[13] See Roxanne Lynn Doty. *The Law into Their Own Hands: Immigration and the Politics of Exceptionalism*. The University of Arizona Press, Tucson, 2009.

[14] Tea Party sympathizers assert that immigration should be decreased and that immigration causes the displacement of U.S. workers, at rates higher than moderate voters, according to a poll conducted by the University of Washington Institute for the Study of Ethnicity, Race, and Sexuality. See http://depts.washington.edu/uwiser/racepolitics.html.

wave of punitive/restrictive legislation more consistent with the anti-welfarist discourse of the mid-1990s, reflected in the immigration and welfare reform laws Congress passed in 1996?

This analysis found that the majority of the recent state-level legislation can be classified as punitive/restrictive. Yet it also found that the long arm of these laws appears to extend only to undocumented immigrants. Legal foreign-born residents, such as asylum seekers, refugees, legal permanent residents, etc. see no similar degradation of rights. They do not face the same punishments that undocumented persons face, and, in fact, this analysis found that support for pro-enforcement legislation did not necessarily preclude a legislature's passage of pro-integration bills to help legal immigrants. In fact, several states have made provisions for citizenship-promotion, English-language education, and refugee services—efforts to help the legal foreign-born—while promoting heavier restrictions and penalties against the undocumented foreign-born.

Rather than manifest outright xenophobia, the state-level legislation signals a bifurcated and ambivalent approach to the management of foreign-born populations. On the one hand, undocumented foreigners face new restrictions brought on by the recent law changes, as well as by the "devolution of enforcement" trend that has beefed up interior enforcement. They may now face pressures from local officials deputized to enforce federal immigration law under 287 (g) agreements or who are partners in the government's Secure Communities program, requiring participating local police to check the fingerprints of all arrested individuals against a Department of Homeland Security (DHS) database. In addition to the stress of possible deportation should they be arrested—though not necessarily convicted—for committing a traffic violation, undocumented migrants must also now contend with the prospect of new state criminal penalties for lacking papers, the central thrust behind the SB 1070 law being imitated nationwide.

By these comparisons, legal foreign-born residents enjoy many more rights and face many fewer restrictions than the undocumented. But this characterization is challenged, too, after taking into account the hardships that punitive/restrictive legislation places on mixed-status households and the heightened discrimination and racism that such laws—and the adverse political climate surrounding their passage—places on all Latino co-ethnics, whether "legal or illegal".[15]

What can the latest wave of punitive/restrictive legislation tell us about anti-immigrant sentiment in the United States? Is this sentiment, of concern but not of too much concern? Is it a blip on a progress chart that in time will culminate in the gradual integration of today's immigrant population, following the trajectory of prior generations? Does the principal benefit of today's punitive/restrictive legislation lay in its theatrical political-symbolic import and its effectiveness as a rallying message at election time?

[15] International Relations and Latino Politics. Meeting held on 15 Oct 2010, at Arizona State University in Tempe, Ariz. From comments from several conference attendees.

While state and local initiatives are limited in immediate scope to their respective jurisdictions, they can have repercussions at the national level. On the one hand, state and local politics affect the positions that national-level politicians are willing to stake their reelection bids on, while political rhetoric can "move the goalposts" closer to or farther from policy objectives. CIR, arguably, is one such goal whose achievement has become even more remote because of the tone of the immigration debate at the local level. And some prognostications suggest that a serious debate on CIR is impossible until at the earliest January 2013 and then only if the Republicans lose control of the House of Representatives and President Barack Obama is reelected. Local and state immigration politics can also have a tangible effect on federal enforcement policy and strategy. For example, local politics conditions support at the ground level for the continuation of "devolution of enforcement" programs such as the 287 (g) and Secure Communities programs. As noted in the recent edited volume *Taking Local Control*, which compiles studies of recent immigrant-related legislative activism in the United States, federal enforcement policy has historically relied on the sometimes tacit and sometimes more overt support of local authorities. But today's enforcement policies appear to take a qualitative step further, explicitly forging binding partnerships.

Analysis of 2010 State-Level Immigrant-Related Legislation

This study analyzed data collected by the National Conference of State Legislatures (NCSL) of state-level immigrant-related legislation passed in the first-half of 2010. The objective of this analysis was to determine what share of the bills conformed to a "punitive/restrictive" definition and what percentage fit rather in an "integrative/beneficial" category. The purpose was to provide a definitive breakdown between these two important categories, in order to determine the aggregate direction of immigrant-related legislation at the state-level. Is most of it "punitive/restrictive" or is it most of it "integrative/beneficial"? In what cases does legislation straddle both categories? Although the NCSL data do subdivide the bills into five or so categories, these topical fields avoid judgment on the essential question of whether a particular bill is designed to make life easier or make life harder for a foreign-born person. At the same time, another objective of the study was to better pinpoint the geographic distribution of the legislation and to identify trends in party composition and legislative outcome.

Methodology

This study assessed immigrant-related state-level legislation that was passed in first-half of 2010, as compiled by the National Conference of State Legislatures. Each bill was evaluated using its NCSL-drafted summary and in consultation with the actual legislation as published on the respective state legislature's website. After initial evaluation, bills were organized into one of three categories. Group A included "punitive/restrictive" legislation, such as bills dealing with enhanced local enforcement, denial of social services and benefits, higher barriers to employment and licensing, and the like. Group B encompassed "integrative/beneficial" legislation, such as bills related to refugee resettlement, funding for English-language classes, and citizenship-acquisition. Bills fitting both groups, such as appropriations, were placed in a Group C.

Some of the NCSL-collected legislation was disregarded for this study. Resolutions, such as a successful motion to institute a Louisiana Irish Week, were thrown out. Entries whose summaries were ambiguously or vaguely worded and legislation that was only obliquely "immigration-related" also were discarded, after consultations of the actual legislation. Dilemmas arose in the study, the greatest having to do with the inadequacy of the monolithic categories to enable sufficient nuance for the different kinds of legislation being passed. For example, Arizona's SB 1070, the strongest pro-enforcement bill passed at the state-level in 2010, was given the same weight in Group A as Florida House Bill 971, which placed a licensing restriction on tow truck operators who contract with the state (in fact, a spectrum may enable a more nuanced visual representation of the different forms of legislation, especially of the enforcement-related kind, the category with greatest variation). The original NCSL data compiled 195 pieces of legislation, which this analysis reduced to 116, also lowering the number of corresponding states from 43 to 37.

The analysis found that 67—or about 58 %—of all bills belonged to Category A, with the remaining 49 evenly split between Group B (24 bills) and Group C (25). The geographic distribution found that the Northeast accounted for the fewest bills with only eight compared against the Midwest (34), the South (43), and the West (31). The geographic quadrant with the most Category A (pro-enforcement) bills was the South with 32, followed by the Midwest and West with 17 and 16, respectively. The Northeast posted only two pro-enforcement bills in the first-half period. For Category B (pro-integration), the Midwest and the West posted the highest number of bills with nine and eight respectively, while the South posted only five and the Northeast two. Southern states passed six times as many Group A bills as they passed Group B bills. In comparison, the other three quadrants reported greater parity between the two dominant categories. Group A bills led Group B bills by only a 2:1 rate in both the Midwest and the West, while in the Northeast both categories had the same number of bills at two. Of the 116 bills, the analysis made the following conclusions:

Most bills favor enhanced enforcement and/or denial of social services to undocumented immigrants.

Approximately 58 % of the bills passed at the state-level in first-half of 2010 conformed to Group A, the category for bills related to enhanced enforcement, denial of social services, and higher barriers for employment and licensing. About 21 % of all bills fit Group B, the "integrative/beneficial" category, and an equal number belonged in Group C.

Geographic Distribution

Southern states account for just under half of all pro-enforcement bills in first-half of 2010.

The states of the South, as defined by the U.S. Census, accounted for 32 of the total 67 Group A bills passed in first-half of 2010. In the time period, the southern states passed six times as many Group A bills as Group B bills (32 versus 5).[16]

In Midwestern and western states, Group A bills outpace Group B bills 2–1. Group A bills surpassed Group B bills by 2–1 in both the Midwest and the West.[17]

The Northeast reports the fewest bills passed in the time period.[18]

The northeastern states passed as many Group A as Group B bills in the time period, two for each category.

Partisan Distribution

Support for pro-enforcement legislation appears bipartisan.

Support for pro-enforcement legislation appeared significantly bipartisan. 27 pro-enforcement bills were passed and signed into law by divided governments, where the legislature and the governor were of different parties or where the legislature was evenly split. Where Democrats controlled both the governorship and the legislature, 14 pro-enforcement bills were passed, but, as of the date of this study, only 10 had been formally enacted, with four awaiting the governor's signature all in Illinois.

Republican governors signed less than a third more Group A legislation into law than their Democratic counterparts: 39–27.

---

[16] The South, according to the Census, comprises Delaware; Maryland; Washington, D.C.; Virginia; West Virginia; North Carolina; South Carolina; Georgia; Florida; Kentucky; Tennessee; Alabama; Mississippi; Arkansas; Louisiana; Oklahoma; and, Texas. However, the following states were excluded from the study either because they were not in session in first-half of 2010 (Texas) or because their legislatures passed no immigrant-related legislation in first-half of 2010, according to the NCSL data (Delaware, North Carolina, and Arkansas). Washington, D.C., is not a state and does not have a state legislature, so it was not captured in the NCSL data. .

[17] The Census defines the Midwest as: Ohio, Indiana, Illinois, Michigan, Wisconsin, Minnesota, Iowa, Missouri, North Dakota, South Dakota, Nebraska, and Kansas. Of these 12 states, only Ohio and North Dakota (because it was not in session) did not record the passage of any piece of immigrant-related legislation in the period. The western states are: Montana, Idaho, Wyoming, Colorado, New Mexico, Arizona, Utah, Nevada, Washington, Oregon, California, Alaska, and Hawaii. Of these states, neither Montana nor Nevada recorded immigrant-related legislation in the time period as they were out of session, and the legislation passed in Wyoming, New Mexico, and Alaska was excluded from this analysis.

[18] The Northeast, by the Census definition, encompasses Maine, New Hampshire, Vermont, Massachusetts, Rhode Island, Connecticut, New York, New Jersey, and Pennsylvania. Immigrant-related legislation was passed in all of these states in first-half of 2010 except for in New Jersey, while the New Hampshire legislation was omitted from this analysis.

The most activist legislatures for immigrant-related legislation appeared to be those in which Republicans controlled the legislature and the governor was a Republican. A large percentage of Group A legislation (26 of 67) and a large share of all legislation (39 of 116) met both of the following two criteria: (1) the originating chamber had a Republican majority; and, (2) the governor was a Republican. Of the 26 pro-enforcement bills that passed, all but one was enacted, and the vetoed bill, Georgia Senate Bill 291, which placed permitting restrictions on immigrant gun owners, went unsigned for a reason unrelated to immigration policy.[19]

Post-2010 Legislation

Although far from exhaustive, this analysis does show the basic patterns and trends that shaped immigrant-related legislation at the state-level in first-half of 2010. The policy thrust for the majority of the legislation was on enhanced enforcement—either through "attrition" and the denial of social services and/or through tougher criminal penalties similar to SB 1070. Geographically, the center of pro-enforcement legislative activism was located closer to the South than to any other region—with the Midwest and the West in not-too-distant second place. And, politically, support for pro-enforcement policies was bipartisan, although the most efficient combination for successful passage appeared to be the duo of a Republican governor and a Republican-controlled legislature. While trends can change, in the short term it appears that these basic characteristics will hold or even harden in 2011 and beyond. Take the following most recent trends in immigrant-related legislation and debate at the state-level:

SB 1070 Copycat Bills

Lawmakers in several states are expected to introduce bills modeled on Arizona's SB 1070, in spite of the fact that a federal court enjoined in July the bill's core enforcement provisions. States where the legislation is popular include those located in politically conservative regions of the country, such as the South, and where long-term immigrant settlement is still considered a recent phenomenon

[19] In a news release, the pro-immigration reform group National Immigration Forum offers seven characteristics for states considering SB 1070-like legislation: (1) A re-elected highly motivated potential bill sponsor, (2) A legislature where a similar bill has already been introduced or that has passed a supportive resolution; (3) A conservative governor and conservative majority in the legislature. National Immigration Forum. Press release. States Take the Lead on Immigration. Katherine Vargas.

dating to the 1990s. Among states where the legislation is expected to be discussed are Georgia, Mississippi, Nebraska, Kansas, Pennsylvania, South Carolina, and Oklahoma. Emboldening legislators to take up bills may be the political bonus to be gained from publicly supporting "get tough" measures on undocumented immigrants. And the absence of a conclusive ruling on the constitutionality of SB 1070 by the U.S. federal judiciary, as well as support by the executive for "devolution of enforcement" policies, may have opened the door wider ideologically for the consideration of such laws. "States will push ahead regardless of the 9th Circuit (court decision upholding the injunction against SB 1070's core enforcement provisions)", Kris Kobach, the new Secretary of State of Kansas said in *The New York Times* article. As of January 2011, Mississippi's state Senate had passed an SB 1070-like bill, while lawmakers in Colorado lawmakers planned to introduce similar legislation, though with some important differences.[20]

Birthright Citizenship Repeal

Assertions that undocumented immigrants are motivated to give birth to "anchor babies" and exploit the U.S. birthright citizenship tradition have fueled a movement to repeal the 14th Amendment. Additionally, efforts are afoot to make statutory changes at the state-level that would deny "state citizenship" to the children of undocumented immigrants, blocking access to state social services, education benefits, and licensing privileges (driver's licenses). Such efforts could symbolise a final race to the bottom for "attrition through enforcement" advocates, considering that many states already have sharply curtailed social services for non-U.S. citizens. Anti-immigrant sentiment appears to inform the positions of some supporters of these measures. One backer of a coordinated movement to repeal citizenship in Oklahoma, Missouri, Pennsylvania, and Arizona said that the goal of the project was to eliminate "an anchor baby status, in which an illegal alien invader comes into our country and has a child on our soil that is granted citizenship automatically", he was quoted as saying in *The New York Times*.

[20] See "Colorado Introduces Arizona-Style Immigration Bill with Notable Differences." Latinovations/La Plaza, 21 Jan 2011. At the same time, support for SB 1070 may prove more valuable on the campaign trail and at the primary stage than once in office. Florida Governor Rick Scott, who took office in 2011, for example, was forced by some accounts to backpedal on promises to back similar legislation, on concerns from lawmakers that a bill would tarnish the state's reputation among Latin American investors. In Virginia's Prince William County, part of the emerging immigrant gateway of metropolitan Washington, D.C., councilman Frank Principle acknowledged in early 2011 that the economic costs outweighed the public safety benefits of implementing new anti-undocumented enforcement provisions. In remarks in the newspaper X he questioned the validity of the underlying arguments for such enforcement provisions: that undocumented immigrant population is more prone to committing violent crime than the general population. See Florida's Anti-Immigration Law Receives Cold Response: La Plaza.

Conclusion

Underlying the intense legislative activity of 2010 has been concerned deeper than dissatisfaction with the government's perceived failure to control the southern border or implement comprehensive immigration reform. Underlying the intense legislative activity of 2010 is the concern and dissatisfaction with the government's inability to conrtol immigration. It can introduce new "foreign" elements into the society. And it can wreak a kind of unexpected creative destruction. At the same time, immigration can also constructively transform communities; it can renew and revitalize the city and the suburb; and it regenerates America's national self—culturally, politically, and economically.

These are the two very distinct visions of immigration that are playing out at the state and local levels in the United States. On the one hand, states with high legal permanent resident populations with long histories of immigrant settlement and where present-day political leaders may themselves be the sons and daughters of immigrants, may have more sanguine outlooks on immigration and greater local demand to implement pro-integration measures. On the other hand, so-called non-traditional immigrant-receiving states, where Latino settlement is new, and those in historically conservative regions, may be more intensely focused on the question of "illegality", responding with measures designed to shun immigrants (denying social services) or sanction them (through new criminal justice penalties). This dichotomy is complicated by differences between certain states and certain local governments, as well as within local governments themselves, such as the conflicts that exist between cities and counties on the merits of enhanced immigration-enforcement powers.

Attitudes toward immigration are highly varied in the United States and differ not only from state-to-state but from state to county and from county to city. Across the country, as this analysis of state legislation has shown, immigration politics are a variegated patchwork, reflecting the diversity of opinion that this controversial subject inspires but also showing the way that it can inhibit the basic issue consensus needed to foster federal-level policy reform. While the growth in state legislation is commonly blamed on federal action, it may be as much a cause of this inaction as an effect.

Chapter 5
SB 1070: Testing the "Frustration" Hypothesis

Meghan McDowell and Doris Marie Provine

Arizona's Support Our Law Enforcement and Safe Neighborhoods Act, popularly known as SB 1070, is the first state law to directly challenge the federal government's claim of plenary power over enforcement of its immigration law. Arizona's law is justifiably famous (or notorious) for that accomplishment. But every milestone has its history. This chapter is about that history, specifically the history of Arizona's efforts to inform the federal government of its concerns as a border state coping with unauthorized immigration. Our study, based on the state/federal dialog over unauthorized immigration that occurred in the two decades prior to SB 1070, provides a backdrop for understanding a bit more about Arizona's motivations in enacting this law.

Journalists typically explain SB 1070 as a product of Arizona's "frustration" with the federal government's apparent inability to control unauthorized immigration from Mexico.[1] The "frustration" framing is loaded with assumptions, some of which are clearly wrong. The frustration hypothesis assumes, for example, that the federal government has been inactive in recent years in seeking to curb illegal immigration and root out violators. This is untrue. The budget of the Border Patrol is larger than it has ever been and so is the number of agents, which has doubled since 2004. The vast majority of the Border Patrol's resources have been deployed on the border with Mexico. The number of deportations to Mexico is also at an all-time high, even as the number of unauthorized immigrants entering the country appears to be declining, as indicated by the fact that border apprehensions dropped from 616,000 to 212,000 between 2000 and 2010 (Medrano 2011). Nor is it

M. McDowell · D. M. Provine (✉)
Justice and Social Inquiry, School of Social Transformation, Arizona State University, 876403, Tempe, AZ 85287- 6403, USA
e-mail: Marie.Provine@asu.edu

[1] A Google search that linked all of the following terms—"frustrated" and "Arizona" and "SB 1070" and "federal government"—produced 62,000 hits.

L. Magaña and E. Lee (eds.), *Latino Politics and Arizona's Immigration Law SB 1070*, Immigrants and Minorities, Politics and Policy, DOI: 10.1007/978-1-4614-0296-1_5,

correct to assume that the federal government has been inattentive to the desire of states to participate in enforcement. In fact, over the past decade, the federal government has been sharing immigration enforcement responsibility with states and localities at a level unprecedented in the past. In short, Arizona's "frustration" with federal immigration enforcement occurs against a backdrop of increasing federal partnerships with local authorities, and in conjunction with escalating and effective federal efforts to detect, deter, and deport people without legal status.

The frustration hypothesis also suggests that Arizona had long waited patiently for a federal "solution" to the problem of unauthorized immigration. Again, this is not the case. Arizona's efforts to control Mexicans and Mexican–Americans in the state include the infamous 1917 Bisbee deportation of over 1,000 workers in railroad boxcars to the New Mexico desert; they were protesting, among other things, the lower "Mexican wage" that had prevailed even before the territory became a state. The Arizona legislature also has a long history of actions hostile to Mexican-origin residents. In 1914, for example, Arizona passed a law requiring 80% of a company's workers to be citizens; the US Supreme Court promptly strucks it down [Traux v Raich 239 U.S. 33 (1915)].

Other legislative efforts include a 1978 ballot initiative to make English the state's official language, which was struck down in the courts. More recently, the target of concern has shifted to immigrants who lack legal status. In 2005, the state denied social services, including English classes, to unauthorized residents, and at the same time reinvigorated its effort—this time successfully—to make English the state's official language. In 2006, Arizona adopted an anti-smuggling statute law that allows smuggled immigrants to be prosecuted as if they are co-conspirators in the smuggling operation; at the same time, it restricted the eligibility of unauthorized immigrants for bail and denied in-state tuition to unauthorized residents over protests by the state's community colleges and universities. In 2008, Arizona imposed sanctions on employers who hire unauthorized immigrants, a case law that was upheld by the US Supreme Court.

Arizona seems to relish opportunities to push the boundaries in the state/federal relationship. The state engaged in lengthy litigation with federal authorities over its English Language Learners program. It has also followed an aggressively independent course in areas unrelated to immigration, such as the adequacy of prison conditions, public funding for elections, the scope of environmental controls, and most recently the imposition of health care costs on the state. As Governor Brewer warned in a March 2011 news conference: "The United States has a federal government, not a national government. For the next 4 years, Arizona will continue to pursue a policy of renewed federalism." She noted that she and the newly elected state attorney general had recently sued the federal government for its "unconstitutional failure to secure the border and to protect Arizona and its citizens against the negative effects of illegal immigration" (Nelson 2011). Arizona is also attempting to create alliances with other states to challenge federal authority to regulate firearms, health care, immigration, and endangered species (Rough 2011).

The "frustration" framing, however ill suited to the Arizona case, is nevertheless useful in reminding us that there is an on-going dialog between states and the federal government in matters pertaining to immigration. While the federal government has long claimed sole responsibility to fashion immigration policy as an aspect of its sovereign power in a world of nation states, the American constitutional plan leaves room for states to exercise some independent authority (see Neuman 1993; Skerry 1995; Filindra and Tichenor 2008; Wells 2004). Issues of immigrant integration, for example, have historically been treated as the province of states and localities.

In contrast to many journalistic accounts that stress conflicting priorities, Newton and Adams (2009) assert that the general pattern has been cooperation between local and federal authorities in immigration enforcement. Where conflict exists, it tends to be over unfunded mandates like REAL ID (Regan 2008; and see Conlan 2006). In shaping policy too, there is a history of dialog. State voices can be heard in debate over immigration policy, because states have the political and institutional power to make their views known, and because the federal government often needs logistical support and cooperation from the local level. Our system of federalism encourages conversation about what each level desires from the other (see Wechsler 1954; Derthick 2001; Nugent 2009).

Political scientists have studied the mechanisms states use to influence Congressional legislation. For example, Dinan (2010) studied the effectiveness of state lobbying efforts in the passage of the Patient Protection and Affordable Care Act of 2010, a law with significant implications for states. In this case, the states had specific concerns on which to focus their efforts. The dialog is likely to range more widely when there is no legislation on the table that might directly affect the fortunes of states. This has been the case with respect to immigration enforcement during most of the period we studied. In this situation, the richest and most consistent source of data on the state/federal conversation is likely to be Congressional hearings that feature testimony by members of Congress on behalf of their constituents and testimony from state and local officials.

The hearings we examined featured state-level complaints about unauthorized immigration and the federal government's failure to address the issue and to pay the costs that the government's lack of control imposes on states and municipalities. The record of public statements, taken as a whole, makes state concerns visible and indicates who is pressing for what kinds of change in federal immigration law. This record helps to clarify whether SB 1070 really is, as claimed, a product of Arizona's long-standing frustration with the unresponsiveness of federal decision makers to its concerns, or whether SB 1070 is better characterized as a preemptive strike, a missile launched without warning to shape public opinion and to help local officials advance their political careers.

There are many opinions about what led Arizona to adopt SB 1070, but there is a dearth of empirical evidence that bears on this question. Our study helps fill this gap. This research also adds a new dimension to the burgeoning literature on immigration-related lawmaking by states and municipalities. Most of this literature has focused on the policies themselves and their likely impact. By moving our focus forward to the complaints that states were making before they took on the task of creating their own immigration legislation, we can gain insight into why and how state laws challenging federal immigration authority come into being.

But how to make sense of the complex overlay of state and federal voices and actions related to unauthorized immigration? It is helpful to think of immigration policy-making as an example of legal pluralism, a concept that recognizes that law can come from many sources at once, and in the process can create multiple and conflicting obligations. Berman (2009) suggests that the roots of legal pluralism extend to the age of empire when conquerors met resistance from long-established communities with their own norms and rules. In our era, legal pluralism provides a way to discuss realms where the prevailing legal norms are murky, because the relevant law comes from more than one direction and the hierarchical ordering is somewhat unclear (Berman 2009, p. 228; see also Michael 2009). Sometimes lack of clarity in legal rules and obligations serves important political ends, such as conflict avoidance. Contemporary legal pluralism scholars owe a debt to Robert Cover (1981) who, a generation ago, argued that law is more than a mechanism of state control—it is also a place for various communities to advance alternative visions.

Immigration enforcement is an apt site for a legal pluralist approach to analysis. This is an area in which the federal government's priorities have often shifted without much notice (Wishnie 2001–2003). In recent decades, the federal government has added to the confusion by attempting to offload some immigration enforcement work to the local level, but it has done so without articulating clear standards or imposing much accountability. Even within the federal government, some members of Congress are at odds with federal administrators, creating a push–pull of confusing messages. Meanwhile, local communities, particularly in the area of policing, have their own priorities. Most urban police departments, for example, attempt to follow a norm of community policing, which is incompatible with vigorous efforts to detect unauthorized residence (Decker et al. 2009). At the same time, the pressure to take action on immigration-related issues at the municipal and state levels has been increasing, and is becoming more widespread as immigrants choose new destinations based on employment opportunities during the past 20 years (Terrazas 2011). Jurisdictions that are side by side may respond in very different ways to new immigrant residents, creating a multi-jurisdictional patchwork of immigration enforcement (Varsanyi et al., 2012). Declining state and local capacity to provide basic social services also exacerbates the situation. For example, as Massey and Sanchez (2010) conclude after surveying rates of indebtedness, unemployment, savings, and other measures of American well-being: "Economic, social, and political conditions have shifted so as to harden categorical divisions between immigrants and natives" (p. 58).

A Brief Review of the Relevant Literature

There is significant scholarly interest in the complex inter-governmental situation that is evolving around immigration enforcement. The informal sharing of enforcement duties that once prevailed between federal immigration-control agents and local police (see McDonald 1997) is being supplemented and sometimes displaced by formal agreements and institutional innovations initiated by the federal government, and by sometimes conflicting local initiatives (Decker et al. 2009). Scholars have dubbed this multi-headed movement toward shared enforcement authority "immigration federalism." Whether these developments should be welcomed or not, however, has been hotly contested. In the law-review literature, for example, scholars have lined up on both sides to argue for (Spiro 1994, 2001; Skerry 1995; Shuck 2007; Rodriguez 2008; Parlow 2007) and against (Wishnie 2001; Olivas 2007) the emergence of local initiatives designed to defect and discourage settlement by unauthorized immigrants.

Social scientists writing in this area have been more focused on mapping the contours of immigration federalism and exploring its implications. Filindra and Tichenor (2008), for example, argue that states have in the past played significant roles in the development of immigration policy, particularly when the federal government has been silent: "States often have been among the first to enter the void—proposing, enacting, and implementing policy innovations and controls amidst inertia at the national level" (p. 3). Miriam Wells (2004) documents the way in which the federal government has long depended on local actors to carry out its law. Others have sought to explain why there is significant variation at the local level (see Ramakrishnan and Wong 2010; Chavez and Provine 2009; Hopkins 2010).

There has been relatively little investigation into the strategic aspects of immigration federalism. Gilette's (1997) exploration at a theoretical level of the conditions that allow states to trump federal authority and promote their own programs is suggestive: "Once we create multi-function governments and allocate responsibilities among them, jurisdictional battles inevitably arise" (p. 1348). He describes the strategies each level can deploy against the other to grab jurisdiction in ambiguous situations. Perhaps most directly relevant to our data are investigations of state and local initiatives that, like SB 1070, implicitly challenge the federal government's claim of plenary power in matters related to immigration policy (see Fleury-Steiner and Longazel 2010; Provine 2009). California's Proposition 187 (Prop. 187) is a good example. This 1994 initiative, adopted overwhelmingly by California citizens, would have cut off almost all social services and educational benefits for residents who could not prove their legal status. A federal court immediately declared it unconstitutional. California's willingness to adopt such a law and the strong support it received have been examined by scholars interested in the degree to which racial anxiety motivated public approval of the measure (Calavita 1996; Jacobson 2008), but to the best of our knowledge, we are the first to examine the discussion between state and federal officials that was taking shape at the time California adopted Prop. 187.

The failure of California's initiative to survive constitutional review has not deterred other states from adopting their own legislation to deter immigrants without authorization from settling or remaining in their jurisdictions. State legislatures began adopting immigration-related laws in significant numbers beginning around 2005, with a steady increase since then. These laws are usually, but not always, opposed to the interests of unauthorized immigrants. As Newton and Adams (2009) observe, many of them simply fill in where the federal government has not yet spoken, sometimes in ways that support immigrant integration. At the same time, some of them, like Hazleton, Pennsylvania's ordinance attempting to prohibit employment and rental to unauthorized immigrants or Arizona's SB 1070 clearly are intended to push for a larger state role in immigration enforcement.

The federal government may have encouraged local interest in immigration legislation with its own efforts to delegate some of the work of immigration enforcement to state and local police. In 1996, Congress created what has been dubbed the "287g program," which provides training for local officers to assist in the enforcement of immigration law. This initial effort to enlist local police as a "force multiplier" in the effort to combat unauthorized immigration has since been expanded to provide a menu of partnering options for law enforcement (ICE 2009). A new and rapidly growing federal program, Secure Communities, is the most extensive of these new federal initiatives. It aims to link all local jails to federal immigration databases and to ease the process of reporting potential immigration violators to federal Immigration and Customs Enforcement (ICE) agents. Forty states had signed onto the program by Spring 2011. The plan is for the program to be in full operation across the United States by 2013.

SB 1070

SB 1070 might appear to be in keeping with the federal effort to involve local police and jail personnel in immigration enforcement. Its mandate that all local policing agencies in the state consider immigration status in their encounters with persons they stop for other reasons appears to be the "force multiplier" that the federal government has said it needs. A police officer who becomes suspicious that the person(s) he or she has stopped lacks legal status must report the situation to ICE agents, transporting the person to a federal facility if necessary. Failure of any police agency to prioritize enforcement in this way makes the agency subject to a citizen suit for damages. To ensure that officers will have a basis upon which to make judgments in enforcing immigration law, legal permanent residents must carry immigration papers, or risk being charged with a state misdemeanor. Other sections of SB 1070 reflect and reinforce the overall goal of the statute, which is stated explicitly: "attrition [of the unauthorized population in the state] through enforcement."

Although the federal government appears to have embraced its own form of "attrition through enforcement" (see Provine and Doty, 2011), it quickly rejected Arizona's decision to enlist local police in the enforcement effort. The Department of Justice sued to block enforcement of SB 1070, which had been scheduled to take effect in July 2010. The government won a preliminary injunction from a federal district court, which was upheld by the 9th Circuit Court of Appeals. But the substance of the suit has not yet been addressed, which leaves. State lawmakers, consistent with their posture in other matters involving challenges to federal authority, were unmoved by the federal government's reaction. State Senator Russell Pearce, a leader in the effort to adopt the law, noted that the 9th Circuit is "the most overturned in the nation" and predicted the US Supreme Court would take up the case and make "the proper ruling" (Ninzel 2011). This stance proved popular with Arizona voters. Republican leaders who voiced support for SB 1070, including the governor, received a boost in their electoral standings. All of them won their bid for office in the November 2010 elections. The U.S. Supreme Court addressed several disputed sections of the statute on June 25, 2012, rejecting all but the crucial section that requires local law enforcement to inquire about immigration status and report suspected illegal immigrants to federal authorities.

Research Problem, Methodology, and Data

The federal lawsuit to block SB 1070 leaves no doubt about the breach it created in federal/state relations. What was that relationship beforehand? Did Arizona communicate its unhappiness with the scope and pace of federal immigration enforcement over time, perhaps increasing its concerns before the passage of SB 1070? How successful have Congressional hearings been in capturing the concerns of the states as they confront unauthorized immigration? And how responsive has the federal government been to these concerns? More generally, we seek to understand the relationship between local, state, and federal lawmakers in legal-pluralist terms that recognize the capacity of each level of the system to have meaningful input into law. This approach has methodological implications, as Berman (2009) notes in his review of contemporary legal pluralist research: "A pluralist account encourages a more microempircal analysis of how… norms are articulated, deployed, changed, and resisted…" (p. 236).

To create the account that follows, we consulted two decades (1990–2010) of Congressional hearings to track the conversation among members of Congress and state and local officials. The hearings we reviewed were selected on the basis of their engagement with unauthorized immigration. In addition to addressing issues related to unauthorized immigration, we only reviewed hearings that featured a *conversation between* members of Congress and state/local officials. If no state/local officials were invited to testify at a given hearing, it was excluded from our analysis. We chose 1990 as a starting point in order to capture whatever debate presaged California's decision to adopt Prop. 187. We broke up the rest of the period under study into segments in order to highlight other possible influences on the discussion. Thus, the 1990–1995 segment highlights the period preceding Prop. 187 (passed in 1994); the 1996–2000 period should reflect the impact of significant changes in federal law that occurred in 1996; the 2001–2005 period allows us to assess whether the terrorist attack on the World Trade Center and Pentagon had an impact on the discussion about unauthorized immigration; lastly, the 2006–2010 period incorporates the flurry of legislative activity on the state and local level.

This material can help us answer the questions we have posed about Arizona's dialog with Congressional committees over the past 20 years. It also helps to answer a broader set of questions about: (a) How local actors frame the need for reforms in federal immigration policy; (b) What is on the table in these discussions; and (c) Who is involved in the conversation. This information also allows us to compare the record of complaints received in the hearings with actions by Congress that could be considered a response to these complaints. Taken together, the hearings provide a context with which to speculate about Arizona's motives in enacting SB 1070.

To select hearings for this analysis, we utilized the Lexis-Nexis database "Congressional Universe." Using this material, we analyzed the prepared statements of witnesses at each hearing. This allowed us to clearly identify the positions of the participants. We decided against relying on our interpretation of the back and forth exchanges between witnesses and members of Congress in light of Laver et al. (2003) recommendation that scholars assess "positions of political actors [using] the texts they generate" (p. 311). For clarification, we also consulted any additional documents submitted for the record, but we did not rely specifically on this material.

Each prepared statement was examined using techniques of conventional content analysis (see Hsieh and Shannon 2005). We developed a thematic categorization schema and hand coded the statements accordingly. We recorded which states and state actors participated, what issues were raised, and whether these issues have changed over time. In total, we reviewed prepared statements from 27 hearings; 12 that took place from 1990 to 1999 and 15 that occurred from 2000 to 2010.

Witnesses were placed into one of five categories: (1) federal officials (e.g. Immigration and Customs Enforcement agents); (2) state officials (e.g. Treasurer for the State of California); (3) members of Congress; (4) citizens (clearly identified as such in the official record); and (5) experts (i.e. professors, demographers, and statisticians). A typical hearing might combine two federal officials, two state officials, six members of Congress, and one or two experts, each of whom prepared statements for the record. Citizens were rarely heard from. Only seven individual citizens participated over the 20-year time period.

State participation was extremely skewed. Overall, 29 states took part at least once during the 20 years of immigration hearings we reviewed. California was by far the most frequent and consistent "voice" in the conversation, with 59 state officials, citizens, or members of Congress from California speaking on behalf of the state from 1990 to 2010. The vast majority of California's participation (43 individuals) is clustered around 1990–1995, the era of Prop. 187. The next most frequent participant behind California was Texas, with 24 participants overall. At least one person representing Texas' interests testified during each time period, but participation surged between 2006 and 2010, when 16 prepared statements were submitted for the record. This increase reflects a national trend beginning in roughly 2005 of increased state legislative activity around issues of immigration reform (see National Council of State Legislators 2011). Florida also submitted 24 prepared statements, but the focus of its participation tended to be narrower than California's. All but two of its statements occurred between 1990 and 1995 and corresponded with the 1994 "Cuban migration crisis" that heightened anxieties related to unauthorized immigration across the state. California and Texas focused their concerns more broadly over problems they perceived with unauthorized immigration and the government's response. The frequency of their participation seems to correspond with periods of moral panic over immigration and undocumented immigrants and fiscal down turn. The remaining high-volume participants were: Arizona (9), North Carolina and New York (7), and Nevada (5). No other state submitted more than four statements during the 20-year period.

In the following sections, we examine the content of the conversation during the hearings, broken down by time periods, to determine what issues were being raised by the states and whether these issues changed from one period to another. We begin with a brief reference to immigration-related events of the period, including federal legislative initiatives. The body of each segment is made up of a narrative, with examples, of the content and character of the issues raised during that segment of time. We pay particular attention to Arizona's role in the conversation, and when Arizona played a role in the period under examination, we discuss it separately.

1990–1995

With nine hearings on unauthorized immigration, this was the most active period we reviewed. These conversations occurred against the backdrop of the perceived failure of the 1986 Immigration Reform and Control Act (IRCA) to achieve one of its principal objectives: preventing workers without legal status from being hired by US employers. Participants in the hearings were unanimous in denouncing the 1986 law and complaining about the continuing flow of immigrants into their states. The discussion never touched on the part the law that is best remembered today, the legalization of roughly 3 million immigrants who were residing in the United States at that time. Daniels (2004) characterizes this period as a time of resurgent anti-immigrant sentiment, but with none of the usual indicators associated with anti-immigrant periods: "the economy was expanding, unemployment was declining, and there was no widely perceived external threat" (p. 239). The first World Trade Center bombing, which occurred in 1993, was, of course, an external threat, but it was not widely perceived as such in the hearings; there were only passing references to it during this 5-year period.

The principal theme in the 1990–1995 hearings was the continuing attraction of the United States to impoverished foreign workers and the need to shut down this "magnet." The magnet metaphor came up 17 times in testimony in this period. New Jersey Representative William Martini's statement prepared for a 1994 hearing is typical:

> Our immigration policies have created a cycle of dependence on the Federal Government. *Like a magnet*, the benefits that illegal immigrants know they will receive when they come to this country act as an incentive to come. Illegal immigrants take advantage of federal programs such as Head Start, Aid to Families with Dependent Children, the Earned Income Tax Credit, Home Energy Assistance, Housing Assistance, WIC, and even the Federal school lunch program. Too often newly arrived immigrants learn to take advantage of these programs instead of contributing to the system. When it becomes easier to receive federal benefits than to work, a cycle of perpetual dependence is created [emphasis added].

While Martini worried about immigrants becoming welfare dependent because of generous federal program, others, such as Florida Representative Porter Goss, saw an unfunded mandate. From Goss's perspective, the federal government was letting immigrants in with lax enforcement, but passing most of the burden onto the states and municipalities:

> Across the nation it has become abundantly clear that the demands on agencies providing services to immigrants far outstrip the resources allocated to them. The federal government has shirked its responsibility, essentially foisting the financial consequences of its failure to control the country's borders onto state and local governments. The bottom line is that taxpayers in the five most highly impacted states (of which my state of Florida ranks third) bear 80 % of the financial burden for the outgrowth of federal immigration policies.

Many participants echoed this point with detailed complaints about the immigrant-related costs of public education and emergency room care and other programs that states are obliged to bear under federal requirements. Indeed, state and local concern over the "skyrocketing" costs associated with "illegal immigration" set the tone of all of these conversations. Materials submitted for the consideration of members of Congress reinforced this theme.[2]

The casting of characters could not have been clearer. An all-powerful federal government, inexplicably and inconsiderately, was laying an unfair burden on the states and local governments, which were powerless to resist these mandates. The federal government was clearly and selfishly shirking its constitutional responsibilities, as Florida Senator Bob Graham complained in a 1994 hearing:

> The federal government has never fully addressed its fundamental responsibility for our nation's immigration policy as enumerated in Article I, Section 8 of the Constitution. That power and singular responsibility was conferred upon the Federal Government by states "to establish a uniform rule of naturalization." Consequently, immigration and naturalization is a core, but often failed, responsibility of the Federal Government. Individual states have no capacity, either under law or in resources, to control access of illegal entrants to our nation. Unfortunately, when the Federal Government does not adequately address its responsibility for illegal immigration, State and local government is often left with the burden of that failure. Until the federal government is required to pay for the results of its own immigration enforcement policies, it has little incentive to get serious about the problem. States and localities, unfortunately, do not have that luxury.

---

[2] For example, California Governor Pete Wilson submitted a fifty-page document for the record titled "The Unfair Burden" that detailed the costs of unauthorized immigration to the state.

This emphasis on the incapacity of the states to control the costs imposed on them might seem ironic, given the passage of California's Prop. 187 in the same year that witnesses voiced many of these complaints. Participants did mention Prop. 187 from time to time, but they appeared to see it as a mark of local outrage with federal neglect rather than as a solution to the problem of unfunded mandates. As Governor Pete Wilson explained: "It was Californians' justified resentment at being mandated by Washington to pay for these services that caused the overwhelming vote for Prop 187 and caused it to be put on the ballot in the first place. It is the very problem that the 104th Congress must cure if we are to achieve an end to this crisis sooner rather than later."

During these hearings, there were frequent demands for reimbursement for the costs the federal government had imposed through its lax enforcement. Almost every testimony raised this issue. The talk was tough. Strategies mentioned to compel federal reimbursement ranged from a lawsuit against the federal government on behalf of the seven states most impacted by unauthorized immigration to an unusual suggestion by then Florida Governor Lawton Chiles. He urged that states be permitted to distribute a federally funded "alien charge card" to unauthorized immigrants to pay for the state and local services they used, such as school and health care.

State and local officials also advocated for "meaningful changes in the availability of public services to illegal immigrants." During a hearing in 1993, Kimberly Belshe, the Deputy Secretary at the California Health and Welfare Agency, outlined this position:

> Controlling the border alone isn't enough. In fact, there is little point in even having a Border Patrol if we're going to continue to reward those who successfully violate U.S. law and enter our country illegally. So the Governor is urging Congress to repeal the federal mandates that require states to provide health care, education, and other benefits to illegal immigrants. We must repeal the incentives that now exist for people to immigrate to this country illegally. *To stem the flow, we must control and turn off the magnet* [emphasis added].

The metaphor of the magnet, according to some speakers, included birthright citizenship. Indeed, an entire hearing in 1995 was devoted to the issue of birthright citizenship during which California Representative Anthony Beilenson argued that granting automatic citizenship to children born on US soil makes illegal immigration "attractive" because it operates as an incentive-reward system. At a different hearing, also held in 1995, California Representative Brian Bilbray addressed birthright citizenship with this argument:

> Children born to illegal alien parents in the United States should not automatically be citizens, as in the current practical interpretation. Automatic citizenship status makes these children, and, by extension, their non-citizen parents, eligible for federal and state benefits. Taxpayers must then pay for the child and unofficially through fraud and abuse, pay benefits to the parents of the child.

The move to criminalize unauthorized immigration began in earnest in 1994 with a hearing devoted solely to issues related to "criminal aliens." It became a consistent theme in hearings from that point forward, though the term "criminal aliens" was never clearly defined by the speakers. The statement of California Representative Anthony Beilenson illustrates two of the problems states complained about in the hearings: the costs to localities of housing noncitizens convicted of crimes; and the possibility of their return after deportation because of lax federal border controls:

> States and local governments have no jurisdiction over immigration law, no authority to deport aliens who are convicted of crimes, and no authority to ensure that those deported are not permitted to re-enter the country, but do have responsibility to incarcerate illegal immigrants who commit crimes.

Beilenson pointed out that states and local governments have been forced to sue the federal government to try and get the government to take custody of several thousand "illegal immigrants." Federal reimbursement for housing them in local facilities, state representatives complained, did not come near matching actual costs. Representative Beilenson told the federal government to expect more demands of this kind from states and localities as they "try to cope with the strain that the federal government's failed immigration policy places on their budgets."

In sum, the proposals for reform during the early to mid-1990s emphasized three basic weaknesses in the federal system: (1) the "magnet" created by federally mandated social services to unauthorized migrants; (2) lack of federal reimbursement to the states for costs associated with extra-legal migration; and (3) inadequate border security to prevent migration from the global south that created burdens on states and municipalities. These complaints emphasized the inability of states and municipalities to act in the enforcement field. If the federal government were to feel the sting of state disapproval, it would be through lawsuits for reimbursement of costs spent on housing criminal aliens.

Where was Arizona in the Conversation?

Arizona was represented in this period by Governor Fife Symington, Senator Jon Kyl, and Representative Bob Stump. Each of them faulted the federal government for failing, in Symington's words, to carry out its "fundamental responsibility to defend borders and guarantee state protection against invasion." The federal government had created a burden so heavy, Symington complained, that states and localities "cannot meet their responsibilities to constituents." The Arizona spokespersons varied in their suggestions for change. Symington stopped short of making specific demands or proposing any reforms. Senator Kyl advocated technological solutions to increase border security and requested an equitable distribution of funds to border states. Representative Bob Stump took a more radical approach: he sponsored legislation that would have placed a moratorium on most forms of legal immigration. Notably, absent from these statements is any warning that the state might be planning initiatives of its own. Surprisingly, there was no discussion of the fact that, along with six other states, Arizona had sued the federal government to force it to reimburse the state for costs associated with unauthorized immigrants (see Verhovek 1994).

1996–2000

The national mood had shifted significantly by the time these hearings were held. Federal policy had also shifted in response to the more restrictive mood. In 1993, the federal government launched Operation Hold the Line in El Paso and in 1994 it initiated Operation Gatekeeper in San Diego to prevent unauthorized immigration from Tijuana, Mexico. Newton (2008) studied Congressional hearings in the period between 1994 and 1996 and found many harsh statements suggesting that immigrants were unworthy of social membership in the United States. In 1996, President Clinton signed into law three pieces of immigration-related legislation that appear to have been designed to respond to public opinion aroused by California's adoption of Prop. 187.[3] These laws wrote stricter detention and deportation policies into law while narrowing humanitarian relief and severely restricting welfare benefits for many noncitizens. They set aside more money for Border Patrol and initiated plans for a wall between the United States and Mexico. The federal government also, for the first time, offered a formal invitation to local police to become involved in immigration enforcement with the 287g program in the Illegal Immigration Reform and Immigrant Responsibility Act. In Wishnie's (2001–2003) words, "The restrictionist immigration agenda was plainly ascendant" (p. 283).

Some of the provisions in the 1996 trio of federal immigration laws were responsive to complaints states had been making in the preceding period, which may help account for why only three pertinent hearings were held during this 5-year span. In these three hearings, state and local officials continued to highlight Washington's failure to "adequately control the border" and "pay the bill" for immigration-related costs incurred by the states. California's Governor Pete Wilson went a step further in advocating an end for all unfunded mandates that force states to give benefits to unauthorized immigrants (illegal aliens), arguing that we need to:

> …establish a national policy which specifies that the federal government can no longer impose mandates on state and local governments by forcing them to provide taxpayer-financed benefits to illegal aliens. The decision should rest solely in the hands of state and local authorities deciding where their resources ought to go.

Another new idea came from Salt Lake County Commissioner Mary Callaghan, who suggested that local police should be authorized to deliver unauthorized immigrants convicted of crimes to federal authorities in order to save incarceration costs:

> We ask that when an individual is brought to the jail on a criminal charge and it is determined that he is an undocumented immigrant, we desire the authority to then assist the INS in transporting that person across state lines to an INS holding facility in Denver or Las Vegas.

[3] The Illegal Immigration Reform and Immigrant Responsibility Act, The Anti-Terrorism and Effective Death Penalty Act, and the Personal Responsibility and Work Opportunity Reconciliation Act (see Nevins 2010; Daniels 2004).

Utah representatives were not interested, however, in enforcing "INS laws." Rather, the idea was to place the burden of "criminal aliens" squarely on the shoulders of the federal government as soon as possible. It is significant that Utah considered the issue of criminal aliens sufficiently important that it asked for this hearing to be held in Utah. The contrast with Arizona could not have been clearer. Arizona did not participate in this period, nor did it ever, in the 20-year period that we examined, hold a special in-state hearing devoted to concerns over unauthorized immigration.

Commissioner Callaghan's comments are consistent with the stance, articulated throughout the 1990s, that the federal government is solely responsible for incarcerating immigrants who enter the country unlawfully and then commit crimes. In the aftermath of 9/11 we will see this position shift in favor of an emphasis on interagency cooperation rather than a strict division of powers between local, state, and federal agencies. The magnet metaphor, so prominent in the first period, is less in evidence, maybe because the 1996 restrictions on federal welfare eligibility and the provision of block grants in some programs were responsive to the magnet argument.

2001–2005

The events of 11 September 2001 reignited the conversation around the US immigration system and renewed calls for comprehensive reform. The 2001 USA Patriot Act, with its authorization of deportation without trial or hearing, was one response to this concern. The conversation between states and the federal government around immigration reflected the new security concerns. Given this, the conversation changed, both in terms of emphasis and suggestions for reform. The seven hearings we reviewed from 2001 to 2005 indicate that post-9/11 state and local concerns were now, for the first time, characterized in terms of issues of technology (i.e. biometrics, fool-proof social security cards, national I.D. cards, and so forth) and terrorism. Notably, unauthorized immigration and terrorism were conflated during the hearings and failure to secure the border became linked to a sense of national, rather than local, vulnerability to an external threat. Comments from Texas Representative John Abner Culberson and California Representative David Dreier illustrate this point:

> I am convinced that our porous borders present the most serious *national* security threat that America faces…I am now convinced that you do not need to go to Baghdad to see the war on terror—you can go to Laredo…The southern border is truly the frontlines of the war on terror because of the threat posed by al-Qaeda and criminal organizations. The world has changed significantly since 1996…As the 9/11 Commission noted, our border security system must be evaluated to ensure that it cannot be taken advantage of by terrorists and criminals.

During the hearings, the emphasis on federal responsibility (and irresponsibility) remained consistent, however, we noted a shift in how state and local participants framed the federal government's shortcomings. 9/11 had entered the conversation about secure borders, and the way the problem was characterized had also changed.

There were fewer generalities and simple calls for more resources than at earlier points in the conversation. The emphasis had shifted to more specific recommendations for change: (1) the lack of an adequate technological infrastructure and (2) lack of interagency cooperation. Members of Congress, representing their states, figured prominently in this discussion. The testimony of Kansas Senator Sam Brownback and Washington Senator Maria Cantwell and Iowa Senator Chuck Grassley exemplify this new emphasis:

> The war against terrorism is a war won by information. The more information we have, the better our chances of winning. The more information our defenders can share, the stronger our line of defenses. The better grasp we have on our immigration procedures and practices, the better we can secure our borders and our safety—Kansas Senator Sam Brownback (2001).
>
> How can we effectively secure our borders from terrorists? By improving the quality and sharing of identity information; improving the screening of foreign nationals seeking entry on US visas; improving the awareness of comings and goings of these foreign nationals as they enter and exit our country; and increasing the number of Border Patrol and immigration personnel at our borders—Washington Senator Maria Cantwell (2001).
>
> We should implement technologies needed to prevent illegal or criminal aliens from entering. We need to create tamper-resistant visas and passports. We need to invest in an effective biometric system and provide the scanners to read the information on border crossing cards—Iowa Senator Chuck Grassley (2001).

Several participants were less sanguine about the capacity of new technology to solve the problem of unauthorized immigration, once again repeating the "magnet" metaphor employed during previous hearings. These speakers returned to the old theme of the attractions of migrating to the United States. As Indiana Representative John Hostettler explained during a 2005 hearing, "We will only be able to assert control over illegal immigration when we can turn off the job magnet that draws most illegal aliens to our country." T.J. Bonner, a union representative for Border Patrol agents concurred adding, "Once the employment magnet is turned off, however, people will soon realize that it is futile to circumvent our immigration laws in hopes of improving their economic lot in life."

As we move into the present era (2006–2010), the ideology underpinning the magnet metaphor would become (re)articulated as "attrition through enforcement." Proponents of attrition through enforcement argued, "The only way to begin to control the illegal immigration influx is to create conditions by which those immigrants will not desire to enter the country illegally in the first place" (Prepared Statement of California Representative David Drier 2006). Attrition through enforcement would gain international notoriety when SB 1070 was signed into law in 2010.

Where was Arizona in the Conversation?

The term "attrition through enforcement" was not part of the conversation in this period, even in the testimony of Arizona representatives, who spoke in two hearings in the 2001–2005 period. In 2001, Representative Jeff Flake issued a joint statement with Delaware Representative Michael N. Castle calling for "the implementation of Sect. 104 of the IIRIRA that mandated the [creation] of a system to provide new machine-readable biometric Border Crossing Cards." Flake and Castle also advocated for an "integrated, computerized entry-exit system [to link] ICE, Customs, Consulates, Universities, and other law enforcement agencies' [databases to] monitor and track students, tourists, and other visa-holders." Their joint statement clearly reflects the post-9/11 sentiment that seeks to improve border security by using technology and increasing interagency information sharing and cooperation.

Senator Jon Kyl's statement during a 2003 hearing on border technology and terrorism is similar. He focused on three ways "terrorists exploit our Nation's visa processing and immigration inspection system," emphasizing the need to employ "better technology," particularly identification cards that "contain a biometric tamper-proof identifier" as a means to prevent the creation and use of fraudulent documents and to deter human smuggling rings.

2006–2010

The key events in this final period of our study were economic and political. By late 2007, the United States was experiencing the worst economic recession since the 1930s. Coupled with the failure to pass comprehensive immigration reform in preceding years, immigrants became—more than in any period studied here—a scapegoat for the nation's sour economic fortunes. Massey and Sanchez (2010) writing to describe this period, note "a reception that is more hostile to immigrants than at any time since the Great Depression. Anti-immigrant rhetoric in the public sphere has reached a crescendo, public opinion against foreigners has hardened, and enforcement budgets and deportations are at record levels" (p. 80). The mood is indicated in part by the rise in anti-immigrant legislation at the state level (see e.g. Chavez and Provine 2009).[4]

We reviewed eight hearings held between 2006 and 2010. This was the second-highest level of activity in the 20-year period we studied, just behind 1990–1995. The prepared statements of state and local representatives continue to reflect one of the main themes of the 20-year conversation between states and the federal government: that the responsibility to secure the US–Mexico border belongs to the federal government alone. We found two important discursive shifts, however. First, there is a perceptible change in the way states describe their own role in dealing with the negative impacts of unauthorized immigration. The constant refrain during the 1990s that the federal government must take *full* responsibility for unauthorized immigrants had been reframed by 2006 to include a threat to "go at it alone" if the federal government continued to fail to meet its responsibilities.

---

[4] According to the National Conference of State Legislatures (2011) in 2010 forty-six states and the District of Columbia passed 208 immigration-related laws and adopted 138 resolutions—reflecting a slight rise in activity from 2009.

In other words, many participants argued that the responsibility to secure the borders belongs to the federal government, but if it cannot meet this responsibility, then it does not have the right to tell states how to deal with unauthorized immigrants that settle in their jurisdictions. Some speakers referred to the rise in state and local legislation as evidence of what one border sheriff called "local solutions to solve local problems":

> Because of [the financial] burdens and the frustrations that recent Administrations, including the present one, have essentially imposed by abdicating enforcement of immigration law, many States and localities have decided to try and fix the problem themselves. They have considered and often enacted legislation aimed at reducing the negative impacts of illegal immigration. According to the National Conference of State Legislatures, as of April 13, 2007, 1,169 immigration-related bills and resolutions have been introduced in the legislature in all 50 states. That is more than twice the number introduced last year. The bills touch on every immigration-related policy, from receipt of public assistance, to education, to voting (Iowa Representative Steve King).

Second, there is a new emphasis in this period on crime along the border—from drug cartels to human smuggling rings. The social construction of the imagined unauthorized immigrant shifts from that of a worker in search of a better life to that of a hardened criminal and/or potential terrorist. Texas Sheriff A. D'Wayne Jernigan, representing the Texas Border Sheriffs Organization at a 2006 hearing on criminal violence along the southern border, explains:

> We have seen the border become more violent and criminally active than at any point in our careers. Our officers rarely encounter the socio-economic illegal alien of the past, but routinely encounter criminal illegal aliens.

Texas Sheriff Sigifredo Gonzalez, Jr. echoed Jernigan's concern:

> We were used to seeing many persons enter the country illegally; however, recently, many of these persons are not longer entering the country to look for legitimate employment. We are now seeing that many of these persons are members of ruthless and violent gangs.

Jernigan went on to point out that the creation of Texas Border Sheriffs Organization "was done out of frustration in what we felt was the inadequacy of our federal government to protect our border in preventing a potential terrorist from entering the country." His comments illustrate the "go at it alone" attitude that merges, somewhat incongruously, with the theme that border crossers are more dangerous than ever and may include potential terrorists.

The now familiar magnet trope was deployed once again to highlight states' concern that the federal government's problems stem, not just from lax enforcement, but also from its failure to eliminate the "magnet" that draws immigrants to the United States. This time the emphasis was on jobs and holding businesses accountable. In his 2007 prepared statement, California Representative Brian Bilbray argued:

> The immigration status quo is intolerable. Not because our immigration laws are broken, but because they are not vigorously enforced. Immigration enforcement has failed primarily because Administrations for 20 years have not enforced sanctions on employers who hire illegal immigrants... The practice of rewarding illegal behavior and ignoring current immigration laws must come to an end.

Later during a 2008 hearing, North Carolina Representative Health Schuler makes a similar point:

> Dishonest employers who seek to exploit low-skilled immigrant labor are the primary cause for the rapid increase in our illegal population. In most cases, the jobs they offer act as a magnet, drawing people over 20-foot walls and through inhumane desert conditions to find work.

Suggestions for reform during this era were, for the most part, consistent with those from earlier hearings. Strategies to eliminate the magnet continued to be emphasized, but with a heightened focus on the right of states to have a greater say in immigration policy and enforcement efforts, particularly in light of the continued federal failure to secure the border and pass comprehensive reform. For example, in his prepared statement Corey Stewart, Chairman of the Prince William County Board of Supervisors, requested "Congress broaden the powers of local government to enforce federal immigration law. Federal legislation needs to clearly enunciate our roles and the relevant authority." Stewart's statement suggests that the post-9/11 emphasis on interagency cooperation has resulted in some confusion over who has "clear legal authority" with regard to immigration policy and enforcement. Despite the confusion, interagency partnership continued to be viewed by several speakers as an integral component of immigration enforcement efforts.

Where is Arizona in the Conversation?

Arizona participated more between 2006 and 2010 than in any other time period. State representatives testified at four Congressional hearings. Much of Arizona's testimony was consistent with the theme of state/federal partnerships. Sheriff Larry Dever of Cochise County reminded the federal government that: "every federal initiative has local consequences. It is critical that local authorities be involved in the early stages of the planning process to assure that these consequences are clearly understood and considered." Arizona Governor Janet Napolitano elaborated on the local consequences theme, without suggesting partnerships between levels in her 2007 testimony. She emphasized the "need for Washington to deliver a law that is both enforced and enforceable. Every day the citizens of my state, Arizona, grapple with the stark reality of an unsecured border." Napolitano went on to characterize the federal failure as exemplifying both "sins of omission" (via ineffective federal policy) and "sins of commission" (via failure to fully fund the SCAAP program, which reimburses states for costs associated with incarcerating unauthorized immigrants who commit local crimes). In her 2008 testimony, Representative Gabrielle Giffords focused on issues of transparency and accountability within the Department of Homeland Security. Along with Representative Bilbray, Giffords introduced "H.R. 5552, the Border Security Accountability Act" in an effort to begin "a thorough assessment of the staffing, equipment, training, and the policies for all the border security functions."

From the perspective of SB 1070, the most interesting contribution from an Arizona spokesperson was Representative Jeff Flake's testimony in a 2007 hearing on the STRIVE Act—a proposal for comprehensive immigration reform. Representative Flake articulated the theme of attrition through enforcement, not as a prediction of what Arizona would do a few years later, but in connection with a general warning about the negative consequences of federal inertia: "Tired of waiting for Congress to act, states are trying to take matters into their own hands." Later in his statement he focuses on what he sees as the real purpose of most state immigration legislation and resulting patchwork of enforcement policies:

> State laws dealing with immigration issues have generally followed a strategy of attempting to encourage immigrants, particularly those without proper documentation, to leave the state *by making life for them untenable*...When Congress fails to act, we run the risk of what we are seeing currently: a patchwork of differing state laws that will be ineffective at providing a comprehensive solution [emphasis added].

Discussion and Conclusion

The constant refrain throughout the 20 years of state/federal hearings examined here is of budget-straining burdens borne by states and municipalities because of the presence of unauthorized immigrants. Constituents were portrayed as outraged, frustrated, and angry about this drain on taxpayer resources. The burdens stemming from unauthorized immigration varied depending on the type of immigrant. "Criminal aliens"—a term that in this context encompasses anyone who has been picked up by the police and held in a local jail—were portrayed as dangerous to the community and expensive to house. Economic immigrants were described as a burden on local social services, though not a threat to the social order.

The concerns about uncontrolled immigration were mostly, but not entirely, economic. Occasionally, speakers mixed in concerns about threats to American culture, as John Andrews, past president of the Colorado Senate, did in his 2007 testimony:

> Right now millions of Coloradans see the invasion of illegal aliens as an urgent problem for our state, and we attribute that problem to the federal government's failure to keep its bargain with Americans everywhere for secure borders and the rule of law. Our schools, our health care system, and our criminal justice system are groaning under this burden. *Our common culture and common language are fraying*. We feel that Washington has let us down [emphasis added].

Concerns about cultural erosion were the exception, however. A few speakers took the opposite tack, expressing admiration for the courage of those who cross the border on foot seeking work, but always in the context of arguments that the border should be more secure. Their rationale was that tighter controls might deter dangerous crossings.

The federal government was faulted for failure to enforce its immigration laws and failure to reimburse states and municipalities for the costs created by lack of enforcement. Against this backdrop, speakers offered various solutions. Border security was a major concern, but so was the "magnet" of jobs and benefits that "attracts" immigrants to try to enter and stay in the United States. The prime magnetic attraction, of course, is employment. But the speakers focused almost as much, surprisingly, on benefits and birthright citizenship as attractants. The two are intertwined in these testimonies—the argument was that American-born children are eligible for benefits that their unauthorized parents consume. Hence, the solution that some speakers offered was to eliminate citizenship for children of unauthorized parents. One speaker went so far as to claim that women frequently come to the United States to have citizen babies who (it was falsely asserted) would then bestow citizenship on their parents.

During almost all of these discussions, unauthorized immigrants were perceived to be Mexican, poor, and unintegrated into American society. The Florida hearings, with their focus on Cuban "boat people" were an exception. There seemed to be an unspoken consensus that unauthorized immigrants could be managed without endangering the rights of legal immigrants. Speakers seemed unconcerned that the dividing line between legal status and its absence might be hard to detect in some cases; there was no reference to the complexity of US immigration laws and the reality of mixed status families and instances of precarious status. Most striking, perhaps, was the assumption that so much rests on legal status—those with it are assets to society, and those without it are a drain.

The issues that speakers addressed changed from time to time in response to external events. National security, for example, emerged as a primary focus of concern after the 9/11 attacks on the World Trade Center and Pentagon. After 2005, the unprecedented activity of states and municipalities in immigration legislation became the basis for warning the federal government about the prospect of patchwork laws. (In the 1995–2000 period California's Prop. 187 served a similar function.) Another change was internal: states adjusted their rhetorical strategy in the later years. In the first decade and a half of hearings, they stressed their *incapacity* to respond to unauthorized immigration, thus putting the moral onus on the federal government to act, or at least to reimburse their costs. In the last 5 years of hearings, advocates stressed the *capacity* of states to legislate in this area, which would create an undesirable patchwork of conflicting laws.

Where does SB 1070 fit into this picture? It could be seen as the logical outgrowth of the "magnet" complaint. Arizona's law is designed to make unauthorized immigration as unattractive as possible, using as many state resources as possible to that end. But no one in these hearings seems to anticipate such a move. Even Representative Flake, who came closer than anyone to articulating the rationale of SB 1070, never linked his concern to law enforcement. His remarks, like those around Prop. 187 and the rise of state legislation generally, were really a warning to the federal government that it needed to act, and act effectively, to prevent an undesirable result.

The hearings we reviewed suggest that Arizona did not warn members of Congress that it was about to break new ground in legal territory with SB 1070. The adoption of this law arose outside of the familiar, comfortable conversation of Congressional hearings. In this way it was unlike birthright citizenship or employer sanctions, which had been focal points a decade before they emerged on the current political landscape. The claim that SB 1070 arose out of Arizona's "frustration" with federal inaction misleadingly suggests a more open and forthcoming relationship with the federal government than actually existed. It is more accurate to characterize SB 1070 as a pre-emptive strike designed to move the national conversation about unauthorized immigrants in a new direction, away from any talk of a "path toward citizenship" toward an enforcement-only approach, and in the process to boost local politicians running on an anti-Washington agenda. Robert Cover (1981) suggests that such confrontational moves have always been part of "the inner logic" of "our federalism." The constitutional plan includes opportunities for cooperation and deference, but also accommodates confrontation and conflict from the states (p. 682).

Cover's observation reminds us that American federalism is the kind of complex arena for political exchange that can best be studied through the lens of legal pluralism. As Berman notes in his review of this literature:

> This is a world in which claims to coercive power, abstract notions of legitimacy, and arguments about legal authority are only parts of an ongoing conversation, not the final determining factors. It is a world in which jurisgenerative practices flower, creating opportunities for contestation and creative adaptation. And although we may not like all the norms being articulated at any given moment, it will do no good to ignore them or to insist on their lack of authority. In a plural world, law is an ongoing process of articulation, adaptation, rearticulation, absorption, resistance, deployment, and on and on (p. 239).

SB 1070 has succeeded in its basic purposes. It has revealed an American public interested in more aggressive enforcement of immigration laws. Donors have sent millions of dollars to Arizona to defend its law and SB 1070 scores well in public opinion polls (Jordan 2009; Pew 2010). As of this writing, five states had adopted similar laws. Discussion of a path toward citizenship, which President Obama proposed in his first State of the Union message, appears to be "off the table." Even the DREAM Act, designed to help long-term youth residents gain legal status, has been voted down. We are indeed in a pluralist legal universe in which one state's legislation, even if rejected by courts, can change a public conversation and perhaps the prospects for other legal reforms. Of course, legal pluralism also contains possibilities for progressive change initiated from an unexpected quarter that moves the national collective consciousness in new directions.

References

Berman PS (2009) The new legal pluralism. Ann Rev Law Soc Sci 5:225–242

Calavita K (1996) The new politics of immigration: 'balanced budget conservatism' and Prop. 187. Soc Probl 43:284–305

Chavez JM, Provine DM (2009) Race and the response of state legislatures to unauthorized immigrants. Ann Am Acad Political Soc Sci 623:78–92

Conlan T (2006) From cooperative to opportunistic federalism: reflections on the half-century anniversary of the commission on intergovernmental relations. Public Adm Rev 66:663–676

Cover R (1981) The uses of jurisdictional redundancy: interest, ideology, and innovation. William Mary Law Rev 22:639–682

Daniels R (2004) Guarding the golden door: American immigration policy and immigrants since 1882. Hill and Wang, New York

Decker SH, Lewis PG, Provine DM, Varsanyi MW (2009) On the frontier of local law enforcement: local police and federal immigration law. In: McDonald W (ed) Immigration, crime and justice. Emerald, Bingley, pp 261–276

Derthick M (2001) Keeping the compound republic. Brookings Institute Press, Washington

Dinan J (2010) State government influence in the congressional policy process: the case of health care legislation in the 111th congress. American Political Science Association, 2010 Annual Meeting Paper. Available at SSRN: http://ssrn.com/abstract=1643301

Filindra A, Tichenor DJ (2008) Beyond myths of federal exclusivity: regulating immigration and noncitizens in the states. American Political Science Association, 2008 Annual Meeting Paper

Fleury-Steiner B, Longazel J (2010) Neoliberalism, community development, and anti-immigrant backlash in Hazleton, Pennsylvania. In: Varsanyi MW (ed) Taking local control: immigration policy activism in US cities and states. Stanford University Press, Pal Alto, pp 73–93

Gillette CB (1997) The exercise of trumps by decentralized governments. Va Law Rev 83:1347–1435

Hsieh HF, Shannon SE (2005) Three approaches to qualitative content analysis. Qual Health Res 15:1277–1288

Hopkins D (2010) Politicized places: explaining where and when immigrants provoke local opposition. Am Political Sci Rev 104:40–60

Jordan M (2009) Donors send millions to defend Arizona law. The Wall Street J. Retrieved 19 April 2011, from http://online.wsj.com/article/SB10001424052702304248704575574461341942940.html

Immigration and Customs Enforcement (2009) News releases: ICE announces standardized 287(g) agreements with 67 state and local law enforcement partners. Retrieved 18 April 2011, from http://www.ice.gov/news/releases/0910/091016washingtondc.htm

Jacobson RD (2008) The new nativism: Proposition 187 and the debate over immigration. University of Minnesota Press, Minneapolis

Laver M, Benoit K, Garry J (2003) Extracting policy positions from political texts using words as data. Am Political Sci Rev 97(2):311–331

Massey DS, Sanchez MR (2010) Brokered boundaries: creating immigrant identity in anti-immigrant times. Sage, New York

McDonald WF (1997) Crime and illegal immigration: emerging local, state, and federal partnerships. National Inst Justice J :2–10

Medrano L (2011) With lawsuit, Arizona tries to stare down Obama on illegal immigration. Christian Science Monitor. Retrieved 11 February 2011, from http://www.csmonitor.com

Michaels R (2009) Global legal pluralism. Ann Rev Law Soc Sci 5:243–262

National Conference of State Legislators (2011) State laws related to immigration and immigrants. Retrieved 3 April 2011, from http://www.ncsl.org/default.aspx?tabid=19897

Nelson G (2011) Gov. Brewer Presses Campaign Against Feds. Arizona Republic, p Z 10

Neuman GL (1993) The lost century of American Immigration Law (1776–1875). Columbia Law Rev 84:1061–1073

Nevins J (2010) Operation gatekeeper and beyond: the war on “illegals” and the remaking of the U.S.–Mexico boundary, 2nd edn. Routledge Press, New York

Newton L (2008) Illegal, alien, or immigrant: the politics of immigration reform. New York University Press, New York

Newton L, Adams BE (2009) State immigration policies: innovation, cooperation or conflict? Publius J Fed 39(3):408–431

Nintzel J (2011) Pearce: ‘SB 1070 is Constitutionally Sound’. Tucson Weekly. Retrieved 18 April 2011, from http://www.tucsonweekly.com/TheRange/archives/2011/04/11/pearce-sb-1070-is-constitutionally-sound

Nugent JD (2009) Safeguarding federalism: how states protect their interest in national policymaking. University of Oklahoma Press, Norman

Olivas MA (2007) Immigration-related state and local ordinances: preemption, prejudice, and the proper role for enforcement. Univ Chic Legal Forum :27–57
Parlow M (2007) A localist's case for decentralizing immigration policy. Denver Univ Law Rev 84:1061–1073
Pew Research Center (2010) Public supports Arizona Law. Retrieved 12 May 2010, from http://pewresearch.org/pubs/1591/public-support-arizona-immigration-law-poll
Provine DM (2009) Justice as told by judges: the case of litigation over anti-immigrant legislation. Stud Soc Justice 3(2):231–245
Provine DM, Doty BE (2012) The criminalization of immigrants as a racial project. J Contemp Crim Justice 27(3):261–277
Ramakrishnan SK, Wong T (2010) Immigration policies go local: the varying responses of local governments to low-skilled and undocumented immigration. In: Varsanyi MW (ed) Taking local control: immigration policy activism in US cities and states. Stanford University Press, Pal Alto, pp 73–93
Regan PM (2008) Opposition to the REAL ID act at the state level: privacy, immigration, or unfunded mandates? American Political Science Association, 2008 Annual Meeting Paper
Rodriguez CM (2008) The significance of the local in immigration regulation. Mich Law Rev 106:567–642
Rough G (2011) Arizona seeking pacts with other states to defy feds. Arizona Republic, pp A1, A5
Schuck PH (2007) Taking immigration federalism seriously. The University of Chicago Law Forum, pp 57–92
Skerry P (1995) Many borders to cross: is immigration the exclusive responsibility of the federal government? Publius 25:71–85
Spiro PJ (1994) The states and immigration in an era of demi-sovereignties. Va J Int Law 121:121–178
Spiro PJ (2001) Federalism and immigration: models and trends. Int Soc Sci J 53:67–73
Terrazas A (2011) Immigrants in new-destination states. Migration Information Source. Retrieved 18 April 2011, from http://www.migrationinformation.org/USFocus/display.cfm?ID=826
Varsanyi MW, Lewis PG, Provine DM, Decker S (2012) A multilayered jurisdictional patchwork: immigration federalism in the United States. Law Policy J 34(2):138–158
Verhovek SH (1994) Texas plans to sue U.S. over illegal aliens costs. The New York Times. Retrieved 18 April 2011, from http://query.nytimes.com/gst/fullpage.html?res=9904E0D7173BF934A15756C0A962958260
Wechsler H (1954) The political safeguards of federalism: the role of the states in the composition and selection of the national government. Columbia Law Rev 54:543–601
Wells M (2004) The grassroots reconfiguration of U.S. immigration policy. Int Migr Rev 38:1308–1347
Wishnie MJ (2001a) Laboratories of bigotry? devolution of the immigration power, equal protection, and federalism. N Y Univ Law Rev 76:493–521
Wishnie MJ (2001–2003) Introduction: immigration and federalism. N Y Univ Ann Surv Am Law 58:283

Cases Cited

Traux v Raich 239 U.S. 33 (1915)

Chapter 6
Effects of SB 1070 on Children

Carlos Santos, Cecilia Menjívar and Erin Godfrey

Although Arizona is perhaps the most visible state to initiate draconian policies to apprehend and deport undocumented immigrants and to deter others from coming into the state, it is not the only one. In spite of costly litigation against SB 1070, economic boycotts to the state, and numerous protests, other states have followed the actions of Arizona legislators. Several states have proposed and passed Arizona-style bills since SB 1070 was signed into law in April 2010 in Arizona. Although polling has found that a majority of people in Arizona and nationwide support the law (Pew Research Center for the People and the Press 2010) (Rasmussen Reports 2010), it has spurred considerable controversy and media attention nationwide, including protests in over 70 US cities (News 2010). Vocal groups around the nation have expressed major concerns related to the potential violation of basic human rights embedded in this law and have called for an economic boycott of the state. And given the considerable negative impact of this boycott on Arizona's

Support of Carlos Santos was provided in part by funds from the School of Social and Family Dynamics at Arizona State University as part of the Lives of Girls and Boys Research Enterprise (http://lives.clas.asu.edu/).

C. Santos
Counseling and Counseling Psychology, Arizona State University, Payne Hall 446 J, MC-0811, Tempe, AZ 85287–0811, USA
e-mail: carlos.e.santos@asu.edu

C. Menjívar
School of Social and Family Dynamics, Arizona State University, Social Science Building 144, Tempe, AZ 85287–3701, USA
e-mail: carlos.e.santos@asu.edu

E. Godfrey
Applied Psychology, New York University, 246 Greene St, 8th floor, New York, NY 10012, USA
e-mail: erin.godfrey@nyu.edu

L. Magaña and E. Lee (eds.), *Latino Politics and Arizona's Immigration Law SB 1070*, Immigrants and Minorities, Politics and Policy, DOI: 10.1007/978-1-4614-0296-1_6,

economy (Jarman 2011), the business communities in several states considering similar legislation have lobbied to strip those bills of provisions that resemble SB 1070. However, in spite of strong opposition from business bureaus and chambers of commerce and threats of boycotts, as of this writing, several other states are considering similar legislation and have passed similar laws. Thus, what has occurred in Arizona, far from exceptional, is emblematic of a new trend in immigration enforcement (Jiménez and López-Sanders 2011).

In this chapter we take a preliminary look at how SB 1070 may influence one slice of social life: the lives of children who, given their ethnicity, might be directly or indirectly affected by this legislation. There have been other efforts to examine the influence of contemporary immigration laws on various aspects of life among immigrant families, including family separation and intergenerational relations (Menjívar and Abrego 2009) (Menjívar 2006), as well as on young Latinos' paths of mobility (Abrego and Gonzales 2010), and on the educational opportunities of immigrants in uncertain legal statuses (Gonzales 2010) (Menjívar 2008). However, the passage of laws such as SB 1070 reverberates well beyond the lives of undocumented immigrants, as the undocumented population is not a separate group easily classifiable and isolated from the documented (or U.S. citizens). Indeed, a hallmark of today's immigration landscape is the presence of what are called "mixed-legal status families," composed of members with various legal statuses, including U.S. born members. It is within this context that we examine some of the possible ways the law touches the lives of young individuals, focusing on how awareness of SB 1070 shapes their views of themselves and of their place in U.S. society.

There are two important features of this legislation that we would like to highlight before we embark in our discussion, as the case we examine here exemplifies both. First, the effects of this kind of legislation have effects well beyond immigrant families, as non-immigrant U.S. born individuals are affected in direct and in indirect ways. U.S. citizen adults and children who live in close proximity to immigrants who are at risk of deportation often feel the effects of these individuals' deportability—that is, the mere *threat* of deportation has consequences, even when not coupled with the *act* of deportation (De Genova 2002). Second, and related, the act of signing bills similar to SB 1070 into law, even when the law is not fully implemented, sends shock waves through communities where immigrants who are at risk of deportation live. This is how the symbolic power of the law exerts influence.

SB 1070 in Context

Although Senate Bill 1070 put Arizona on the map with regard to controversial immigration laws, it is not the only law in the state intended to reduce the presence of approximately 400,000 undocumented immigrants in the state. Nor is Arizona the only state in the country that has passed similar measures. Ostensibly in response to the federal government's inaction on immigration law reform, state-level laws have been gaining traction since the mid 2000s. For instance, in 2005 there were 300 bills introduced and 38 immigration-related laws throughout the country; by 2007 the numbers had increased to 1,562 bills and 240 laws (Hegen 2008). These actions have taken the form of policies involving English as the official language, attacks on bilingual education, anti-affirmative action legislation, and municipal policies that make it illegal for landlords to rent to undocumented immigrants, or for day labourers, presumably undocumented immigrants, to seek work at street corners. Several of these measures aim to make illegal certain practices that presumably attract immigrants to their states, such as the hiring of undocumented immigrants or the provision of social services to undocumented immigrants. But it is already illegal, by federal law, to knowingly or willingly hire undocumented immigrants, or to provide social services to undocumented immigrants, which state-level measures seek to cut, thus making many of these measures redundant. However, the symbolism in the passage of these laws is potent enough to influence behaviors, perceptions, and a sense of self among those affected (directly and indirectly).

The long string of legislative actions of which SB 1070 is part include some of the most noted local-level laws, such as Proposition 200 ("Protect Arizona Now" or "Arizona Taxpayer and Citizen Protection Act"), a voter-approved initiative passed in 2004 to require proof of eligibility to receive social services such as, retirement, welfare, health, disability, public or assisted housing, post-secondary education, food assistance, unemployment or similar benefits that are provided with appropriated funds of state or local governments, and to require state and local workers to report immigration violations to federal authorities in writing. Most of these provisions were already federal law, making Proposition 200 largely redundant. In 2006, Arizona voters approved Proposition 100, which denies bail to undocumented immigrants accused of felonious crimes, Proposition 102, which bars undocumented immigrants from collecting punitive damages in civil lawsuits, Proposition 103, which makes English the official language of the state, and Proposition 300, which denies in-state college tuition to immigrants who cannot produce proof of permanent legal residence or citizenship, and bars undocumented immigrants from accessing subsidized child care and adult education programs (Arizona Legislative Council 2006). And in 2007, Arizona passed the Legal Arizona Workers Act (which went into effect on January 1, 2008), a measure to identify and punish businesses that "knowingly" and "intentionally" hire unauthorized workers (already federal law since 1986), with the suspension of a business license or its revocation for a second offense, which also requires all employers to electronically verify whether employees are legally eligible to work.

Within this heightened legal climate came SB 1070, which Governor Jan Brewer signed before television cameras on April 23rd, 2010. Among its key provisions is the mandate that local police check the immigration status of any person they reasonably suspect of being in the country illegally as part of every lawful stop, detention, or arrest. Prior law in Arizona, and the law in most other states, does not mandate that law enforcement personnel ask about the immigration status of those they encounter. In fact, many police departments discourage such inquiries to avoid deterring immigrants from reporting crimes and cooperating in other investigations (Cooper and Davenport 2010). Among other provisions, the law also makes it illegal for undocumented workers to seek work in public places; it specifies that in addition to a federal violation, a person is guilty of trespassing if she or he is present on any public or private land and cannot produce proof of legal residence, and allows law enforcement agents to arrest a person without warrant if there is probable cause to believe the person has committed a public offense that makes the individual removable from the United States (State of Arizona Senate Bill 1070). On July 29th 2010, a federal judge blocked the most controversial portions of the law (on hold for 2 years during litigation but subsequently upheld by the U.S. Supreme Court; it is now the law), but others went into effect immediately, such as making it illegal to stop a car to pick up a day laborer.

The objective of this series of laws, in Arizona and in other states, does not seem to be to directly decrease the number of undocumented immigrants in the state, as this responsibility remains within the purview of federal law, but to make "attrition through enforcement" the local policy. This means that conditions for immigrants in a particular state are made so inhospitable that they deter and discourage immigrants from coming in and create enough of a disincentive for those already in the state to leave voluntarily, or "self deport." Thus, it is believed that hundreds, perhaps thousands, of undocumented immigrants have left Arizona; this population is believed to have decreased from 2008 to 2009 from 500,000 to 400,000 (Passel and Cohn 2010).

Importantly, SB 1070, and the state-level laws that preceded it, does not stand in a legal vacuum, as previous laws that were passed since 2004 in Arizona are still in place, as well as those that exist at the federal level, particularly the Illegal Immigration Reform and Immigrant Responsibility Act (IIRIRA) of 1996 that has facilitated the deportation of thousands through the 287(g) agreement. Indeed, Maricopa County (the most populous county in the state) was one of the most vigorous users of 287(g) agreement, a federal program that sought to identify for deportation undocumented immigrants who committed serious crimes, but that was used mostly to conduct raids (or workplace inspections, as these operations are called) in businesses where Latino immigrants work or to carry out traffic stops in the neighborhoods in which they live (or crime suppression sweeps, as they are referred to). Thus, the passage of SB 1070, in conjunction with the laws that preceded it, affects Latino communities within a broader legal context, having a multiplier effect. While the effects of SB 1070 reverberate through Latino communities in Arizona, the 2008 "employer sanction law" is still in effect, the same time that workplace raids and traffic stops were conducted as part of the 287(g) agreement. What sets SB 1070 apart from current federal and other state-level laws is that during the time the most controversial portions of this law were on hold, its effects were felt far and wide, even beyond the state of Arizona, as fearful immigrants in other states looked to Arizona to assess what could happen in their states next (Saenz et al. 2011). Thus, it is the effect of this symbolic power that we examine here.

SB 1070 and Child Well-Being

While media and scholarly attention has been paid to national public opinion as well as the legal and policy ramifications of SB 1070, less attention has been paid to how Latinos and other minorities living in Arizona perceive and experience this law. There have been media accounts of the repercussions that the passing of the law has had on Latinos, immigrants, and non-immigrants alike, including not reporting crimes to the police in order to avoid contacting authorities, not visiting physicians or hospitals even in emergency situations so as to avoid detection, changing driving habits and staying home more often, and weighing the pros and cons of sending children to school (González 2011). However, we have very little systematic information about these and other potential consequences, particularly among the youth population—many of whom are citizen children of immigrant parents. An important area in which to begin to explore the consequences of immigration legislation is in perceptions that those potentially affected might form of themselves and of their place in society. This is particularly fruitful to examine among youth for whom identity formation is a critical developmental task. In this regard, awareness of SB 1070 may be related to important psychological outcomes among youth. Early adolescence is a critical period marked by important developmental changes, including biological transitions, shifts in interpersonal relationships, increased capacity for complex, abstract and dialectical thought, and increased emphasis on identity formation, racial/ethnic experiences, civic engagement, and self-esteem (Watts and Flanagan 2007). Thus, it is important to understand the links between the passing of this legislation and these aspects of psychological development during this critical developmental period.

In this chapter we examine relationships between early adolescents' awareness of SB 1070 and their perceptions of themselves and of their place in U.S. society. The aim of this preliminary analysis is to demonstrate the potential impact of the passage of SB 1070 on key psychological aspects of youth's development and encourage greater consideration among researchers and policymakers of these unintended psychological consequences for youth. Their experiences are key in capturing future potential effects of this and similar pieces of legislation around the country, as these youngsters constitute the fastest growing segment of the U.S. population, and their experiences today can have important repercussions for tomorrow's social, demographic, political, and economic prospects. Given that according to 2010 Census figures nearly one in four children in the country are Latino, their social and economic integration is fundamental for the future of the nation.

And as we mentioned earlier, an important feature of SB 1070 is that the law, as it was written, did not take full effect immediately, as a federal judge placed on hold for two years several of its key provisions. However, the symbolic act of signing this bill into law has had multiple consequences, which points to the powerful messages behind these legal actions. Thus, the effects on children we examine here are not necessarily linked to the most controversial provisions in the law but to the *passage* of the law, and how the mere awareness of the law can have serious repercussions for those affected. Below, we present the data and methods we use to explore these relationships, followed by a discussion and implications of the findings thus far.

Data and Methods

The current study uses survey data to begin a systematic examination of youth's awareness of the recent immigration act in Arizona, SB 1070. The study was conducted among racially and ethnically diverse youth in a middle school located in the greater Phoenix, Arizona region. Despite being located in a state where public schools have recently been forced to end ethnic studies classes, this middle school is welcoming, and in fact, is primarily composed of diverse children in terms of immigrant generation, race, and ethnicity. The sample size for the study was 726 middle school students. We secured an 84.9 % participation rate in the middle school where this study was conducted. The school serves primarily low-income students. According to the state's department of education, 81.1 % of the student population at the school was categorized as "economically disadvantaged" using parental income as a proxy in 2010 (Arizona Department of Education, National School Lunch Program, and School Breakfast Program 2011). The average age of participants was 12.4 years (SD = 0.97), about equally divided between male (52 %) and female (48 %).

Participants were European American (17 %), African American (17 %), Native American (10 %), Asian American (3 %), Latino/a, mostly Mexican–American (49 %), Mixed[1] (4 %). The percentage of participants who reported speaking either Spanish-only or both Spanish and English at home was 51 %. Approximately 14 % of participants reported being separated from both parents at some point in their childhood for longer than 6 months for an average of 2.6 years (SD = 1.8). In terms of immigrant status, 13 % of participants are first generation immigrants (i.e., foreign-born), 40 % are second generation immigrants (i.e., at least one parent is foreign-born), and 47 % are third generation (i.e., both parents and child are U.S. born). Thus, the sample in the present study consists of ethnically and racially diverse middle school students who are predominantly citizens of the United States (87 %). It is important to note that this sample is not representative of the national or state population of youth and therefore the results cannot necessarily be generalized to the broader population. However, as large-scale surveys typically do not focus on this age range and do not assess youth's perceptions of themselves and their role in U.S. society, this sample provides a unique opportunity to begin to explore the psychological implications of immigration legislation, such as SB 1070, among youth for whom the passage of the law was a particularly prominent part of civic and social life.

[1] Those in the mixed category mostly reported having at least one parent who is of Latino/a origin.

Procedure

Students were recruited from all grades in the school (i.e., 6, 7, and 8th grade). During recruitment, youth were informed about the study by their teachers and provided with a packet in either English or Spanish containing information and parental consent forms to take home to their parents. Prior to collecting survey data, students' assent was also obtained. Surveys were administered during two class periods (approximately 90 min) deemed least disruptive to students' learning by the principal and social studies teachers. Survey questions were read out loud to the class while students answered them individually. Survey administration was supervised by two to four trained research assistants. Protocols were administered in English and survey administrators circulated throughout the classroom answering questions to ensure comprehension. All survey administrators remained in the classroom while students filled out the protocol and collected the survey at the end of each administration.

To ensure confidentiality, each survey had an identification number on it. Once students filled out paper work to note their unique identification numbers, all identifying information apart from the unique identification numbers was separated to further ensure confidentiality. All surveys were spot-checked upon completion during each administration period. After completion of the survey, each student received a rubber bracelet with the project's name embossed on it.

Measures

Awareness of SB 1070. Participants were asked the following question: "How aware are you of the recent act called SB 1070 in Arizona related to immigration issues?" and were asked to rate how aware they were on a five-point Likert scale ranging from *Not at all aware* (1), *A little aware* (2), *Somewhat aware* (3), *Very aware* (4), *Extremely aware* (5).

American identity. Participants completed a measure of American Identity (Phinney and Devich-Navarro 1997) that assesses participants' sense of being American. They were asked to rate how much they agree with statements such as "I think of myself as being American.", and "I feel good about being American." Response options are on a five-point Likert scale ranging from *Strongly disagree* (1), *Disagree* (2), *Neither agree or disagree* (3), *Agree* (4), *Strongly agree* (5). Cronbach's α was 0.92 in the present study.

Perceived ethnic discrimination. Participants completed a measure of perceived ethnic discrimination from authorities (Whitbeck et al. 2001), which assessed adolescents' experiences with ethnic discrimination from authorities. Participants were asked to rate how often they experienced discrimination on a four-point Likert scale from *Almost never* (1), *Sometimes* (2), *Often* (3), *Very often* (4). Items include: "How often have others suspected you of doing something wrong because of your ethnicity?" and "How often has the police hassled you because of your ethnicity?" Cronbach's α for this scale was 0.69 in the present study.

Self-Esteem. Self-esteem was assessed using the Rosenberg Self-Esteem Scale (RSES) (Rosenberg 1965). It is considered a general measure of self-esteem, and was developed for use with middle and high school students (Whitbeck et al. 2001). It consists of 10 items on a 5-point Likert scale ranging from *Strongly disagree* (1) to *Strongly agree* (5). Students indicate their agreement or disagreement with items such as "I feel that I have a number of good qualities" or "I feel I do not have much to be proud of". The RSES demonstrated strong internal reliability in the present study; Cronbach's α was 0.83.

Results

As a first step toward understanding the relationships between awareness of SB 1070 and identity development, perceptions of discrimination, and self-esteem, we calculated a series of bivariate Pearson's correlations. Results revealed that awareness of SB 1070 was significantly positively associated with perceptions of ethnic discrimination from authorities, but negatively related to American identity. Additionally, self-esteem was significantly positively related to American identity. Finally, ethnic discrimination was negatively associated with American identity (see Table 6.1).

To adjust these relationships for demographic characteristics that may be related to awareness of SB 1070, we then conducted a series of multiple regression analyses controlling for age, gender and family structure. The results of these analyses indicated that generation of immigration, American identity and perceived ethnic discrimination from authorities were all significantly related to awareness of the SB 1070 act. First-and second-generation adolescents reported greater awareness of SB 1070 than adolescents who are third generation ($b = 0.59$ (0.19); $p = 0.003$; $\beta = 0.13$ and $b = 0.48$ (0.15); $p = 0.002$; $\beta = 0.15$, respectively). In addition, there was a negative relationship between American identity and awareness of SB 1070 ($b = -0.07$ (0.03); $p = 0.020$; $\beta = -0.09$). Early adolescents who reported greater awareness of the law also reported a weaker sense of being American. Follow-up analyses revealed that this association was significantly moderated by generation of immigration: the negative relationship between SB 1070 awareness and American identity was *stronger* among first-and second-generation youth than among youth in the third or later generation ($b = -0.21$ (0.09); $p = 0.02$; $\beta = -0.09$ and $b = -0.13$ (.06); $p = 0.04$; $\beta = -0.10$, for first- and second- generation youth, respectively).

Table 6.1 Correlation Results

	Awareness of SB 1070	Self-esteem	Ethnic discrimination	American identity
Awareness of SB 1070	–			
Self-esteem	0.04	–		
Ethnic discrimination	0.12**	−0.04	–	
American identity	−0.13**	0.10**	−0.12**	–

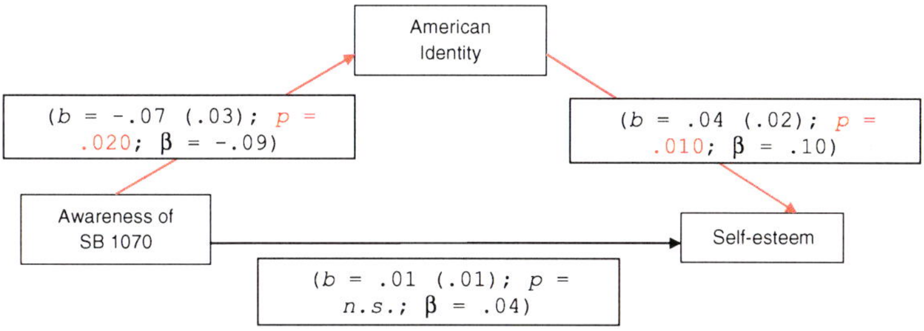

Fig. 6.1 Indirect effects model between awareness of SB 1070, American identity and self-esteem

This relationship was not moderated by race/ethnicity, however, suggesting that this negative association was similar for youth of all racial/ethnic backgrounds in the sample. Finally, we found a positive association between perceptions of discrimination from authorities, and awareness of SB 1070 ($b = 0.28$ (0.11); $p = 0.011$; $\beta = 0.10$). Early adolescents who reported higher awareness of the law perceived greater discrimination from authorities. This association was not moderated by either generation of immigration or race/ethnicity. No significant relationship between self-esteem and awareness of SB 1070 was found. However, controlling for adolescents' awareness of the law, we found that American identity was positively associated with self-esteem ($b = 0.04$ (0.02); $p = 0.010$; $\beta = 0.10$).

Finally, given the negative relationship between awareness of SB 1070 and American identity and the positive relationship between American identity and self-esteem, we explored the possibility that awareness of SB 1070 was indirectly related to adolescent's self-esteem through its relationship with American identity (see Fig. 6.1). We tested for this indirect relation using the product of coefficients technique presented by Sobel (1982). As indicated in Fig. 6.1, the direct relationships between awareness of SB 1070 and American identity and between American identity and self-esteem (controlling for awareness of SB 1070) were both significant. In addition, the indirect relationship between awareness of SB 1070 and self-esteem via American identity was significant using the Sobel (Sobel 1982) test ($b = -0.004$ (0.002), $p < 0.05$). These results suggest that adolescents who report higher awareness of SB 1070 report a weaker sense of being American, which in turn is associated with diminished psychological health (i.e., lower levels of self-esteem).

Discussion

In the midst of the immigration debate in Arizona and elsewhere, there is a missing story about the potential psychological consequences of legislation like SB 1070. Yet, the psychological wellbeing of immigrant youth is of paramount importance to our nation. Immigrant youth (i.e., youth from birth through age 17, with at least one foreign-born parent) make up the fastest growing segment of the U.S. population (Tienda and Haskins 2011). Our study was conducted in a middle school with a sizeable immigrant youth (i.e., first and second generation) population. Most of these youth are U.S. citizens, and according to federal estimates, significant numbers of them are likely living with at least one unauthorized parent.[2] Although immigrant youth represented a slight majority of our sample (53 %), a significant number of youth were third generation and beyond (47 %).The school where our study took place offers an important context to examine the effects of immigration reform. The population of the school is similar to other diverse urban schools in the United States, and reflects a growing diversity in American education. Indeed, the youth in our study, and the youth in other diverse U.S. schools, are learning and living alongside youth of diverse immigrant generations and legal statuses. This reality forces us to examine how immigration issues not only affect immigrant youth directly, but also their peers, and the local culture of schools where youth of diverse backgrounds interact. Importantly, the psychological well-being of immigrant, and non-immigrant youth alike, is critical to the development of human and other forms of capital necessary for success. And health outcomes contribute to economic opportunities. Unhealthy workers are less productive, cost more and earn less in their lifetime (Perreira and Ornelas 2011). Thus, by promoting the wellbeing of immigrant and non-immigrant children, we can ultimately improve the economic prospects of the next generation of Americans.

This study sought to examine more closely the unique experiences of immigrant children and their peers by using a psychological measure of wellbeing, assessing children's awareness of the SB 1070 legislation in Arizona, their perceptions of discrimination from authorities, and their sense of being American. Our findings indicate that awareness of SB 1070 had a small but significant negative association with youth's sense of being American, and that this weakened sense of American identity resulted in a small but meaningful reduction in psychological wellbeing (i.e., lower levels of self-esteem). In addition, our results suggest that this negative relationship was stronger for first- or second-generation adolescents of all racial and ethnic backgrounds. While this finding may not be surprising given the nature of the legislation, it has potential long-term implications for the development of personal and national identity among a large and rapidly growing group of youth in the United States, the majority of whom are U.S. citizens. Because the data are cross-sectional, we cannot be certain that awareness of SB 1070 *caused* these decreases in American identity and psychological wellbeing. However, these results point to the possibility that SB 1070 may have negative repercussions for outcomes that are key aspects of the developmental period of early adolescence and have long-term consequences for development. As mentioned earlier, youth's psychological wellbeing plays a critical role in their later emotional, educational, and occupational outcomes. In addition, developing a sense of positive national identity may contribute to later levels of civic engagement and political participation. Thus, our study among a diverse sample of youth

[2] An estimated 4 million immigrant youth live with unauthorized parents, and are U.S.-born citizens (Passel and Cohn 2010).

from the state of Arizona provides some initial evidence that legislation like SB 1070 may be associated with aspects of psychological development that are important to the long-term economic and democratic strength of the state and the nation as a whole. Although these results are preliminary, they suggest that researchers and policymakers should continue to track and explore how laws such as SB 1070 may have unintended influences on youth development.

It is important to note that the association between awareness of SB 170 and American identity was not moderated by race/ethnicity. Thus, our findings are not specific to Latino children— although a main, implicit or explicit, purpose of the law is to identify undocumented Latino immigrants. The associations we found between awareness of SB 1070, American identity and self-esteem were detected in a sample of racially and ethnically diverse youth–including white youth who attend highly diverse schools. On one hand this is not surprising given that these youth live in environments where their peers belong to groups that are, implicitly or explicitly, a target of this act. There are various mechanisms through which peers can exert influence on wellbeing (e.g., co-rumination has been looked at as one mediator of depression contagion among friends) (Rose et al. 2007). Thus, it seems plausible that white youth in settings that are highly diverse are affected by the punitive and discriminatory culture promoted by acts like SB 1070. On the other hand, it is striking that SB 1070's negative psychological consequences were also detected among white children as it reveals the law's reach beyond those who belong to groups that it directly targets—this is how the long arm of the law extends to have unforeseen consequences. Indeed, discriminatory messages perceived and embedded in legislation like SB 1070 may possibly affect children either directly or indirectly. And this is an area where the "unintended consequences" of the law may need further study, as our results point to potential effects of this legislation on community dynamics, ethnic and racial relations, as well as possible new forms of coalitions and communities.

The positive association we found between awareness of SB 1070 and perceptions of discrimination is also important. This result suggests that the children in our study may perceive a hostile environment from authorities around them in light of practices that are seen and perceived as discriminatory, such as the SB 1070 legislation. However, since these data are cross-sectional, it may also be that youth who already perceive a hostile environment from authorities may be more attuned to legislation such as SB 1070. Nonetheless, this positive association suggests that awareness of SB 1070 and perceptions of discrimination from authorities may work together to contribute to a general sense of distrust among youth. Future research should endeavor to explore this relationship in more detail and determine the causal relationship between them. This is particularly important given that SB 1070 awareness and perceptions of discrimination may act in accordance to further complicate key outcomes among children such as academic engagement. Research examining the effects of discrimination on schooling among Latino youth has reported various negative outcomes such as lower grade point averages, poor self-esteem, increases in school drop-out, and lower generalized academic wellbeing (DeGarmo and Martinez 2006) (Greene et al. 2006) (Martinez et al. 2004).

Academic success is critical for these youth's academic future and career opportunities, and research suggests that outcomes in academic domains during adolescence are followed by similar outcomes in later stages of development (Henderson and Dweck 1990). School dropout rates for Latino adolescents constitute an alarming 2.4 times that of white non-Latino students, and 1.6 times that of black non-Latino students (U. S. Department of Commerce (n.d.) Current population survey (October 1972–2004). These statistics underscore the importance of understanding the factors that contribute to the academic engagement of Latino youth, particularly when research by the Pew Hispanic Center also has found that young Latinos and their parents are fully cognizant, even more than other ethnic and racial groups, of the benefits of a college degree (Pew Hispanic Center 2009). Given the established literature linking experiences of discrimination with academic dis-engagement, our finding that SB 1070 awareness was linked to perceptions of discrimination lead us to believe that SB 1070 may also result in poorer academic engagement (although this association remains to be tested in future analyses). These findings point to the social and economic costs of this legislation, as it affects the long-term trajectories of Latino youth, who by sheer numbers alone not only constitute the fastest growing segment of the U.S. population today and of its future labor force but will likely shape the kind of society the United States will be in the future.

Additionally, our findings parallel those of a recent report by the Pew Hispanic Research (cited in Massey 2007) in which young Latino respondents were the most likely to either have experienced or known of someone who has experienced discrimination because of their race or ethnic group. Legal status has certainly become a central axis of stratification (Jiménez and López-Sanders 2011; Lopez et al. 2010; Menjívar 2006) and legislation like SB 1070 accentuates the effects that legal status has, particularly with regard to perceptions of discrimination. A Pew Hispanic Center study (Lopez et al. 2010) found that of various factors that lead to discrimination, 36 % of Latino respondents ranked immigration status as the most important, outranking skin color (21 %), language skills (20 %) and income and education (17 %). Similar to the findings in our study, these figures highlight the negative effects of current immigration laws that exacerbate perceptions of discrimination based on legal status, a characteristic shared by a large group of individuals.

Laws like SB 1070 have the potential to reverberate negatively in the lives of diverse youth well beyond its intent of stopping undocumented immigration. The results of this study suggest that SB 1070 may foster an environment where immigrant youth and their peers are distrustful of authorities. Our study of immigrant youth and their peers suggests that their identity as Americans may be undermined by punitive and discriminatory acts like SB 1070, although the majority of these youth were American citizens. Interestingly, right wing rhetoric that emphasizes so-called American values and traditions (e.g., as evident in the English-only education movement), seems to be doing a disservice to its mission by encouraging acts and laws that have consequences for how U.S.-born youth see their country. Ironically, these acts undermine the very principles of American identity and love for the country that these groups promote. Failing to act runs the risk of raising adults who are distrustful of their nation and unidentified with its political force.

Finally, an important factor to consider is the long-term effect of legislation such as SB 1070 on the perceptions of young individuals as they become adults and active members of their communities. Perceptions of exclusion or of not fully belonging, even when they are U.S. citizens, are amplified by pieces of legislation like SB 1070 across the country, and can affect how individuals think of their position in society, and what their rights and responsibilities are. Thus, laws like SB 1070 carry important repercussions for political participation, citizenship, and membership more generally. The unintended consequences of similar legislation can create a marginalized segment of the population with fewer rights (and responsibilities) and a tiered system of citizenship that accentuates and exacerbates the effects of other forms of social stratification. The aim of this chapter was to begin to demonstrate some of the unintended consequences of SB 1070 among a small sample of youth in Arizona. We hope this work can serve as a call for both researchers and policymakers to more fully and systematically consider the influence of such legislation on the development of our nation's youth.

References

Abrego LJ, Gonzales RG (2010) Blocked paths, uncertain futures: the postsecondary education and labor market prospects of undocumented youth. Journal of Education for Students Placed at Risk, 15(1):144–157

Arizona Department of Education, National School Lunch Program and School Breakfast Program (2011) Child nutrition programs: percentage of free and reduced reports. Retrieved from Arizona Department of Education website: http://www.ade.az.gov/health-safety/cnp/frpercentages/free-reducedpercentage_OCT10.pdf

Arizona Legislative Council (2006) Ballot proposition analyses. http://www.azleg.state.az.us/2006_Ballot_Proposition_Analyses/

Cooper JJ, Davenport P (2010) Immigration advocacy groups to challenge Arizona law. The Washington Post. Retrieved May 12, 2011 from: http://www.washingtonpost.com/wp-dyn/content/article/2010/04/24/AR2010042402200.html

De Genova N (2002) Migrant "illegality" and deportability in everyday life. Ann Rev Anthropology 31:419–447

DeGarmo DS, Martinez CR Jr (2006) A culturally informed model of academic well-being for Latino youth: the importance of discriminatory experiences and social support. Fam Relat 55(3):267–278

Gonzales RG (2010) More than just access: undocumented students navigating the post-secondary terrain. J College Admission 206:48–52

González D (2011) Senate bill 1070: 1 year later. The Arizona Republic, 23 April

Greene ML, Way N, Pahl K (2006) Trajectories of perceived adult and peer discrimination among Black, Latino, and Asian American adolescents: patterns and psychological correlates. Dev Psychol 42(2):218–238

Hegen D (2008) State laws related to immigrants and immigration: January 1—July 30, 2008. Retrieved from National Conference of State Legislatures website: http://www.ncsl.org/print/press/immigrationlegislationreport.pdf

Henderson VL, Dweck C (1990) Motivation and achievement. In: Feldman SS, Elliott GR (eds) At the threshold: the developing adolescent, Harvard University Press, Harvard, pp 308–329

Jarman M (2011) Valley feels loss of migrant money. The Arizona republic. Retrieved May 12, 2011 from: http://www.azcentral.com/arizonarepublic/business/articles/2011/04/23/20110423biz-1070retail0423.html

Jiménez TR, López-Sanders L (2011) Unanticipated, unintended, and unadvised: The effects of public policy on unauthorized immigration. Pathways. The Stanford Center for the Study of Poverty and Inequality, Stanford, pp 3–7

Lopez MH, Morin R, Taylor P (2010) Illegal immigration backlash worries, divides Latinos. Pew Hispanic Center http://pewhispanic.org/files/reports/128.pdf

Martinez CR, DeGarmo DS, Eddy JM (2004) Promoting academic success among Latino youths. Hispanic J Beha Sci 26(2):128–151. doi:10.1177/0739986304264573

Massey DS (2007) Categorically unequal: the American stratification system. Russell Sage, New York

Menjívar C (2006) Liminal legality: Salvadoran and Guatemalan immigrants' lives in the United States. Am J Sociol 111(4):999–1037

Menjívar C (2008) Educational hopes, documented dreams: Guatemalan and Salvadoran immigrants' legality and educational prospects. Ann Am Acad Political Social Sci 620(1):177–193

Menjívar C, Abrego L (2009) Parents and children across borders: legal instability and intergenerational relations in Guatemalan and Salvadoran families. In: Foner N (ed) Across generations: immigrant families in America. New York University Press, New York, pp 160–189

CBC News (2010) Arizona immigration law sparks huge rallies. Retrieved May 12, 2010 from: http://www.cbc.ca/news/world/story/2010/05/01/arizona-immigration-law-protests.html

Passel JS, Cohn D'V (2010) U.S unauthorized immigration flows are down sharply since mid-decade. Pew Hispanic Center Report

Perreira KM, Ornelas IJ (2011) The physical and psychological well-being of immigrant children. Future Child 21(1):195–218

Pew Hispanic Center (2009) Between two worlds: how young Latinos come of age in America. Washington http://pewhispanic.org/files/reports/117.pdf

Pew Research Center for the People and the Press (2010) Public supports Arizona immigration law: democrats divided, but support provisions. Retrieved May 12, 2011 from: http://pewresearch.org/pubs/1591/public-support-arizona-immigration-law-poll

Phinney JS, Devich-Navarro M (1997) Variations in bicultural identification among African American and Mexican American adolescents. J Res Adolescence 7:3–32. doi:10.1207/s15327795jra0701_2

Rasmussen Reports (2010) Most Arizona voters still support immigration law. Retrieved May 12, 2011 from: http://www.rasmussenreports.com/public_content/politics/general_state_surveys/arizona/most_arizona_voters_still_support_immigration_law

Rose AJ, Carlson W, Walter EM (2007) Prospective associations of co-rumination with friendship and emotional adjustment: considering the socioemotional trade-offs of co-rumination. Dev Psychol 43:1019–1031

Rosenberg M (1965) Society and the adolescent image. Princeton University Press, Princeton

Saenz R, Menjívar C, Juanita S, Garcia E (2011) Arizona's SB 1070: Setting conditions for violations of human rights here and beyond. In: Judith Blau, Mark Frezzo (eds) Sociology and Human Rights: A Bill of Rights for the Twen-ty-first Century. pp 155–178, Sage/Pine Forge Press, CA

Sobel ME (1982) Asymptotic confidence intervals for indirect effects in structural equation models. Sociol Methodol 13:290–312

State of Arizona Senate Bill 1070 (2010) 49th Legislature 2nd Sess

Tienda M, Haskins R (2011) Immigrant children: introducing the issue. Future Child 21(1):3–18

U. S. Department of Commerce (n.d.) Current population survey (October 1972–2004). Available from National Center for Educational Statistics Web site, http://nces.ed.gov

Watts R, Flanagan C (2007) Pushing the envelope on youth civic engagement: a developmental and liberation psychology perspective. J Community Psychology 35:1–14

Whitbeck L, Hoyt D, McMorris B, Chen X, Stubben J (2001) Perceived discrimination and early substance abuse among American Indian children. J Health Soc Behav 42:405–424

Chapter 7
Attrition Through Enforcement and the Elimination of a "Dangerous Class"

Luis F. B. Plascencia

Introduction

The enactment of Arizona's Support Our Law Enforcement and Safe Neighborhoods Act (SB 1070) on April 23, 2010, and its amendment 7 days later (HB 2162), accentuated the political debate within Arizona and beyond on the question of migration and migrants, particularly from Mexico.[1] By July 9, 2010 seven lawsuits had been filed challenging the law, particularly the authority of the state to require state and local law enforcement agents to verify migration status of individuals suspected of violating federal migration laws—an argument for the exclusive "preemptive" power of the Federal government over the regulation of migration. The legal challenges also alleged that the Act would foster the "racial profiling" of persons deemed to be Latinos/Mexicans, including multiple Native American communities in Arizona.[2]

[1] This essay draws on some of the thinking that was presented in a one-page column that discusses the concept of attrition through enforcement; see Plascencia 2010.

[2] *Frisancho v. Governor Brewer* (4-27-2010); *Salgado v. Governor Brewer* (4-29-2010); *National Coalition of Latino Clergy and Christian Leaders v. State of Arizona, Governor Brewer* (4-29-2010); *Escobar v. Governor Brewer* (4-29-2010); *Friendly House* et al.*/ACLU/NILC/MALDEF v. Whiting* et al. (5-17-2010); *U.S. Department of Justice v. State of Arizona, Governor Brewer* (7-06-2010); and *LULAC* et al.*/Center for Human Rights and Constitutional Law v. State of Arizona, Governor Brewer* (7-09-2010). A key contention raised by all the lawsuits is the position that the historical preemptive powers of Article 1, Sect. 8, Clause 3, the "Commerce" clause, in the U.S. Constitution, as defined by multiple Supreme Court rulings, grants the federal government the power to regulate migration. Thus, under this logic, the State of Arizona does not have the power to mandate the verification of migration status of persons deemed not to have authorization to be present. The one unchallenged exception being those law enforcement entities that are certified under the 287(g) provision of the Immigration and Nationality Act, as authorized by the 1996 Illegal Immigration and Immigrant Responsibility Act (IIRIRA) enacted by President Clinton.

L. F. B. Plascencia (✉)
Social and Behavioral Sciences, Arizona State University,
W. Salter Drive 9900, Peoria, AZ 85382, USA
e-mail: luis.plascencia@asu.edu

L. Magaña and E. Lee (eds.), *Latino Politics and Arizona's Immigration Law SB 1070*,
Immigrants and Minorities, Politics and Policy, DOI: 10.1007/978-1-4614-0296-1_7,

On July 28, 2010 a federal district court judge issued a temporary injunction halting the implementation of the key provision of the law—the enforcement verification provision—but other provisions became effective after the ruling. In response, the state filed a request for an expedited review by the Ninth Circuit Court of Appeals. The latter rejected the request, but held a hearing on November 1, 2010; and on April 11, 2011, the three-judge panel issued its opinion upholding Judge Susan Bolton's July 28, 2010 ruling.[3] Governor Janice K. Brewer announced the state's appeal to the U.S. Supreme Court on November 22, 2011.

Although the above legal and policy questions are central to the juridical challenges to SB 1070/HB 2162, and will inform their review by the U.S. Supreme Court, the juridical questions are but one element in the broader political debate.[4] A critical issue that has been overshadowed by the juridical foci is the political aim of Arizona's SB 1070. Most commentators and academic analysts who have examined the law have focused on the juridical questions regarding the preemptive federal powers over migration or the alleged "racial profiling" that will result from the law,[5] and so have largely overlooked the momentous policy enunciated in the statute.[6] The introduction in the bill asserts the following: "The legislature declares that the intent of this act is to make attrition through enforcement the public policy of all state and local government agencies in Arizona." And although Governor Brewer made no reference to the intent of the law in her statement accompanying the signing, nor has said much about it in the multiple subsequent press conferences, her signature enacted that policy. Consequently, since April 23, 2010, the public policy in Arizona that is supposed to guide the actions of all public entities across the state, from local libraries, municipal police and fire departments, K-12 public schools, public hospitals, to state universities, and all state agencies, is attrition through enforcement. Thus, the attrition through enforcement political discourse merits greater attention than it has received to date.

---

[3] United States v. State of Arizona *et al.* (2011).

[4] The amendments made by HB 2162 subsumed the text of SB 1070, thus technically the debate is about HB 2162, and not SB 1070 since it was replaced by the former. However, in order to avoid the awkward notation of SB 1070/HB 2162, the essay uses "SB 1070" to simplify the reading.

[5] On the question of "racial profiling" and SB1070/HB2162, much of the debate has focused on whether the enacted measure will *lead* to "racial profiling." Those in favor of the law take the position that it will not lead to racial profiling because racial profiling is already against the law, and the amendments in HB2162 will prevent it. Those opposing the law argue that the law will *lead* to racial profiling. What is overlooked by both sides is that there is recent, documented evidence that "racial profiling" *has been taking place* in Arizona and likely continues. See *Veronica Arnold* et al. *v. Arizona Department of Public Safety,* et al. (2006), a lawsuit filed in 2001; and the three mandated reports by the University of Cincinnati Policing Institute, (2007, 2008, and 2009). The data make it quite clear that racial/ethnic "minorities" are treated differently if stopped.

[6] The one notable exception is the chapter by the political scientist Roxanne Doty, in her recent book (2009). Professor Doty cogently argues that attrition through enforcement strategy can be interpreted, following the work of Giorgio Agamben, as a form of "exception," a "politics of exceptionalism." This essay offers a different interpretation.

The more recent Arizona legislative actions in 2011 regarding the omnibus SB 1611 (a comprehensive bill that expands the restrictions on livelihoods and public resources for migrants), the companion "birthright" bills (SB1308 and 1309) which are aimed at producing a challenge to the birthright provision in the 14th Amendment that sponsors hope will lead to an eventual favorable ruling on the part of the Supreme Court, as well as several other bills being considered, are sequels to SB 1070. They are not only chronological sequels, but also can be thought of as measures to solidify Arizona's public policy: attrition through enforcement. Consequently, the discussion here should be thought of as a preliminary effort to examine the policy articulated in SB 1070, and thus an analysis that will need to be reexamined in the context of the post-SB 1070 measures.

This chapter aims to examine the genealogy of the concept and discourse of attrition through enforcement, and discusses some of its limitations. It argues that the concept is an influential and politically charged notion that relies on a particular construction of informally authorized migrants (i.e., what is commonly referred to as "illegal/undocumented" migrants), a construction that distorts the complexity of the historical and contemporary migration processes, and of federal policy on such migrants.[7] The essay presents an interpretation for its emergence, support, and its larger political aim in the final section of the essay.

Attrition through enforcement has become a prominent and influential discourse across the nation since 2006, as evident from the multiple municipalities (e.g., Hazleton, Pennsylvania, Illegal Immigration Relief Act 2006) and states that have explicitly and implicitly embraced it as a kind of "common-sense" approach to "illegal immigration." Republican State Representative Randy Terrill, the primary sponsor of Oklahoma's HB 1804 (2007), for example, has repeatedly noted that he fully supports attrition through enforcement and that that was the aim of HB 1804, yet the bill does not have the language found in SB 1070.[8]

In order to promote a fuller understanding of SB 1070, and avoid some of the common problems in analyses of SB 1070, discussions that place the Act as the starting point for the "anti-immigrant" actions in Arizona, this chapter first summarizes the federal and state division in the regulation of migration and migrants, and then discusses the pre- and post-Operation Gatekeeper (1994) actions adopted in Arizona. It then turns to a discussion of the genealogy and limitations of the concept of attrition through enforcement.

---

[7] For a fuller discussion of the term "informally authorized" migrant, see Plascencia (2009). The proposed term is based on a critique of the commonly deployed labels of "illegal" or "undocumented" migrant; while not without limitations, it aims to overcome the common limitations of the aforementioned labels.

[8] Among the key provisions of HB 1804 were measures to restrict public resources, the issuance of driver's licenses, required law enforcement official to detain and coordinate with ICE, criminalized harboring, and required employers to use E-Verify. The trajectory of HB 1804 followed a similar path to that of SB 1070: the governor enacted it, lawsuits were filed against it, a Federal District judge issued an injunction against key parts, it was appealed to the Denver circuit, and the circuit court returned it to the District judge.

The Federal-State Arrangement

Since the early 1990s, states and local communities in the United States have been engaged in intense policy debates regarding the presence and impact of migrants, particularly individuals labeled "illegal/undocumented" migrants (e.g., California's 1994 Proposition 187).[9] States, counties, and municipalities across the nation have enacted a wide array of policies aimed at regulating migration through measures targeted at migrants. The majority of such actions are exclusionary and encompass a wide spectrum of policies such as: English-only legislation, restricting marriage licenses, requiring landlords to verify the migration status of renters, elimination of in-state tuition for students without a social security number, restricting driver licenses, prohibiting the public funding of day labor sites, restricting use of consular identification cards, and others (Plascencia 2008). In addition, state prisons, county sheriff offices, and local police departments have sought certification by U.S. Immigration and Customs Enforcement (ICE) under the 287(g) provision in the Immigration and Nationality Act, which grants certified state and local entities authority to investigate migration status of individuals stopped or under custody.

An important aim of most such measures is to reduce access to public resources—resources that are deemed to properly belong to "citizens" and "taxpayers"—and thus eliminate the presence of persons thought not to have a formal basis for being present in the United States, nor deserving of Constitutional rights. In other words, persons who are present but are defined as not belonging; a process producing what Simmel (1950) labeled "the stranger," or what Badiou (2004) characterizes as the simultaneous process of inclusion and exclusion, being present but excluded.[10]

Although most measures have been exclusionary, some local governments have taken opposite actions, enacting ordinances such as "city of refuge" measures, "don't ask, don't tell" police department policies, encouraged the use of consular identification cards, and one city, New Haven (CT), even issued city identification cards to informally authorized migrants (Hansen 2007–2008; Ridgley 2008; Villazor 2010). This also has included opposition on the part of some local law enforcement officials and departments to 287(g) certification and local enforcement of migration laws on the grounds that their duty to 'serve and protect' their respective communities is compromised when local residents fear reporting crimes committed against them, or fear reporting crimes they have witnessed (Gascón 2009; Police Executive Research Forum 2011; Williams 2009).

Some policymakers and scholars have interpreted the above actions as representing a 'new devolution' of federal powers to state and local governments (Fix

[9] California's 1994 Proposition 187, approved by voters, has been widely examined in academic and law journals, chapters in migration policy books, including a book devoted to its analysis (Ono and Sloop 2002). The courts overturned most of the provisions; one provision that was not overturned was the item providing for enhanced criminal penalties related to fraudulent production and use of identification documents.

[10] Leo Chávez labels elements in the debate as constituting part of the national "Latino threat narrative" (2008).

and Tumlin 1997; Hartley 2007; Zimmermann and Tumlin 1999). In particular, they tend to interpret such actions as being stimulated by the passage of the Personal Responsibility and Work Opportunity Reconciliation Act (PRWORA), the Antiterrorism and Effective Death Penalty Act (AEDPA), and the IIRIRA (Illegal Immigration Reform and Immigrant Responsibility Act)—President Clinton enacted all three in 1996. The PRWORA excluded non-citizens, including Lawful Permanent Residents (also known as "green card" holders), from most means-tested public assistance programs, though allowed states discretion to include some formally authorized migrants who met the5-year ban on benefits set by Congress (Freeman et al. 2000; Freeman and Plascencia 1999).

The latter two Acts expanded the category of "aggravated felony," which in turn significantly reduced who would be granted asylum, permanent residency, U.S. citizenship, as well as grounds for preventing deportation (renamed "removal" in 1996). Under IIRIRA, the retroactive inclusion of crimes that may have been committed, even if the event took place decades before and the migrant had already served the mandated incarceration or probation time, had two important consequences. First, it increased the number of migrants classified as "criminals" and thus the total number of persons subject to removal. This has produced a subtle conceptualization of removals by ICE. It has allowed ICE to claim a high success in removing "criminals," an action that on its face many "conservatives" and "liberals/progressives" would support. Thus individuals who in everyday discourse might be thought of as persons "who have paid their dues" to society, are classified as "criminals" and become subject to removal, along with those who are under custody for committing a crime.[11] Second, it expanded the role of local law enforcement entities in identifying and locating such "criminals" through the 287(g) certification provision in the Act.[12] The criminalization of migrants is an important element in the constitution of migrants as a "dangerous class" (Brace 1872), a dimension further discussed below.

While there is no doubt that the enactment of the three statutes expanded the articulation between state/local and federal policy-making regarding migrants, and the enacted changes are major policy transformations, when viewed historically, they can be considered a continuation and expansion of long-standing practices, rather than newly instituted actions. State and local governments have a long

---

[11] A recent review of ICE Secure Communities apprehension data by the journalist Daniel González showed that 66 % of those apprehended and removed had committed low-level crimes, or had no criminal record (González 2011).

[12] The result of these practices has been that migrants who are otherwise 'law-abiding' persons are transformed into "criminals" as a result of minor infractions such as operating a car with a non-functioning tail light; and so it is the infraction that results in a 'probable cause' to stop the vehicle, and then leads to the inquiry regarding migration status. If the person is deemed to be subject to removal, the local law enforcement entity will retain the person in custody, and so the individual is transformed into a "criminal." If an ICE agent takes custody of the person and offers the option of "voluntary departure" and the individual accepts rather than requesting a removal hearing, then ICE can take credit for having removed a "criminal." Such a removal is considered that same as if ICE had taken custody of a county prisoner convicted of a felony and removed that person from U.S. territory.

history of enacting policies aimed at regulating migration and migrants, in both *de jure* and *de* facto forms (Higham 1963[1981]; Kalnay 1941; Klebaner 1958; U.S. Immigration Commission 1911).

From the Colonial Period to the Nineteenth Century, local governments possessed wide powers regarding the regulation of entry, removal, and granting of citizenship. The Immigration Act of 1882 was the first major action toward the federalization of migration. While policy was set at the federal level after its enactment, state migration bureaus carried out the actual implementation of federal policies. It was not until the 1891 Immigration Act that the regulation of entry and removal became an exclusive federal activity. However, the federalization of migration control did not mean that state and local governments were prohibited from regulating migrants within their jurisdictions; they continued to do so as long as enacted regulations did not contradict Constitutional guarantees such as "equal protection," "due process."

State governments, under the authority of the Tenth Amendment, can take action in policy areas not explicitly delegated to the federal government. Consequently, state and local governments have a long history of enacting policies aimed at regulating needed but unwanted migrants residing in their respective jurisdictions (Pfaelzer 2007; Plascencia 2001; Plascencia et al. 2003a, b). Such policies can be grouped into two broad categories: citizenship-based and migrant-based measures. Citizenship has a long history of being used to exclude migrants from a broad set of public and private resources. Non-citizens have been prohibited from owning farmland, fishing, selling soft drinks, owning a dog, owning a gun, removing garbage, etc. One mechanism that has been and continues to be used is the requirement of citizenship in occupational licenses; specifically those deemed to part of state "police powers" such as teachers, law enforcement officers. Since occupational and business licenses are largely regulated by states, state governments have significant latitude in determining the requirements they can impose on applicants. In addition, states continue to exclude non-citizens from multiple state public resources such as student scholarships, farm loans, appointment to governmental bodies, placing mining claims, etc. In the first half of the Twentieth Century, many labor unions also excluded non-citizens from their membership (Summers 1946).

State and local governments have also adopted measures that do not explicitly require U.S. citizenship, indicate that they are aimed at migrants, or have a migration-related end, yet their context suggests otherwise. In other words, some policymakers have used the power to regulate migrants as an indirect means to regulate "immigration." Included among such migrant-based measures are actions such as restricting hair styles (Chinese queue), adult education classes, restriction on livelihoods, requiring full understanding of English to serve on a jury, some identity theft laws, and others.[13] Moreover, local law enforcement entities have an

[13] An informative discussion of restrictions in one city (San Francisco) against Chinese, such as the queue, "cubic air" requirements in room occupancy, operation of laundries, and others can be found in Courtney (1956). For a sustained discussion of cases regarding Chinese laundries, see Bernstein (1999).

established history of directly participating in efforts to regulate migration, despite the recognized preemptive powers of the federal government in this policy area. Some of the prominent efforts include the role of county sheriff and local police department personnel in aiding major migration control efforts such as the Immigration and Naturalization Service (INS) deportation efforts in the 1930s (Balderrama and Rodríguez 2006), the implementation of President F.D. Roosevelt's Executive Order 9066 to remove and intern persons of Japanese descent (both citizens and non-citizens), the implementation of the INS 1954 "Operation Wetback" (García 1980), the implementation of Operation Jobs in 1982 (Plascencia 2011), the informal joint Border Patrol and El Paso Police Department foot patrols between 1980s and 1992, and the multiple workplace raids from the 1970s to at least 2008.

Based on annual data compiled by the National Conference of State Legislatures (NCLS) since 2005, states and local governments have generated a large volume of migration-related legislation. In 2005 there were close to 300 state bills introduced, and 38 enacted; by 2007 over 1,500 bills were proposed and 240 adopted. The latter year represents an important threshold: in that year, all 50 state legislatures considered and adopted efforts to control migration, principally through efforts aimed at migrants. By November of 2009, all 50 states had debated a combined total of 1,500 bills, passed 222 laws, and adopted 131 resolutions, Alaska and Massachusetts were the only two states that did not approve or adopt migration control measures. And for 2010, NCLS reports that "more than 1,400 were introduced, 208 laws were enacted, 10 were vetoed, and 138 resolutions were adopted for a total of 346" juridical actions (NCLS 2011). The level of action at the state level highlights the saliency of the issue of migration among state policy makers.

County and local policy makers have also been engaged with efforts to regulate migration and migrants. While no single entity has replicated the efforts of NCLS in tracking local ordinances, law journal articles analyzing specific ordinances, and news media coverage of major legal challenges, index a significant level of concern. Between May 2006 and July 2007, according to Fair Immigration Reform Movement, close to 160 cities and counties in 33 states had sought such efforts. While comparable data do not exist for 2008–2010, the issue of migration control remains key for local policy makers. One indicator of this is the number of state and local law enforcement entities that have obtained 287(g) certification.

According to ICE, between 2002 and 2009, a total of 66 local law enforcement entities had signed a memorandum of agreement, the majority of which are county entities. However, what is noteworthy is the number added in 2007 (22) and 2008 (30). And as of October 2010, ICE reports that it has 71 agreements in 25 states (ICE 2011). It should be noted that although ICE claims great success in establishing "partnerships" with local law enforcement entities across the nation, the data suggest a less rosy picture. Particularly when one observes that there are 3,143 counties in the United States, 48 continental states, and 276 cities with populations of 100,000 or more; and that some entities have canceled their agreements with

ICE, such as Massachusetts in 2007. What is also obscured by the total number of agreements (71) is that 18 (25 %) of these are represented by two states, Arizona (9) and Virginia (9), that California with the nation's largest population (an estimated 37.3 million) and a substantial migrant component accounts for only three agreements, and New York City, the nation's most populous city (approximately 8.4 million) and a city with a large migrant population from across the globe has chosen not to formally "partner" with ICE.[14]

The diversity of measures that have been considered, while important in themselves for what they indicate about the articulation between federal, state, and local regulation of migration, need to also be contextualized within the population they aim to control. The majority of the legislative efforts are aimed at Latino migrants in general, but specifically Mexican-origin migrants, particularly those labeled "illegal/undocumented" migrants. Law professor Michael A. Olivas, a prolific scholar who has examined migration and education law for over two decades, arrived at the following conclusion regarding restrictionist state and local measures[15]:

> I believe that most of the current local and state ordinances, even as they are sometimes undifferentiated and aimed in a vague way at perceived 'foreigners,' are primarily aimed at excluding and stigmatizing immigrants of Mexican heritage, whether citizen, undocumented, or ascribed-undocumented. I believe such prejudice is clearly aimed at Mexicans, real or imagined (2008, p. 104).

Olivas's conclusion echoes similar views expressed by other scholars who have examined the formation of anti-migrant discourses in the United States and the near synonymous association between "Mexican" and "illegal/undocumented" migrant (Chávez 2001; Fernández and Pedroza 1981; Heyman 1998, 2001; Santa Ana 2002). The mast to the anonymous Attrition Through Enforcement website is explicit about the association made between the concept and Mexicans (Fig. 7.1).

---

[14] In the case of Arizona, the following entities have a 287(g) agreement with ICE: Arizona Department of Corrections, Arizona Department of Public Safety, City of Mesa Police Department, City of Phoenix Police Department, Florence Police Department, Maricopa County Sheriff's Office, Pima County Sheriff's Office, Pinal County Sheriff's Office, and Yavapai County Sheriff's Office (See ICE 2011). It also should be noted that the absence of a formal agreement with ICE does not mean that local police do not communicate or coordinate activities with ICE.

[15] It should be noted that the label restrictionist, as used here, should not be interpreted as indexing a homogeneous or monolithic set of individuals or organizations within states, but rather a general orientation toward migration and migrants. The common element among individuals and organizations labeled "restrictionist" is a general position on the need to reduce migration to the United States, particularly from Asian and Latin American nations, and the support of arguments that allege a net negative impact of migrants on the social fabric of the nation and its economic wellbeing. On the other hand, "pro-migrant" individuals and organizations are also conceptualized as representing diverse perspectives; such entities tend to support arguments that allege a net-positive gain to the nation.

Fig. 7.1 *Source* http://attritionthroughenforcement.com/Home/tabid/36/Default.aspx

Consequently, state and local efforts to regulate migration and migrants are not simply about the protection of public resources, they appear to be associated with ongoing states of despair and anguish about the nation, about membership and belonging. In other words, sociopolitical anxieties about the circle of membership—the demarcation between the US and the THEM[16]—including fears about the future racial/ethnic composition of the United States, fear of the loss of a presumed monocultural nation, and the prominence and political status of the increasing Latino population.[17] The strategy of attrition through enforcement can be thought of as representing an approach that effectively integrates and depends on such anxieties, and promotes a horizon that is appealing to some, but one that is not likely to materialize.

Arizona, Pre-operation Gatekeeper

Most contemporary discussions of SB 1070, both by journalist and academics, tend to locate it as the starting point or as part of a 'new' anti-migrant wave that emerged in Arizona in 2010. What is overshadowed in the common narrative is the long-standing concern with migrants, as well as the more recent precursors to SB 1070. Space does not allow a full discussion of the multiple nineteenth and twentieth century examples of restrictionist state actions taken, particularly after 1880,

---

[16] Some of the prominent perspectives on this distinction are found in Bennett 1992, Buchanan 2002, Huntington 2004, Limbaugh 1992; as well as among television and talk-show radio personalities such Glenn Beck, Lou Dobbs, and others.

[17] The notion of a "presumed monocultural nation" refers to the common perspective that the United States has since its founding had a single culture, and single language. While English is the *de facto* national language, this is different from assuming that no other languages or cultures have existed in the territory that now comprises the United States of America. The multiple Native American communities and languages in the continental states, Alaska, and Hawai'i, for example, that existed prior to 1776 and continue to exist to the present, suggest that the United States has always been a multicultural nation. It is a diversity that has historically proved valuable. Choctaw speakers in World War I, and later Apache, Comanche, Meskwaki, Navajo, and other Native American communities, as well as Basque, played a major role in the outcomes of World War I and II.

however, brief mention of some of these is useful as a way to underscore the need for a more comprehensive understanding of SB 1070 and its deep roots.[18]

Two months short of its 2-year anniversary as a new state in the Republic (December 14, 1914), George W.P. Hunt, Arizona's first governor, enacted the "Act to Protect the Citizens of the United States in Their Employment against Noncitizens of the United States, in Arizona." Its contemporary sounding title matches contemporary concerns. The principal provision stated:

> Section 1. Any company, corporation, partnership, association or individual who is, or may hereafter become an employer of more than five (5) workers at any one time, in the state of Arizona, regardless of kind or class of work, or sex of workers, shall employ not less than eighty (80) per cent qualified electors or native-born citizens of the United States or some subdivision thereof (*Truax V. Raich* 1915).

The measure aimed to secure an affirmative action employment position for U.S. born citizens, particularly those defined as "White native" population,[19] in the state, irrespective of qualifications; and it imposed a set of sanctions on employers who violated the law, and on employees who falsely claimed U.S. citizenship in seeking employment.

Mr. Mike Raich, a native of Austria and resident of the state, was dismissed from his job as a cook at a restaurant in Cochise County, and on December 15, 1914 filed a lawsuit contesting his firing. The case progressed to the U.S. Supreme Court, and on November 1, 1915, the Court ruled that Arizona's action violated the equal protection afforded by the 14th Amendment, which specifies "nor shall any State deprive any person of life, liberty, or property, without due process of law; nor deny to any person within its jurisdiction the equal protection of the laws." Mr. Raich, a non-citizen "person" under the construction of the Amendment, benefited from the protections afforded by the Constitution.

In 1915, the state also considered a provision in the Claypool-Kinney bill, a measure that on the surface was a 'public health/occupational safety' proposal that required persons working in hazardous jobs to speak and write in English. Employer opposition to the measure prevented its passage. Some Mexican-origin

[18] Meeks (2007) and other historians have noted that the year 1880 marks an important transition for Arizona's economy and social relations. The observation is that with the accelerated economic development that took place in that year, the immigration of European-descent individual also increased substantially, and so the combined effect was to make racial/ethnic boundaries more fixed. Prior to 1880, Spanish/Mexican elite had significant control over political and economic resources, and so the smaller European descent community maintained generally good relations with both the Mexican and Native American communities in the state; including intermarriage.

[19] "White native," "white," "American citizen," and "old stock" were common labels used in the late 1800s and early 1900s to refer principally to individuals with Cornish, English, Irish, and German origins. Other persons of European descent such as Italians, Spaniards, and those from Eastern Europe were not considered full members of the broader "white" community. This racialized scheme positioned Mexicans below these two groups, and Native Americans below Mexicans (Meeks 2007).

observers interpreted the proposed bill as an effort to exclude Mexicans from working in the state's copper mines—a key sector in Arizona's economy. And 2 years later (1917), the state copied California's 1913 "Alien Land Law," thus prohibiting "aliens ineligible to naturalize because of race" (i.e., Japanese and other Asians, including Punjabi Sikhs) from owning agricultural land in Arizona (Lowe 1976).

From the pre-World War I years and continuing through the present, various historians have described the difficult sociopolitical experience of racialized communities, specifically African Americans, Chinese Americans, Mexican Americans, Native Americans, Punjabi Sikhs, and others, as they sought to access economic, social, and political opportunities in Arizona, particularly in the Phoenix area. Their full integration into society in Arizona was hampered by state and local laws and practices that upheld anti-miscegenation measures, residential segregation, employment discrimination, Jim Crow measures in public facilities and accommodations, and others.[20] A central element in some of the ordinances and practices was the concern with the presence and impact of non-citizens ("aliens," "strangers"), particularly with the sizeable growth of the Mexican-origin community.

Exclusions, as Badiou (2004) has insightfully articulated, can simultaneously occur with inclusions. The above exclusions support this view. The completion of the Roosevelt Dam in 1911, a product of the federal 1902 Reclamation Act, secured a stable water supply and fostered a substantial increase in acreage devoted to cotton—another one of Arizona's core commodities. The expanded acreage required a proportional increase in labor; cotton growers, in violation of the 1885 Contract Labor Act (23 Stat. 332), recruited Mexican workers for cotton picking in Arizona.[21] Mexican migrants were welcomed by the cotton sector, and contributed to the growth and wealth of the state; other sectors opposed such recruitment, though benefited from the economic multiplier effect and revenues to the state from the increased cotton production. The passage of the restrictive 1917 Immigration Act (39 Stat. 874), with its literacy and increased head tax requirements, and the entry of the U.S. into World War I, led Arizona cotton growers to demand a waiver to the 1885 and 1917 laws. The U.S. Secretary of Labor was pressured to interpret the Ninth Proviso in the 1917 Act as granting him the power

---

[20] Some of the relevant sources that examine forms of exclusion based on the racialization of individuals in Arizona include the following: Dimas (1991), Dean and Reynolds (2006), Leonard (1992), Lowe (1976), Luckingham (1994), Meeks (2007), Whitaker (2005). The classic book by the historian Higham (1963[1981]), *Strangers in the Land: Patterns of American Nativism* 1860–1925, provides a detailed description of federal, state, and local policies enacted against "aliens" in U.S. history.

[21] The 1885 Contract Labor prohibited all recruitment of foreign workers for jobs in the United States, and imposed a hefty fine on employers of $1,000 for each offense. Southwest agricultural employers, including some in Arizona, ignored the law, and boundary enforcement officials made limited effort to enforce it. Congress amended the 1885 Act several times, though it remained in effect until repealed by the 1952 McCarran-Walter Act (66 Stat. 163). The best discussion of the 1885 Act is found in Orth (1907).

to waive both Congressional actions.[22] Arizona cotton growers welcomed the federally authorized contract workers from Mexico.[23] A similar though larger scale effort was implemented over 22 years, from 1942 to 1964. The combined impact of these policies is significant. They served to foster a sustained migration from Mexico to Arizona, increased the presence of Mexican-origin persons in the state, and solidified the integration and inclusion of Mexican labor in the state's economy. The aforementioned is a historical context that is absent in the discussions by architects and supporters of attrition through enforcement; their narrative assumes that labor migration operates as a neo-classical, micro-economic process wherein the individual is the unit of analysis, and the State and employers do not have significant roles in the process. It is also ahistorical: actions and policies in the past are not included as important to the understanding of contemporary policies.

Arizona Post-gatekeeper

There is no doubt that Arizona was impacted by the political decision to implement Operation Gatekeeper in the Tijuana-San Ysidro boundary area in October 1994.[24] President Clinton's elections-driven decision produced a lasting impact on the national and state politics on migration, as well as on the loss of lives of thousands of migrants who have behaved in ways not predicted by then INS Commissioner Doris Meissner and her advisors. Commissioner Meissner's assumption that treacherous geography, accompanied by personnel-intensive boundary watch, would effectively eliminate the desire of individual to improve the opportunities for themselves and their children, at the same time that U.S. employers encouraged the migration and granted jobs to those that succeeded, was utopian. The treacherous terrain of the Sonora desert appears to have reduced a fraction of the volume, but did not eliminated it as hoped for by the Clinton and subsequent Administrations. The net impact of the stated policy of "prevention through deterrence" was to shift the historically high level of migrants seeking to enter California, to Arizona. By the second half of 1995, the Tucson Border Patrol sector was reporting a high level of apprehensions, and Arizona ranchers adjacent to Sonora were expressing their alarm and displeasure with the turn of events.

---

[22] The Ninth Proviso contract labor program can be considered the first "bracero program;" although it was predated by smaller U.S.-Mexico arrangements, and followed by the much larger programs associated with World War II that operated between 1942 and 1964. A forthcoming essay examines the historiography of the WWII program.

[23] The 1920 Hearings by the Committee on Immigration and Naturalization in the House of Representatives (U.S. House of Representatives 1920) are a noteworthy source for deciphering the views of major Arizona leaders such as then Congressman Carl Hayden on the important need met by Mexican migrants in the economic growth and wellbeing of Arizona.

[24] For insightful discussions of the boundary enforcement efforts that predated and contributed to the implementation of Operation Gatekeeper, see Dunn (1996, 2009). A book length discussion of Operation Gatekeeper can be found in Nevins (2010).

State and local elected official in Arizona reacted by enacting policy measures aimed at regulating migration and migrants. Thus starting in 1996, a series of ordinances and actions were implemented to address the migration into Arizona that resulted from Operation Gatekeeper. Table 7.1 summarizes some of the policy actions that were implemented in response to the issue[25]:

Table 7.1 underscores the view that it is erroneous to interpret SB 1070 as the start of an "anti-immigrant" trend in Arizona, and instead suggests that SB 1070 is better understood as a measure that expanded previous measures, and explicitly articulated an underlying idea in policy actions enacted between 1996 and 2010. But as SB1611 and other proposed measures make clear, SB 1070 is not a terminal policy action; it is a prequel to other attrition through enforcement initiatives.

Attrition Through Enforcement: Tracing its Genealogy

The exact origin and author(s) of the concept of attrition through enforcement are not clear. However, the two principal promoters are quite clear: the Center for Immigration Studies (CIS), particularly its Executive Director, Mark Krikorian; and Kansas's Kris Kobach, listed as "Of Counsel" (and previously as Senior Counsel) with the Immigration Reform Law Institute (IRLI), formerly a law professor at the University of Missouri at Kansas City School of Law, and elected as Kansas's Secretary of State in November 2010. The Southern Poverty Law Center lists CIS and IRLI as part of the John Tanton "network" of anti-migrant organizations, along with the Federation for American Immigration Reform (FAIR), Numbers USA, U.S. English, Negative Population Growth (NPG), and others.[26]

In 2004, Kobach authored a policy brief for CIS that outlined his argument that state and local police "possess the inherent authority to arrest aliens" for both criminal and civil violations of federal migration laws as part of a "unified approach" to halting "terrorists" (2004). This was followed by the release of two short CIS policy newsletters that outlined the concept of attrition through enforcement, the first in May 2005 (Krikorian 2005) and the second on April 2006 (Vaughan 2006). During the period covered by the two CIS briefs, Kobach

[25] Table 7.1 does not include the bills proposed but not enacted. Former Governor Janet Napolitano (2003–2009) vetoed some of the measures proposed. Her appointment to the post of Secretary of the Department of Homeland Security (DHS) by President Obama, allowed Governor Janet K. Brewer to assume the position of Governor.

[26] The Southern Poverty Law Center (SPLC) has developed an ongoing set of reports on John Tanton and the organizations and activities he has initiated and supported since the 1980s (see htt p://www.splcenter.org. Their initial report, "Puppeteer," described the effective political strategy that John Tanton, M.D. formulated (SPLC 2002) and the links to the Pioneer Fund, an organization labeled by SPLC as a "white supremacist" funding entity. Moreover, although IRLI does not note its connection to other organizations in the "network," FAIR has indicated that IRLI is "FAIR's legal affiliate" (FAIR nd). The SPLC has classified FAIR as one of the 1,000 "hate" groups in the continental United State for 2010.

Table 7.1 Arizona measures to regulate migration and migrants

Years	Policy action	Brief description
1996	Driver licenses	Required proof of U.S. citizenship or authorized presence
1997	"Chandler roundup" ["looking Mexican"]	Chandler police department and INS apprehension of individuals 'suspected' of being present without formal authorization; U.S. citizens and Permanent Residents are detained[1]
2000	Proposition 203, english for children	Limits English as a Second Language (ESL) instruction
2004	Proposition 200, protect Arizona now	A multi provision statute targeted at non-citizens; included provisions regarding voting, public benefits, mandates state employees to report persons suspected of being present without authorization, and others
2005	Day labor law (H.B. 2592)	Prohibits local government from constructing or maintaining a day labor site used by "aliens" who are "not entitled to lawful residence"
2005	"Coyote" law (anti-smuggling)	Aimed at reducing human smuggling; though used to charge "undocumented" individuals with 'self-smuggling'
2006	Proposition 100	The law denies bail to "undocumented" persons
2006	Proposition 300	Denies in-state tuition for students without a social security number ("undocumented" students)
2006	Proposition 103, english-only	Asserts that Arizona's official language is English, and mandates all official actions to be conducted in English
2007	HB 2779, FLEA/LAWA, employer sanctions	Allows for the cancellation of "licenses" of businesses that employ persons without employment authorization
2010	HB2281	A measure to prohibit ethnic studies programs
2010	SB1070/HB2162	Establishes the policy of attrition through enforcement; requires local law enforcement officials to verify migration status, and other provisions
2011	SB 1611; SB 1308, SB 1309; et al	Not enacted

See Romero and Serag (2004–2005), Romero (2006) for a detailed discussion of the event published a lengthy discussion on his argument on the "inherent arrest authority" (also referred to as "inherent authority") of local police departments to enforce federal immigration law in Kobach 2005–2006, and a short law journal article in Kobach 2007–2008, that present academic descriptions of the concept of attrition through enforcement (Kobach 2005–2006, 2007–2008).[27] Although a number of the anti-migrant organizations, such as Numbers USA, FAIR, and the anonymous authors of the web site Attrition Through Enforcement,[28] have expressed their support for the concept, these sources appear to rely on the language and/or concepts found in documents released by the CIS, and those authored by Kobach.

Attrition through enforcement encompasses a set of political positions and policy prescription aimed at eliminating the presence of migrants perceived to be a danger to the United States economy and society, particularly to states and local communities. The core premises, as outlined in the CIS and Kobach documents, including his Congressional testimony (Kobach 2005, 2006, 2009), are the following:

1. It is a "rational," "alternative," "third way" to solve the nation's "illegal immigration" problem (including the presence of "illegal aliens"): it is an alternative to the "false choices" of either granting "amnesty/legalization" to the estimated 10–12 million migrants deemed to constitute the "unauthorized" population, or implementing a draconian mass removal of such persons;
2. It is a realistic and doable action: it simply builds and expands on numerous other efforts already being implemented such as workplace raids, expansion of Border Patrol, criminalization of unauthorized re-entry, E-Verify, Social Security Administration No-Match letters, the "Special Registration" efforts aimed at Muslims, Secure Communities, and state and local restriction on public benefits;
3. It is the consistent application of existing laws and law enforcement tools: upholding the "rule of law" will lead to broad public support and weaken the opposition from un-named "loose border" or "open border" activist organizations and individuals;
4. It will result in the "self-deportation" on the part of "unauthorized" migrants: migrants are "rational" beings, and so when confronted with limited access to jobs and public and private resources (e.g., housing, driver licenses, medical care), they will "naturally" "deport themselves";
5. It is a key strategy that state and local governments can implement: state and local governments have the authority to implement a wide array of restrictions/exclusions on the "unauthorized" migrant population, such as prohibiting the private rental of housing, prohibiting municipalities from adopting 'city of refuge', and/or police departments from enacting 'Don't Ask, Don't Tell' ordinances, eliminating

[27] Kobach's article cites Vaughan's policy brief, but not Krikorian's. A somewhat odd fact given that Krikorian published the earlier brief which appears to be the first use of the notion, and Kobach invokes the concept of "self-deportation," which Krikorian used in the 2005 policy brief.

[28] See http://attritionthroughenforcement.com.

in-state tuition for migrants without a social security number, redefine birthright citizenship for U.S.-born children of "unauthorized" migrant parents; and
6. The incorporation of local law enforcement entities across the country in enforcing federal migration laws, based on their "inherent authority," will serve as a "force multiplier" in the twofold task of preventing "terrorism" and reducing the presence of "illegal immigrants."

The neutral-sounding concept, similar to the "prevention through deterrence" predecessor under the Clinton Administration in the implementation of Operation Gatekeeper and subsequent boundary enforcement efforts, is a notion with significant implications for the wellbeing of communities, particularly those defined as ethnic-Mexican communities.[29] To their credit, the architects of the concept were able to formulate a common-sensical sounding discourse that on the surface appears to be a kinder, gentler form for addressing the nations "immigration problem" in the absence of a federal "comprehensive immigration reform." Through the integration of commonly supported notions of upholding the "rule of law," anti-terrorism efforts to assure the public safety and security of the nation, and state and national policy concerns regarding migration and migrants, with an alleged set of "well established" legal principles, the architects, particularly Kobach's contribution, produced a discourse that many state and local policy makers readily adopted. In 2010, Arizona enacted attrition through enforcement as "the public policy of all state and local government agencies in Arizona." Thus, attrition through enforcement is more than an academic issue that scholars can spill much ink to talk among themselves and fill the pages of law and academic journals; it is a policy that merits a more substantial understanding of its premises and assumptions.

The Bybee-I Memo, OLC April 2002

To understand why the promotion and adoption of the concept of attrition through enforcement, as well as one of its central tenets, came to fruition, it is important to examine two important documents and their particular developments: (a) the secretive U.S. Department of Justice, Office of Legal Counsel (OLC), April 3, 2002 memo to Attorney General John D. Ashcroft, and (b) Attorney General Ashcroft's Prepared Remarks of June 6, 2002.[30] The former document is titled "Non-preemption of the authority of state and local enforcement officials to arrest aliens for immigration violations," and was authorized by Jay S. Bybee, Assistant Attorney General in the OLC (President G.W. Bush appointed Jay S. Bybee in

[29] The concept of prevention through deterrence masked that the policies and actions that were developed could and did result in the deaths of an estimated 200 migrants per year.

[30] The OLC 2002 Memo is available at http://www.aclu.org/immigrants-rights/olc-memo-state-and-local-law-enforcement-immigration-laws-1; and Attorney General Ashcroft's prepared remarks can be found at http://parstimes.com/news/archive/2002/Ashcroft.html.

2003 to the Ninth Circuit Court of Appeals). The April 2002 memo (Bybee-I) was followed 4 months later by the OLC August 1 memo, more commonly known as the "Bybee Memo," "Torture Memos", or "Standards for Conduct for Interrogation under 18 U.S.C. 2340–2340A." A comparative discussion of the Bybee-I and Bybee-II memos would be instructive, however, what is relevant here is not the comparison of the content, but their parallel policy process and the eventual court interventions that made both memos public.

Both memos represent formulations of federal policy by the Executive Branch, they led to policy actions guided by the authority of the memos, and were kept secret. The American Civil Liberties Union (ACLU) and other organizations filed Freedom of Information Act (FOIA) requests for both memos. A redacted version of the Bybee-I memo was released by the Justice Department on July 22, 2005; the Central Intelligence Agency (CIA) and Justice Department (DOJ) released the "harsh interrogation techniques" documents on April 15, 2010. What is also noteworthy is that the CIA and DOJ released the *full content* of the torture memos, but DOJ released a redacted copy of the 2002 OLC memo in which 3 of the 13 pages contain only a small portion of text—thus the full content of the first memo remains unknown to the public.[31]

Based on the proceedings of the Federal District Court and Second Circuit Appellate Court that heard the ACLU et al. FOIA request,[32] Kobach was central to the development and drafting of the April memo, as well as the promotion of the core ideas such as when he "sort of summarize[d]" the contents of the memo in March 2003 at a meeting of the FBI's Criminal Justice Information Services Advisory Board, a meeting attended by some state and local law enforcement representatives. The portion of the memo made public reveals two core arguments: One, previous OLC memos (i.e., 1989 and 1996) that restricted state and local law enforcement entities from enforcing civil immigration violations are deemed to be "mistaken" and represent "misplaced" interpretations of case law and statutes; and Two, that based on a concept that states are "sovereign entities," that Congress has not statutorily refused to receive 'assistance' from the states, and a 'correct' reading of case law, states possess an "inherent authority" to arrest "aliens" suspected of having violated criminal and **civil** provisions in migration law (my emphasis).

The April OLC memo came to symbolize the presumed correct interpretation of law, and was followed by communication from Attorney General Ashcroft to some chiefs of police indicating that, based on Department of Justice OLC

---

[31] The legal arguments pursued by the Department of Justice to keep the memo secret were: first, that the memo was an internal pre-decision document and did not constitute a policy adopted by the Department or other federal agencies; second, in the appeal they added the argument that the memo should remain secret because it represented a document related to the attorney-client privilege. The appellate court rejected both arguments, though it allowed the Department to redact some information in the memo.

[32] See *National Council of La Raza*, et al. *v. Department of Justice*, No. 03 Civ. 2559 (LAK), U.S. District Court, S.D. New York (2004), and *National Council of La Raza*, et al. *v. Department of Justice*, 411 F3d. 350 (2005).

opinion, they had the "inherent authority" to begin arresting "aliens" suspected of violating not only criminal provisions, but also civil provisions of migration law. But when ACLU and other migrant-rights organizations, as well as members of Congress, sought to request copies of the new policy, the DOJ refused to release the memo because it was an internal confidential document, and did not represent policy.

The prescribed policy in the April 2002 OLC memo surfaced 2 months later in the prepared remarks by Attorney General Ashcroft (June 6, 2002). On that date, Ashcroft made public the implementation of the National Security Entry-Exit Registration System (NSEERS; more commonly known as the Special Registration program). The principal individuals required to register are persons from 24 nations in the Middle East and North Africa, nations with a significant Muslim populations. What is relevant here is that Ashcroft's comments made an explicit association between terrorism and state and local spaces, including an association between "terrorist" and "the border"[33]:

> In this new war, our enemy's platoons infiltrate our borders, quietly blending in with visiting tourists, students, and workers. They move unnoticed through our cities, neighborhoods, and public spaces. Their tactics rely on evading recognition at the border and escaping detection within the United States. Their terrorist mission is to defeat America, destroy our values and kill innocent people (Ashcroft 2002).

Toward the end of his remarks, Attorney General Ashcroft drew upon a point later elaborated by Kobach and CIS, the idea that the existence of "650,000 police officers" in the nation could contribute to the identification of "aliens" who had violated the mandated Registration (Ashcroft 2002). In other words, local police officers working independently or in partnership with ICE through the 287(g) program, would allow the substantial expansion of personnel tracking individuals suspected of violating the Special Registration requirements as well other immigration laws. Kobach refers to this as the "force multiplier": "The more than 650,000 police officers nationwide represent a massive force multiplier" (Kobach 2004, p. 1; see also Kobach 2005–2006). What should be noted here, however, is that the focus of Kobach's 2004 essay is on "stopping terrorist," thus the push for state and local law enforcement entities, in this reiteration, is for the use of their "inherent authority" to apprehend "terrorist." His testimony to Congress in 2005 and 2006 position state and local enforcement, including the 287(g) program, as central to anti-terrorism (Kobach 2005, 2006).

---

[33] Among scholars specializing on the Mexico-United States boundary area, it has long been observed that the national discourse on United States boundaries has coded the Mexico-United States political boundary as "the border." From journalist, academics, policy makers, to human rights and pro-migrant groups along the 2,000-mile southern boundary, many among these have developed a taken-for-granted speech act regarding the southern boundary; that boundary has been encapsulated as "the border." The hegemonic position of the linguistic term disavows the social reality about the multiple U.S. political boundaries—e.g., the Canada–United States 4,000-mile boundary, the Alaska–Canada boundary, the coastal U.S. borders, and the coastal boundaries of island possessions such as Hawai'i and Puerto Rico, etc.

The final relevant point made by Ashcroft in his 2002 prepared remarks, is his reference to the April OLC memo and the aims of the announced policy:

> When federal, state and local enforcement officers encounter an alien of national security concern who has been listed on the NCIC [National Crime Information Center] for violating immigration laws, federal law permits them to arrest that individual and transfer him to the custody of the INS [Immigration and Naturalization Service]...The Justice Department's Office of Legal Counsel has concluded that this narrow, limited mission that we are asking state and local police to undertake voluntarily—arresting aliens who have violated criminal provisions of Immigration and Nationality Act **or civil provisions** that render an alien deportable, and who are listed on the NCIC—is within the **inherent authority of the states**. The Department of Justice has no plans to seek additional support from state and local law enforcement in enforcing our nation's immigration laws, **beyond our narrow anti-terrorism mission** (Ashcroft 2002; my emphasis).

Ashcroft foregrounds the change in policy that erases the DOJ's previous distinction between criminal and civil violation of migration provisions, and asserts the concept of the inherent authority of states to arrest persons suspected of such violations; he also observes that the suggested states' use of that inherent authority is focused on "anti-terrorism."

An important point here is that Kobach's and CIS's subsequent elaboration of the principle of inherent authority gradually shifts to a concern focused on the power of state and local governments to restrict private and public resources from persons suspected of being present without formal authorization. In other words, the inherent authority concept becomes the central rationale for attrition through enforcement, and in the process the dangerous "alien" replaces the figure of the "terrorist." And by 2009, Kobach added a supportive element to the aforementioned: state and local enforcement of federal immigration laws is also aimed at "protecting unemployed U.S. citizens" (Kobach 2009). According to Kobach:

> The final purpose that Sect. 287(g) achieves in many jurisdictions is the removal of unauthorized aliens who are occupying jobs that would otherwise go to U.S. citizens or to aliens authorized for employment in the United States...This objective is served in **Maricopa County** as well...Removing unauthorized alien employees from the United States **creates jobs for U.S. citizens** the very next day (Kobach 2009, p. 12; my emphasis).

The fact that Kobach does not provide any support for his assertion is notable, but what is more important is that the 2009 arguments link economic concerns within the national recession, with the "inherent authority" rationale. Attrition through enforcement is thus infused with an economic/employment rationale, and becomes a tool to address real economic difficulties encountered in states and local communities across the nation. The promotion of attrition through enforcement as a readily available option that state and local policy makers could adopt to improve economic conditions, evolved into a common-sensical "third way" to simultaneously eliminate the presence of "unauthorized" migrants, and create "jobs for U.S. citizens," as well as reduce the presumed costs associated with the former. Stated differently, the restriction on forms of livelihood, housing, medical care, driver licenses, in-state tuition, marriage licenses, birth certificates, etcetera, have the 'logical' aim of leading to "self-deportation;" and once the unwanted class of individuals leave, then U.S. citizens will be able to enjoy the benefits and riches being 'stolen' by a "dangerous class." Attrition through enforcement is the policy solution aimed at accomplishing this.[34]

Limitations in the Discourse

Several legal scholars have developed substantive critiques of Kobach's legal reasoning and argumentation in the OLC 2002 memo, his Congressional testimony, and law journal writings (American Immigration Lawyers Association 2002; Keblawi 2003–2004; Olivas 2008; Pham 2004; Wishnie 2004)[35]; detailed descriptions of these are consequently not included here. What is worth noting is the consistent view among a number of his law school peers and fellow attorneys, that Kobach's propositions and arguments are neither convincing nor supported by case law or legal practice. More specifically, the foundational premise of attrition through enforcement (premise number six above) regarding the "inherent arrest authority" of state and local law enforcement entities to enforce provision in immigration law is characterized as 'inherently' or 'deeply' flawed, particularly the argument addressing civil provisions.

And although not intended as an analysis of Kobach's argumentation, a recent Congressional Research Service (CRS) report to Congress on the authority of state and local police to enforce immigration law notes a more complex picture. The CRS notes that while the Appellate Courts of the Ninth and Sixth Circuit have ruled on the side of federal preemption, the Tenth Circuit court has issued rulings that appear to support the position that local entities "have implicit authority to investigate and arrest persons for *either* criminal or civil violations of federal immigration law" (CRS 2010, p. 10; their emphasis). Their conclusion is a more nuanced picture than that argued in the April 2002 OLC memo, or the multiple places where Kobach argues that his interpretation is "well established," "widely recognized," supported by "abundant" and "solid" case law," and the correct one—the argument undergirding the primary provision in SB1070.

The July 6, 2010 lawsuit filed by the U.S. Department of Justice against the State of Arizona (in response to SB1070/HB2162) makes clear that the federal government's position, without referencing the 2002 OLC memo, is that states do not possess an inherent arrest authority; the federal government retains its

[34] The linking of a migration enforcement action with jobs for U.S. citizens is not new. The Hoover Administration's implementation of mass deportations in the late 1920s and early 1930s articulated the same argument (Balderrama and Rodríguez 2006). The argument was again repeated during the implementation of Operation Jobs in 1982 (Plascencia 2011). In both instances, though for different reasons, the promise of jobs for U.S. citizens remained a political assertion with a positive popular appeal.

[35] It should be noted that the AILA (American Immigration Lawyers Association) document has as its focus the proposed rules for the NSEERS program, however, the rules duplicate the inherent arrest authority argument, thus its comments are relevant.

preemptive powers. After describing the special case created by Congress for the 287(g) program, the lawsuit notes:

> But the opportunity that federal law provides for participation by state and local officials does not mean that states can enact their own immigration policies to rival the national immigration policy; the formulation of immigration policy and balancing of immigration enforcement priorities is a matter reserved for the federal government. Such regulations do not fall within the state's traditional police powers and remain the exclusive province of the federal government (*United States v. Arizona*: 13).

It is this critical juridical/political interpretation that the Court of Appeals in the Ninth Circuit is currently reviewing, and that the U.S. Supreme Court will eventually issue an opinion on. Yet irrespective of the pending judgments, what should not be lost is the problem in Kobach's proposition that the "inherent arrest authority" of local entities is unproblematic, and well established, and that the April 2002 OLC proves it.

The limitations in Kobach's interpretations are also evident in the principal state and local cases that have dealt with questions of state/local powers to regulate migrants and exclude their access to resources, and which he litigated. A review of these cases shows that the most of the respective courts did not find his arguments convincing, and ruled against his clients.[36] These facts, however, have not necessarily reduced the attraction of Kobach's promotion of "inherent authority" or attrition through enforcement. His status as a law school professor appears to have aided the promotion and adoption of these, despite the significant criticisms from established law school professors and immigration attorneys, as well as ACLU attorneys; and now the same federal agency that employed him during 2002 and 2003.

There are several limitations in the concept of attrition through enforcement. The first of these is the ahistorical nature of the concept. As noted above, the argument completely eschews all historical processes that have been key in establishing the foundation for migration, both in violation of law, and accordance with law. Some examples of the processes were noted above. Second, the argumentation is premised on an alleged clear distinction between "legal" and "illegal" migrants in federal law. Yet there is a long list of historical and contemporary exceptions that have allowed migrants to enter without formal authorization such as the discretion of migration officials not to enforce the 1885 Contract Labor Law in the Southwest from 1885 to 1952; the 1948 and 1954 'Open Border incidents;' the contemporary 'Dry Foot, Wet Foot' policy that grants Cuban nationals who

---

[36] In the cases of *Lozano v. Hazleton*, PA (local regulation of private rental housing and other provisions); *Gray v. Valley Park*, MO (a local employer sanctions case); *Villas v. Farmers Branch*, TX (local regulation of private rental housing); *Day v. Bond* (in-state tuition for "unauthorized" migrant students); and *Martínez v. University of California Board of Regents* (in-state tuition). However, in the minor case of *Freemont v. Kotas*, a case involving the opposition of the City of Freemont (a city with a population of about 25,000) to a proposed anti-migrant voter initiative, a state court ruled that voters could proceed with their initiative. In the case against SB1070, a federal court ruled against the principal provision; this could also be counted as an additional preliminary loss for Mr. Kobach.

manage to evade Coast Guard or Customs officials and enter via water or land, permanent residency and a 'path to citizenship,' even though they arrived without any documents authorizing their entry; the granting of entry under humanitarian and foreign policy issues. In addition, there are multiple federal policies that recognize the presence of "unauthorized" migrants and allow for their integration into U.S. society (Plascencia under review). One of the less known ones, but a specially noteworthy one, is 8 U.S.C. §1440, the statute, with origins dating back to the Civil War, that allows the granting of U.S. citizenship to "...an alien or a noncitizen national...**whether or not he has been lawfully admitted** to the United States for permanent residence" (my emphasis). The provision has allowed "undocumented" migrants performing military work during defined conflict periods, including under the present 'war on terrorism,' to be granted U.S. citizenship.[37]

Third, the CIS and Koback writings avoid addressing the role of employers in providing jobs to individuals without employment authorization; the jobs that presumably will be offered to U.S. citizens after attrition through enforcement measures take effect. While I am not suggesting that employer sanctions are a solution, what I am indexing here is that the argumentation for attrition through enforcement disavows a social reality that is central to understanding the presence of persons they define as the problem that must be solved. If one accepts the argument that a key objective of state and local enforcement of civil and criminal violations of immigration law is 'to create jobs for U.S. citizens,' then local police and sheriffs could use their "inherent authority" to simply go door to door in affluent neighborhoods and review the presence of unauthorized domestic workers, develop a plan to visit *all* employers in the city and state, and review the I-9 s for every employee. Furthermore, while visiting employers, state and local law enforcement officers could also review if employers are abiding with federal wage and hour laws, OSHA workplace safety laws, DOL agricultural worker laws, EEOC employment discrimination laws, EPA regulations, as well as the U.S. tax code. Such 'assistance' to the federal government would greatly augment the "massive force multiplier" effect. Employers found to be illegally employing persons without employment authorizations, or violating federal criminal and civil statutes could be immediately arrested or cited for violating IRCA's employer sanctions provision, as well as the Legal Arizona Workers Act (LAWA). Employers violating the non-immigration laws could be detained and promptly reported to the respective federal agency. These options are noted to foreground

[37] It is notable that scholars and others assuming a restrictionist position, particularly a strong anti "amnesty" position, almost never make reference to the federal "amnesty" granted to Cuban nationals, to migrants that qualify under 8 U.S.C. §1440, or to the "Registry" provision that dates back to 1929 (and revised several times since then) and allows the granting of Permanent Residency to migrants who may have entered without authorization but have been successful at remaining undetected and being law-abiding residents. Mr. Kobach has expressed his position on the DREAM Act as being an action that will provide an unwanted amnesty (a "sleeper amnesty") (Kobach 2007).

the problematic nature of the logical extension of the application of what CIS and Kobach argue is the alleged inherent authority of state and local law enforcement entities.

Arizona's actions, moreover, have shown that local and state inherent authority will not likely be applied to employers; they are granted amnesty for violating the rule of law. There are two clear examples of this. The first is the enactment of the LAWA in 2007 that took effect in January 2008. The LAWA was promoted as an urgently needed measure to address the economic and social crisis posed by the large number of Arizona employers who were in violation of the federal restriction enacted by President Reagan in 1986 (IRCA), and who were employing an unknown but sizeable workforce of persons without employment authorization—presumably depriving U.S. citizens of jobs. The LAWA enacted an employer sanctions provision, and provided for the cancellation of operating "licenses" for the law-breaking employers. Over the slightly more than three years since it took effect, the Arizona Attorney General's office reports that only two employers have been charged with initial violations of the law (Water World, Glendale, AZ, December 2009; and Danny's Subway, Inc., Phoenix, March 2010).[38] SB1070, moreover, enacted an additional level of protection for Arizona employers: employers can invoke "entrapment" protection if they 'unknowingly' hired persons without employment authorization who were working with law enforcement officials; thus, SB1070 simultaneously seeks to punish migrant workers and protect employers who violate the state's LAWA.

A second example is the results of the workplace raids ("investigations") conducted by Maricopa County Sheriff Joe Arpaio. As of March 2011, 43 workplace raids and traffic stops have been conducted over the recent years, and 465 "undocumented" migrants have been arrested; employees possessing an invalid ID are charged with "identity theft," a class-four felony. However, none of the known employers employing the apprehended individuals have been charged with violation of the LAWA. The result is a plainly odd situation since the Sheriff's office news releases and newspaper coverage of the workplace raids generally provide the name and address of the employer (e.g., Scottsdale Art Factory, 7407 East Greenway, Scottsdale, Arizona 85260, 1-800-292-008; January 28, 2009, 60 arrested and 40 charged with identity theft). The result is that the Sheriff's office, the County Attorney, and the public know who the law-breaking employers are, but the employers are not charged with violating the state's employer sanctions law even though unauthorized employees were removed from the specific premises of the employers. It also appears that Maricopa County residents have selected not to file the readily available complaint form against the known employer violators—an option made available under the LAWA. These examples suggest that the notion of 'upholding of the rule of law,' as discussed by the CIS and Kobach,

[38] http://www.azag.gov/LegalAZWorkersAct/CourtOrders.html.

overlook *de facto* flexibility in its application, the sensitivity allotted to employers in violation of state and federal law, and the forms of amnesty that can emerge.

A fourth limitation in the attrition through enforcement discourse is the sleigh of hand in the promotion of the concept, and incomplete disclosure in Kobach's writings. In Kobach's writings, one finds that the two primary sources of authority for the idea that states and local law enforcement entities possess an "inherent arrest authority" are the 2002 OLC memo (Bybee-I) and the June 2002 prepared remarks of Attorney General Ashcroft regarding the NSEERS program. What is occluded is the fact that Kobach was key in the formulation of the OLC memo (or perhaps may have been the principal author), the Attorney General's prepared remarks simply draw on the OLC memo, and the legal fight that ensued to make the memo public.

The result of the aforementioned is that Kobach's arguments place great weight on inherent authority and attrition through enforcement, and cite the 2002 OLC memo as the foundation for the legal authority. Consequently, he is principally citing himself as the source for the legal authority that he relies on. In testimony provided to Congress and in other writings, he has not acknowledged that he authored the 2002 OLC, or provides details regarding his role in the production of that memo. This is also the case when he notes the examples of state and local governments, or private parties, who have sought to adopt restrictions (e.g., *Lozano v. Hazleton*, PA), He does not disclose his direct involvement in promoting the ordinances, or that he was paid to defend the particular case when it was challenged in court. The development of Arizona's SB1070 was aided by the support of Kobach as Senior Counsel at the IRLI. He was also hired by the Maricopa County Sheriff's office and the Maricopa County Attorney's office as an "immigration expert;"; these contacts in addition to his interaction with State Legislators for Legal Immigration (SLLI), have facilitated his interaction with Arizona State Senator Russell Pearce, a central figure in the enactment of SB1070.

The limited personal documents that have been made public suggest that Kobach had an important role in advising Senator Pearce of the 'legal soundness' of the "inherent authority" of state and local governments to enforce criminal and civil violations of immigration law—the central provision of SB1070. Kobach and Mike M. Hethmon (Director and General Counsel of the IRLI) played an important role in crafting the amendments to SB1070 that produced HB2162, and in making public a strategy on how SB1070 could actually be used. In an e-mail made public, Kobach communicates the following to Senator Pearce:

> Russell,
> I discussed all of the changes with Mike Hethmon and he concurred. But there is one additional point that he suggested—which you will certainly agree with. When we drop out "lawful contact" and replace it with "a stop, detention, or rest [sic], in the enforcement of a violation of any title or section of the Arizona code" we need to add "or any county or municipal ordinance." This will allow police to use violation of property codes (i.e., [sic] cars on blocks in the yard) or rental codes (too many occupants of a rental accommodation) to initiate queries as well.

I have not received anything from the people on the phone this afternoon. Please ensure that they make this addition as well. Thanks! Kris (Kobach 2010).

The enacted HB2162 incorporates the two ideas.[39]

The suggested strategy makes clear that the alleged inherent arrest authority of state and local law enforcement entities is not solely focused on stopping or detaining persons suspected of being "terrorist" or violating a federal criminal or civil violation of immigration law who are stopped or detained in a public place such as a highway, street, park, commercial parking lot. Instead, it is suggested that potential residential infractions become the vehicle and justification for then inquiring into migration status. What is left unstated is that the strategy is a class- and racial/ethnic group-based scheme. Local police seeking to carry out the provisions in the law would know where to find such property code violations—the neighborhoods were lower-income Mexican descent and other racialized minorities live; affluent neighborhoods would remain outside the gaze of police. Such a scheme intrinsically contradicts Governor Brewer's assertion in enacting HB2162, wherein she notes that the "new amendments make it crystal clear and undeniable that racial profiling is illegal, and will not be tolerated in Arizona" (Brewer 2010). The 2007–2009 practices of the Arizona Department of Public Safety (University of Cincinnati Policing Institute 2007, 2008, 2009), and specific inclusion of "county and municipal ordinances," reinforce the actuality and increased possibility that SB1070/HB2162 will intensify the potential of "racial profiling" within the attrition through enforcement strategy.

Discussion

Having explored the development of the concept of attrition through enforcement, and some of its limitations, I now turn to the more difficult issue of seeking an explanation for why Arizona leaders, with support from many residents, pursued the adoption of the 1996–2010 policies, including SB1070. On the assumption that actions pursued by actors must at important levels make sense to the actors, the proposed interpretation seeks to integrate immediate concerns about the impact of the funneling of migrants from the Tijuana-San Ysidro corridor to Arizona after 1994, with relevant broader socioeconomic processes in the United States. Such a perspective seeks to move away from an exclusive focus on individuals, and instead seeks to explore the role of social processes, including power relations,

[39] HB2162 reads as follows: "B. For any lawful **stop, detention or arrest** made by a law enforcement official or a law enforcement agency of this state or a law enforcement official or a law enforcement agency of a county, city, town or other political subdivision of this state **in the enforcement of any other law or ordinance of a county, city or town or this state** where reasonable suspicion exists that the person is an alien **and** is unlawfully present in the united states." The bolded text represent the changes inserted by HB2162; and the plain text is the original language in SB1070.

that shape how individuals may interpret and respond to what they perceive as harmful or beneficial factors to society.

The above discussion and the context of the events suggests that adoption of the 1996–2010 measures in Arizona to regulate migration and migrants encompass actions that were adopted in response to specific factors. I suggest that three important issues motivated the support for the enacted policies: economic trends, demographic trends, and political formulations. I will first summarize the relevant elements in the three issues, and then will seek to link them together into an overall interpretation.

The current "Great Recession" has not only highlighted immediate concerns with household income, employment, and tenuous house ownership due to recent speculation in land and house construction, as well as the collapse of mortgage-based investment portfolios, it also has drawn attention to long-standing economic trends, particularly the pattern of inflation adjusted average hourly earnings. The Bureau of Labor Statistics, Congressional Budget Office (CBO), as well as multiple non-profit entities such as the Economic Policy Institute, have noted the fact that when adjusted for inflation, the average hourly earnings of U.S. workers have been essentially flat since 1980, some argue that this pattern dates back to the early 1970s. Thus, U.S. workers have been struggling to maintain an impossible standard of living, based on their earnings. U.S. households adjusted to their precarious life by adding income earners (if possible), and making up the difference with credit. The Great Recession underscored the inherent limitation of such a strategy—the loss or reduction in income, as well as the devaluation of houses, forced many household to loose their primary asset, their houses. Arizona real estate researchers estimate that 40 % of house owners are living in houses whose value is less than the amount owed. This has created a degree of anguish and uncertainty about the present and the future; including the possibility that children will have a lower standard of living than the parents.

These problematic economic conditions have likely created a deep uncertainty and insecurity for many residents in Arizona. Gusterson and Besteman, and the contributors to their book, label this the "insecure American" (2010). The insecure Arizonan confronts an uncertain condition. Such insecure conditions facilitate the production of an environment that seeks a culprit, a source that can be identified as a principal cause of the economic problems. The "illegal/undocumented" immigrant has become such a subject, a "dangerous class" of strangers. The emergence of the concept of attrition through enforcement dovetailed well with the anguish and desperation to reverse the economic conditions. Its aim to harness all state and local governmental sources to restrict forms of livelihood, driver licenses, medical care, K-12 public education, in-state tuition, etc., with the goal to produce self-deportations and 'create jobs for U.S. citizens' has become a social project that many Arizonans support. Framed in this way, it can be argued that there is a specific rationality in the support for attrition through enforcement: it is a desire to possess economic certainty. But what it fails to take into account is the actual dynamics of labor markets, the historical foundation of migration patterns, the transnational nature of labor and commodity production, as well as the federal tax laws that incentivize corporations to close facilities and relocate production to places with lower labor costs.

The second major factor is the concern with the demographic trends in the state and the nation. At the end of the 1970s, some journalist, corporations, and public officials began to refer to the 1980s as "the Decade of the Hispanic." The designation drew attention to early demographic projections for the 1980s. At the release of the 1990 decennial census, the Bureau of the Census announced that the Latino population had increased by 53 %, an increase from 14.6 to 22.4 million, during the 1980s; representing about 9 % of the total population. By 2000, U.S. Latinos increased by 57.9 % (in contrast to the 13.2 % growth for the total U.S. population) with 35.3 million Latinos, or 12.5 % of the total U.S. population. According to the Pew Hispanic Center, based on the Census data released to date for 33 states, Latinos account for 58 % of the growth in those states, with a combined total of 38.7 million (Passell and Cohn 2011). The Bureau of the Census estimated that in 2010 there would be 47.8 million Latinos, an increase of 12.5 million between 2000 and 2010. Finally, the Bureau's longer-term projections estimate that in 2050 Latinos will comprise 24.4 % of the total U.S. population. The prospects of a nation with one out four individuals being of Latino-descent, and persons of Mexican-origin being the single largest component, has produced an alarming concern among some groups of individuals and political leaders.[40]

The Bureau of the Census's March 2011 release of the initial redistricting data for Arizona shows an overall growth of 24.6 % for the 2000–2010 period, and an increase of 17.3 % for the non-Latino population. The Latino proportion of the population has grown from 18.8 % in 1990 to 25.3 % in 2000, and now it is estimated at 29.6 %; its rate of growth from 2000 to 2010 was 46.3 %. Of the total state population of 6.4 million, Latinos make up 1.9 million.

Irrespective of the exact total, numerous organizations and individuals have since the late 1970s expressed concern with the demographic transformation of the nation. John Tanton, the prime figure in the creation and funding of organizations such as FAIR, CIS, IRLI, U.S. English, and others, has expressed his personal concern that 'immigration is a demographic issue,' and for the loss of the political and social position of 'white-Americans.' As reported by the Southern Law Poverty Center, their tally of "hate"/"nativist" groups reached the 1,000 mark in 2010, and a common thread in many of these groups is the concern with the demographic decline of "white" individuals.[41]

---

[40] I should note that the reaction has not been homogeneous. Corporations and the military are two segments that have responded by reconfiguring their approach to the demographic transition. Since the 1990s, the Department of Defense has been clear that the military of the future, and the defense of the nation, will depend on Latino participation. Kobach's essay for the Heritage Foundation refers to the DREAM Act as "rewarding lawbreaking" and a "nightmare" (2006). Yet his discussion ignores that the Department of Defense is one of the sustaining supporters of the DREAM Act; for DOD it is not a nightmare, it is a reality it embraces.

[41] See http://www.splcenter.org/get-informed/intelligence-report/browse-all-issues/2011/spring, as well as SPLC (2002).

Echos and reiterations of the demographic "peril" posed by the changing demographic profile in the United States, particularly the role of Latinos, are also found among prominent scholars: Schlesinger (1992), Huntington (2004). At the center of their arguments is a certain anguish about the loss of a past; a past that is not fixed chronologically, but is lamented as being lost. Susan Stewart's observation, drawing on a Lacanian concept of "lack," regarding nostalgia is relevant here:

> Nostalgia…is always ideological: the past it seeks has never existed except as narrative, and hence always absent, that past continually threatens to reproduce itself as a felt lack… [N]ostalgia wears a distinctly utopian face, a face that turns toward a future-past, a past which has only ideological reality (1984, p. 23).

The notion of attrition through enforcement appears to be a solution to eliminate a "dangerous class," achieve the self-deportation of that class, and once the process is completed, a way to regain a nostalgic ideological past. The nostalgia embedded in the measures enacted between 1996 and 2010, seems to suggest a past that presumably possessed an accepted demographic profile, a past wherein "non-whites" were present but less visible in the demographic and political landscape.

The final relevant element is a political formulation that has evolved since the 1960s. It is a formulation that is concerned with the political status of "non-Whites," particularly the Mexican-origin and Native American communities in the state. In the case of Native Americans, it should be recalled that the language of "subject to the jurisdiction thereof" in the 14th Amendment (1868), was interpreted as not applicable to Native Americans, thus they did not benefit from the birthright citizenship provision. It was not until the 1924 Indian Citizenship Act that most Native Americans were recognized as U.S. citizens; yet in the case of Arizona, U.S. citizens of Native American descent were not allowed to vote until 1948. Moreover, it was not until the passage of the 1965 Voting Rights Act that many state and local strategies to restrict voting among "minorities" were removed, and it was this that allowed racialized communities to more fully assert their political positions in the ballot box, and in seeking public office.

The net outcome of the last five decades of voting rights cases has been the opening of the political circle in Arizona; Latinos in particular have been able to increase their participation in school boards, city councils, county boards of supervisors, state House of Representatives, the Senate, and the Office of the Governor. A contemporary reading of the 2004 Proposition 200 with its added restrictions on voting, the two English-only measures, and the birthright bill under consideration, suggests that an important but unstated point of contention is the contemporary and future political power of Latinos in the state. To the extent that it grows, driven in significant ways by the demographic changes, it undoubtedly holds an increasing potential to shape the outcome of voter initiatives and who is elected to office. California's experience illustrates the possibility of shifts in political environments that can follow important demographic trends.

Together the economic trends, demographic trends, and political formulations have combined to produce an important and radical phenomenon. It is a process that aims to achieve a political goal: the goal of eliminating the presence of a particular class deemed to be dangerous to the state. The aim of attrition through enforcement is to create a set of social conditions so inhospitable that human life becomes intolerable. Through the removal of access to livelihoods and as many public resources as possible, the strategy strips subjects of elements that make life possible.

Scholars have formulated various labels to describe parallel processes. The Harvard sociologist Orlando Patterson coined the concept of "social death" (1982) in the context of analyzing the symbolic and power operation of slavery. Sjoberg et al. (1984), Sjoberg (1996) and his colleagues, in their effort to examine the operation of bureaucracies, formulated the sociological concept of "social triage" to explain how a bureaucracy, and the broader society, "sacrifices" the "disadvantaged". The anthropologist Arjun Appadurai hypothesizes that a significant number of the world's experience with forms of "ethnic cleansing" and other forms of violence against minorities encompass a "fear of small numbers" (2006). He postulates the counter-intuitive notion that much ethnic cleansing and other forms of "predatory identities" are grounded on the "fear of the weak," and are linked to anxieties about national identities. The concept of "social suffering," as a product of political, economic, and institutional power, is also a parallel (Kleinman et al. 1997). Lastly, the work of Michel Foucault and Giorgio Agamben, specifically their formulation of the concept of "biopolitics," can also be included as efforts to examine forms of exclusion. All of these conceptual efforts draw attention to how individuals and communities assert their superior position of power to regulate a defined class of individuals. The level and form of violence vary, but the goal is similar: to eliminate the presence of a racialized group defined as dangerous to the existing power relations.

Although all of the above authors provide important insights regarding the operation of exclusion, and this sheds light on the notion of attrition through enforcement, I now venture to propose an explanation for what else may be in operation in Arizona. My hypothesis draws on the insights presented by Georges Bataille and Alexander Kojève. In the case of the former, the notion of "expenditure" and sacrifice are central to his analysis of society (Bataille 1985; Richardson 1998), and in the latter, his detailed reformulation of Hegel's *herr-knecht* (translated as master–slave, or master-servant) power relation (Kojève 1947 [1969]).

What I want to suggest is that the general European-descent endorsement of the juridical actions taken between 1996 and 2010, including SB1070, represents an example, borrowing Durkheim's term, of "effervescence," more specifically an expenditure of effervescence. It is an effervescence grounded in the combined economic insecurity and fear of a demographic future—a fear of 'small numbers' now, but a number that will be 'a large number' in the future. Embedded in this fear is the trauma and horror of becoming a 'small number' in the future; and perhaps the fright of the uncertainty of how it will be treated as a 'small number.' As suggested by Kojève, the master in the master–slave relationship has an ongoing fear of the weaker subject and of what the slave may do if the relationship ends and the master is no longer the master. Patterson discusses this tension with specific historical material related to actual slavery.

Bataille's discussion of the 'principle of loss' is applicable to both the demographic and political factor noted above. The concern with the future demographic profile and a changed political landscape, as reflected in the notion of attrition through enforcement, can be thought, as already suggested, as an overriding anguish about what has been "lost." What is perceived to have been lost is a nostalgic ideological past that represents an idealized world where individuals 'knew their place' and behaved accordingly. It was a time, to use the past vernacular, "native Whites"/"Americans" generally held a superior position in the state, and 'non-Whites' respected the power relations that sustained that superiority.

Finally, attrition through enforcement, drawing on Bataille's central concept of sacrifice, can be considered an important political sacrifice. The 'dangerous class' faces a triple sacrifice. As a result of the multiple state exclusions, they must sacrifice their human life if they choose to remain; if they choose to 'self-deport,' they must sacrifice whatever roots and assets they may have accumulated in Arizona; and they must recognize that they are the sacrificial subjects of attrition through enforcement. On the other hand, the sacrificers, like all other sacrificers, must have something to gain; something they desire through the violence imposed on the sacrificial objects or subjects. For Kojève, there is a central desire that operates in the *herr-knecht* relationship:

> To be human, man must act not for the sake of subjugating a thing, but for the sake of subjugating another Desire…The man who desires a thing humanly acts not so much to possess the thing as to make another recognize his right…to that thing, to make another recognize him as the owner of the thing. And he does this…in order to make the other recognize his superiority over the other (1947 [1969], p. 40).

In the case at hand, we can say that attrition through enforcement is a form of political sacrifice that has constructed a sacrificial subject—the Mexican "illegal/undocumented" migrant—but has a more foundational aim than simply promoting self-deportations, or recovering a nostalgic past. Perhaps the process of political sacrifice seeks to re-assert a state and national identity, a way to claim community, to search for economic security, and to retrieve an imagined community that is perceived to have been lost.

References

American Immigration Lawyers Association (2002). Comments on proposed rule titled "registration and monitoring of certain nonimmigrants," http://www.aila.org/content/default.aspx?bc=1016%7C6715%7C8921%7C10552%7C7153

Appadurai A (2006) Fear of small number: an essay on the geography of anger. Duke University Press, Durham, NC

Ashcroft J (2002) Attorney general prepared remarks on the national security entry-exit registration system (June 6). Available at http://www.parstimes.com/news/archives/2002/ashcroft.html

Badiou A (2004). Infinite thought: truth and the return of philosophy In: Feltham O, Clemens J (eds) (trans: Feltham O, Clemens J). Continuum Books, London

Balderrama F, Rodríguez R (2006) Decade of betrayal: mexican repatriation in the 1930s. University of New Mexico Press, Albuquerque, NM
Bataille G (1985). Visions of excess: selected writings, 1927–1939. In: Stoekl A (ed) University of Minnesota Press, Minneapolis
Bennett WJ (1992) The de-valuing of America: the fight for our culture and our children. Summit Books, New York
Bernstein DE (1999) Lochner, parity, and the Chinese laundry cases. William Mary Law Rev 41:211–294
Brace CL (1872) The dangerous classes of New York, and twenty years' work among them. Wynkoop and Hallenbeck, New York
Bewer JK (2010) Statement by Governor jan brewer. (April 30). http://azgovernor.gov/dms/upload/PR_043010_StatementGovBrewer.pdf
Buchanan PJ (2002) The death of the West: how dying populations and immigrant invasions imperil our country and civilization. Thomas Dunne Books, New York
Chávez L (2008) Latino threat: Constructing immigrants, citizens, and the nation. Stanford University Press, Stanford
Chávez LR (2001) Covering immigration: popular images and the politics of the nation. University of California Press, Berkeley
Congressional Research Service (2010) Authority of state and local police to enforce federal immigration law (september 17). Library of Congress, US
Courtney W (1956). San Francisco's anti-chinese ordinances, 1859–1900. Ph.D dissertation. University of San Francisco
Dean DR, Reynolds JA (2006). Hispanic historic property survey: final report. Phoenix. Historic Preservation Office, City of Phoenix, AZ. Available at: http://phoenix.gov/HISTORIC/ethnicsvys.html
Dimas PR (1991) Progress and a Mexican American community's struggle for existence: Phoenix's golden gate barrio. Ph.D dissertation, Arizona State University
Doty RL (2009) The law into their own hands: immigration and the politics of exceptionalism. The University of Arizona Press, Tucson, AZ
Dunn TJ (2009) Blockading the border and human rights: the El Paso operation that remade immigration enforcement. University of Texas Press, Austin, TX
Dunn TJ (1996) The militarization of the US-Mexico border, 1978–1992: low-intensity conflict doctrine comes home. Center for Mexican American Studies, The University of Texas at Austin, Austin, TX
FAIR (Federation for American Immigration Reform) (nd). "SB1070, Support Our Law Enforcement and Safe Neighborhoods Act: A Detailed Look," http://www.fairus.org/site/PageNavigator/sb1070_resource_center
Fernández C, Pedroza LR (1981) The border patrol and news media coverage of undocumented Mexican immigration during the 1970s: a quantitative content analysis in the sociology of knowledge. The University of Arizona, Tucson
FIRM (Fair Immigration Reform Movement) (2007) Overview of recent local ordinances on immigration http://www.fairimmigration.org, and http://www.ailadownloads.org/advo/FIRM-LocalLegislationDatabase.doc
Fix ME, Tumlin K (1997). Welfare reform and the devolution of immigrant policy. New Federalism, Series A, No. A-15. The Urban Institute, Washington, DC
Freeman GP, Hurtado-Ortiz M, Plascencia LFB (2000) Work and welfare among latino immigrants in California and Texas. Policy Brief. In: Claremont CA (ed) The Tomás Rivera policy institute
Freeman GP, Plascencia LFB (1999) The impact of the 1996 welfare act: food stamps and immigrants in El Paso. Policy Brief. The Tomás Rivera Policy Institute, Claremont, CA
García JR (1980) Operation wetback: the mass deportation of Mexican undocumented workers in 1954. Greenwood Press, Westport, CT
Gascón G (2009). Testimony, hearing on public safety and civil rights implications of state and local enforcement of federal immigration laws. Subcommittee on immigration, citizenship,

refugees, border security, and international law, and subcommittee on constitution, civil rights, and civil liberties, U.S. House of Representatives (April 2). Washington, DC. http://judiciary.house.gov/hearings/hear_090402.html
González D (2011) Federal immigration program mainly nets low-level criminals, analysis says, Arizona Republic (March 9). http://www.azcentral.com/news/articles/2011/03/09/20110309arizona-immigration-analysis.html
Gusterson H, Besteman C (eds) (2010) The insecure American: how we got here and what we should do about it. University of California Press, Berkeley, CA
Hansen JM (2007–2008) Sanctuary's demise: the unintended effects of state and local enforcement of immigration law. The Scholar: St. Mary's Law Review on Minority Issues 10:289–331
Hartley RC (2007) Congressional devolution of immigration policymaking: a separation of power critique. Duke J Const Law Public Policy 2:93–157
Heyman JMcC (1998) Finding a moral heart for U.S. immigration policy: an anthropological perspective. American Anthropological Association, Arlington
Heyman JMcC (2001) Class and classification at the U.S-Mexico border. Hum Organ 60(2):128–140
Higham J (1981) Strangers in the land: patterns of American nativism 1860–1925. Atheneum, New York
Huntington SP (2004) The hispanic challenge. Foreign policy no. 141 (March–April):30–45
ICE—Immigration and Customs Enforcement (2011) Mutually signed agreements (71) as of 10/29/2010, http://www.ice.gove/news/library/factsheets/287g.htm#signed-moa
Kalnay F (1941) The new American: a handbook of necessary information for aliens, refugees, and new citizens. Greenberg Publisher, New York
Keblawi J (2003–2004) Immigraiton arrests by local police: inherent authority or inherently preempted?, Catholic Univ Law Rev 53:817–853
Klebaner BJ (1958) State and local immigration regulation in the United States before 1882. Int Rev Soc Hist 3:269–295
Kleinman A, Das V, Lock M (eds) (1997) Social suffering. California University Press, Berkeley, CA
Kobach KW (2010) E-mail: "one more change!" April 28, 2010, 7:42 p.m. From "Kobach, Kris W." to russellpearce, rpearce@azleg.gov. http://wonkroom.thinkprogress.org/wp-content/uploads/2010/04/kobachemail.jpg
Kobach KW (2009) Testimony, hearing on public safety and civil rights implications of state and local enforcement of federal immigration laws. Subcommittee on immigration, citizenship, refugees, border security, and international law, and subcommittee on constitution, civil rights, and civil liberties, U.S. House of Representatives (April 2). Washington, DC. http://judiciary.house.gov/hearings/hear_090402.html
Kobach KW (2007–2008) Attrition through enforcement: a rational approach to illegal immigration. Tulsa J Comp Int Law 15:155–163
Kobach KW (2007) A sleeper amnesty: time to wake up from the DREAM act. Backgrounder (September 13). The Heritage Foundation, Washington, DC
Kobach KW (2006) The senate immigration bill rewards lawbreaking: why the DREAM act is a nightmare. Backgrounder (August 14). The Heritage Foundation, Washington, DC
Kobach KW (2005–2006) The quintessential force multiplier: the inherent authority of local police to make immigration arrests. Albany Law Rev 69:179–235
Kobach KW (2005) The 287(g) program: ensuring the integrity of America's border security system through federal-state partnerships. Testimony, house committee on homeland security, subcommittee on management, integration, and oversight (July 27). http://frwebgate.access.gpo.gov/cgi-bin/getdoc.cgi?dbname=109_house_hearings&docid=f:28332.pdf
Kobach KW (2004). State and local authority to enforce immigration law: a unified approach for stopping terrorist. Backgrounder. Center for Immigration Studies, Washington, DC
Kojève A (1947 [1969]). Introduction to the reading of hegel. Basic Books, New York

Krikorian M (2005) Downsizing illegal immigration: a strategy of attrition through enforcement. Backgrounder (May). Center for Immigration Studies, Washington, DC
Leonard KI (1992) Making ethnic choices: California's Punjabi Mexican Americans. Temple University Press, Philadelphia, PA
Limbaugh III, Rush H (1992) The way things ought to be. Pocket Books, New York
Lowe RE (1976) The Arizona Alien land law: its meaning and constitutional validity. Ariz State Law J 253–276
Luckingham B (1994) Minorities in phoenix: a profile of Mexican American, Chinese American, and African American communities, 1860–1992. The University of Arizona Press, Tucson, AZ
Meeks EV (2007) Border citizens: the making of Indians, Mexican, and Anglos in Arizona. University of Texas Press, Austin, TX
National Conference of State Legislatures (2011). Immigration policy project, 2010 immigration-related laws and resolutions in the sates (January 5). Data from 2005 to 2010 are available at http://www.ncsl.org/default.aspx?tabid=21857
Nevins J (2010). Operation gatekeeper and beyond: the war on "Illegals" and the remaking of the U.S. Mexico boundary. Routledge, New York
Olivas MA (2008) Lawmakers gone wild? College residency and the response to Professor Kobach. South Methodist Univ Law Rev 61:99
Ono KA, Sloop JM (2002) Shifting border: rhetoric, immigration, and california's proposition 187. Temple University Press, Philadelphia, PA
Orth SP (1907) The alien contract labor law. Polit Sci Q 22(1):49–60
Passell JS, Cohn D (2011). How many hispanics? Comparing new census counts with the latest census estimates. Pew Research Center/Pew Hispanic Center, Washington, DC. http://pewhispanic.org/reports/report.php?ReportID=139
Patterson O (1982) Slavery and social death: a comparative study. Harvard University Press, Cambridge, MA
Pfaelzer J (2007) Driven out: the forgotten war against Chinese Americans. Random House, New York
Pham H (2004) The inherent flaws in the inherent authority position: why inviting local enforcement of immigration laws violates the constitution. Florida State Univ Law Rev 31:965–1003
Plascencia LFB (under review) The web of exception: the production and erasure of marginality of 'undocumented' mexican migrants in the United States
Plascencia LFB (2011) Operation Jobs (I and II). In: Arnold K (ed) Anti-immigration in the United States: a historical encyclopedia. ABC-CLIO/Greenwood Press, Santa Barbara, CA
Plascencia LFB (2010) Immiserization in Arizona—attrition through enforcement. Anthropol News 51(7):47
Plascencia LFB (2009) The "undocumented" Mexican migrant question: re-examining the framing of law and illegalization in the United States. Urban Anthropol 38(2–4):375–434
Plascencia LFB (2008) Whom shall we punish, whom shall we help?: Arizona's war of position on migration. In: Paper presented at the 2008 annual conference of the American anthropological association (November 19–23)
Plascencia LFB, Freeman GP, Setzler M (2003a) The decline of barriers to immigrant economic and political rights in the American States, 1977–2001. Int Migr Rev 37(1):5–23
Plascencia LFB, Freeman GP, Setzler M (2003b) The decline of barriers to immigrant economic and political rights in the American States, 1977–2001. Int Migr Rev 37(1):5–23
Plascencia LFB (2001) "State, county and municipal legislation," in encyclopedia of American immigration, vol 2. M.E. Sharpe, Armonk, NY, pp 518–522
Police Executive Research Forum (2011) Police and immigration: how chiefs are leading their communities through the challenges. Washington, DC
Richardson M (1998) Georges bataille—essential writings. SAGE, Thousand Oaks, CA
Ridgley J (2008) Cities of refuge: immigration enforcement, police, and the insurgent genealogies of citizenship in U.S. sanctuary cities. Urban Geogr 29(1):53–77
Romero M (2006) Racial profiling and immigration law enforcement: rounding up of usual suspects in the latino community. Crit Sociol 32(2):447–473

Romero M, Serag M (2004–2005) Violation of Latino civil rights resulting form INS and local police's use of race, culture and class profiling: the case of the chandler roundup in Arizona. Clevel State Law Rev 52:75–96
Santa Ana O (2002) Brown tide rising: metaphors of latinos in contemporary American public discourse. University of Texas Press, Austin
Schlesinger AM Jr (1992) The disuniting of America. W.W. Norton & Co., New York
Simmel G (1950) The stranger. In: Wolff KH (ed) The sociology of Georg Simmel. The Free Press, New York, pp 402–408
Sjoberg G, Vaugan TR, Williams N (1984) Bureaucracy as a moral issue. J Appl Behav Sci 20(4):441–453
Sjoberg G (1996) The human rights cahllenges to communitarianims: formal organizations and race and ethnicity. In: Sciulli D (ed) Macro socio-economics: from theory to activism. M.E. Sharpe, Armonk, NY, pp 273–297
Souther Poverty Law Center (2002). "Puppeteer" intelligence report issue 106 (Summer). http://www.splcenter.org/get-informed/intelligence-report/browse-all-issues/2002/summer/the-puppeteer
Stewart S (1984) On longing: narratives of the miniature, the gigantic, the souvenir, the collection. The Johns Hopkins University Press, Baltimore, MD
Summers C (1946) Admission policies of labor unions. Q J Econ 61(1):66–107
University of Cincinnati Policing Institute (2009). Traffic stop data analysis study: year 3 final report. Prepared for the Arizona department of public safety (Nov 1). Cincinnati, OH
University of Cincinnati Policing Institute (2008). Traffic stop data analysis study: year 2 final report. Prepared for the Arizona department of public safety (Nov 20). Cincinnati, OH
University of Cincinnati Policing Institute (2007). Traffic stop data analysis study: year 1 final report. Prepared for the Arizona department of public safety (Nov 1). Cincinnati, OH
U.S. House of Representatives (1920), Committee on immigration and naturalization. Temporary admission of illiterate mexican laborers. Hearings, 66th congress, 2nd session. Washington, Government Printing Office, DC
U.S. Immigration Commission (1911). Volume 39, Part 4, state immigration and alien laws. Reports of the immigration commission, 61st congress, 3rd session, document no. 758
Vaughan J (2006). Attrition through enforcement: a cost-effective strategy to shrink the illegal population. Backgrounder (April). Center for Immigration Studies, Washington, DC
Villazor RC (2010) 'Sanctuary Cities' and local citizenship. Fordham Law J 37:573–598
Williams H (2009) Testimony, hearing on public safety and civil rights implications of state and local enforcement of federal immigration laws. Subcommittee on immigration, citizenship, refugees, border security, and international law, and subcommittee on constitution, civil rights, and civil liberties, U.S. house of representatives (April 2), Washington, DC. http://judiciary.house.gov/hearings/hear_090402.html
Wishnie MJ (2004) State and local enforcement of immigration laws. Univ Pennsylvania J Const Law 6:1084–1115
Whitaker MC (2005) Race work: the rise of civil rights in the urban west. University of Nebraska Press, Lincoln, NE
Zimmermann W, Tumlin KC (1999). Patchwork policies: state assistance for immigrants under welfare reform. Occasional paper number 24. The Urban Institute, Washington, DC

Case and Statutes Cited

Truax v. Raich, 239 U.S. 33 (1915)
Plyler v. Doe, 457 U.S. 202 (1982)
Gonzales v. City of Peoria [AZ] 722 F.2d., U.S. Court of Appeals, Ninth Circuit (1983)
National Council of La Raza, et al. *v. Department of Justice*, No. 03 Civ. 2559 (LAK), U.S. District Court, S.D. New York (2004)
National Council of La Raza, et al. *v. Department of Justice*, 411 F3d. 350 (2005)

Veronica Arnold et al. *v. Arizona Department of Public Safety,* et al., *No. CV-01-1463-PHX-LOA*
Lozano et al. v. City of Hazleton, Case No: 07-3531, U.S. Court of Appeals, Third Circuit (2010)
United States v. State of Arizona et al, Case 2:10-cv-01413-NVW (2010)

1885 Contract Labor Law (23 Stat. 332)
1917 Immigration Act (39 Stat. 874)
1952 McCarran-Walter Act (66 Stat. 163)
8 U.S.C. §1440

Chapter 8
Immigrant Informal Labor in Times of Anti-Immigrant Rage: Insights from Greater Phoenix

Francisco Lara-Valencia and Jacob Fisher

Comprising 25 cities and towns, in 2003 Greater Phoenix was the 13th largest metropolitan area in the U.S. in terms of gross production and the third largest in the southwest only after Los Angeles-Long Beach and Orange County in California (Mayors 2004). Between 1993 and 2003, the Greater Phoenix's economy grew in average 8.2 % annually, a rate that placed this area among the ten most rapidly expanding metropolitan economies in the U.S (Mayors 2004). High-wage occupations led this growth, followed by medium-wage paying jobs in the high-tech, aerospace/aviation, biotechnology, and software industries (MAG 2005). Due to its location within one of the major transportation corridors in North America, Greater Phoenix is also becoming a hub in the trade resulting from the North American Free Trade Agreement (NAFTA). Overall, Arizona exported US $14.9 billions worth of goods in 2005, with Mexico and Canada being the two largest trade partners (GPEC 2007). Overall, Greater Phoenix is the focal point in the transition of the State of Arizona from a resource-based production economy to a more technologically driven and externally oriented regional economy.

In parallel to such economic transformation, Greater Phoenix is undergoing a rapid demographic transition. In 2010, Phoenix's population reached 3.8 million after growing an average of 3.4 % annually during the 5 previous years (Census 2011). The most important component of this growth has been the expansion of the Latino or Hispanic population that contributes more than 50 % of current demographic change in the area (MAG 2005). Over the past 5 years, this

F. Lara-Valencia (✉)
School of Transborder Studies, P.O. Box 873502, Tempe, AZ 85287-3502, USA
e-mail: fcolara@asu.edu

J. Fisher
Fisher Architecture and Planning, 9th Omarim St. Omer industrial Park, OMER 84965, Israel

L. Magaña and E. Lee (eds.), *Latino Politics and Arizona's Immigration Law SB 1070*, Immigrants and Minorities, Politics and Policy, DOI: 10.1007/978-1-4614-0296-1_8,

population grew an average of 7.2 % annually, increasing its share in the total population from 25.1 % in 2000 to 29.2 % in 2005. According to the 2005 American Community Survey, 612,850 of Phoenix's residents were born outside the U.S. and of these 181,853 entered the country in 2000 or later (Census 2007). The share of the foreign-born population in 2005 (16.1 %) was more than twice that in 1990 (7.3 %), with the bulk of the new immigrants coming from Latin America (72.8 %), principally Mexico and Central America, followed by immigrants from Asia (12.9 %) and Europe (11.1 %).

As this chapter will argue, economic growth and social change in Greater Phoenix are two intimately intertwined processes. Growing labor demand, especially in occupations requiring few skills and paying low wages, is met with a steady supply of workers from Mexico and other less developed countries that migrate seeking relatively higher salaries across borders. By articulating the two sides of the labor market, migrant workers fill jobs that resident workers are unwilling to fill because they are filthy, dangerous, and poorly paid. In addition, migrant workers not only fill gaps in the Greater Phoenix's labor market, but they also create new businesses, raise the productivity of other workers, and reduce internal inflationary pressures. Nonetheless, this process is not exempt of contradictions and has produced a heated debate mainly because unauthorized workers from Mexico and Central America are one of the main sources of this labor. In short, four factors are at the forefront of the dispute about immigration in Arizona.

First, even though some citizens in Arizona may value the contribution of these immigrant workers to the stability of the job market, the perception that immigrants represent a fiscal burden and a risk to non-immigrants communities is the dominant element in the public narrative on immigration. Second, rising violence resulting from drug trafficking and human smuggling in the Mexican border is a growing concern among Arizona's citizens as politicians had successfully linked labor immigration with those activities. Third, the growing pervasiveness of immigrants in the labor market increases the fear of job displacement among those native workers facing unemployment in a stagnant state economy. Fourth, the inability of the U.S. federal government to implement immigration reform has fuelled the enactment of aggressive state laws and local policies rejecting the presence of immigrant workers in Greater Phoenix and other cities in Arizona.

Amidst this debate, a fact that is hardly noticed by the general public and even by specialized observers is that immigrant labor markets are rife with exploitation, social exclusion, and violation of basic human rights. Perhaps the most vulnerable to these miseries is the segment of informal workers that congregate on street corners, store fronts, parking lots, and churches seeking to be hired for a temporary job. Also known as day labor, this type of informal employment became an important component of the personal and household care and hospitality industries in Greater Phoenix in the past two decades; but also without doubt is the most visible form of informalization accompanying current change in Greater Phoenix. An important characteristic of informal labor markets is its connection with immigrant neighborhoods because the role played by community networks in recruiting, screening, and sanctioning day labor and providing shelter to unauthorized workers (Sassen 2000). In consequence, day labor work sites tend to develop a situation of spatial dependency that reinforces the ethnic character of neighborhoods and fosters the formation of urban landscapes which are distinctively segregated.

This chapter explores the pattern of geographical distribution of day labor hiring sites in the Greater Phoenix area focusing in particular on the social composition of the surrounding residential areas. It also analyzes the implication of recent anti-immigration laws and policies in Arizona in the dynamics of informal labor markets and immigrant communities. Following a review of the literature concerned with economic informalization and day labor, the chapter continues with the description of the methods and data sources used to explore the spatial dimension of day labor work in Greater Phoenix. The analysis explores the correlation between day labor hiring sites and neighborhood characteristics, especially their concentration of Hispanic and foreign-born populations, as well as their level of social-spatial segregation. Then, neighborhoods containing day labor hiring sites are explored to detect patterns in the size and organizational characteristics of these sites. Finally, we use a typology of day labor hiring sites as a heuristic device to speculate about the impact of anti-migrant policies on migrant communities.

Background

The research on day labor in the United States is relatively young. Many of the studies in the field tend to describe the characteristics of the market, and seldom get to the point where a theoretical framework for understanding the day labor phenomenon has been established. Most of the literature produced during the 1990s suggested a relationship between the 'ethnic enclave' and informal economy (Bohley 1990; Castells and Portes 1989). In this discussion, the role of immigration in the informal economy is central. While some argue that the share of immigrants from particular ethnic groups in informal activity is significant (Castells and Portes 1989; Portes 1995; Sassen 1989), others argued the opposite (Williams and Windebank 1998). However, the informal economy, that day labor is part of, is not only associated with immigration from the third world but also with global market forces, globalization of the financial market, and its effect on the formation of international labor market. Sassen (2000) argued that "much of the multiculturalism in large cities is much a part of globalization as is international finance" (p. 80). The increasing mobility of capital affects the formation of labor markets and the regulation of global labor force. The employment of immigration workers is a component of capital mobility. In general, capital mobility contributes to the formation of an international labor market. More specifically, the economic restructuring associated with the current phase of capital mobility has generated a large supply of jobs and casual labor markets that facilitate the informal employment of disadvantaged foreign workers, along with the creation of a formal demand for high-level skilled workers (Sassen 1991, p. 32).

One of the main issues in the debate on informal economy in advanced and developing countries is its relation to the formal economy. One side of the debate sees the informal economy as a separate and marginal economy not directly linked to the formal economy. In this dichotomy, the informal sector is that of the poor and unemployed, while the formal economy is that of those employed in better paid occupations in regulated activities. Critics of the dualistic view argue that formal and informal economies are not separated but rather symbiotic components of the market system. This structural perspective suggests that the informal economy is subordinated to the formal sector and helps mainstream activities in the urban economy to survive and expand as required by the market cycle. Sassen suggested a process of informalization caused by (1) growing disparities in the distribution of income and wealth and the corresponding inequalities in consumption levels and (2) the inability of small entrepreneurs to keep up with competition for productive resources, including space, services, and labor, from the leading sectors of the urban economy (Sassen 1989). Williams and Windebank (1998) suggested that informal employment, including various types of unpaid work, is complementary to formal economic activities and always has a role to play in maintaining living standards of particular communities. An important implication of this hypothesis is that informal activities result from a process that responds to the needs of the local economy. Therefore, the informal sector in highly developed countries, like the U.S. and several European nations, is not a phenomena imported from less developed countries, but an internal process resulting from endogenous structural changes occurring at the local level (1997).

An important dimension of the restructuring of labor markets is the role that communities play in the operation of informalized economic activities. Through the formation of networks, communities are able to communicate the existence of job opportunities and match a particular demand for workers with the appropriate set of skills. In the case of immigrant communities, these networks frequently provide basic communication skills, educate on work etiquette, and afford a minimum standard of security. This amounts to the creation of a parallel regime where the community replaces labor markets in the functions of recruiting, screening, and training workers. It also creates a spatial dependency between certain informal activities and the place that shelters these communities. Therefore, informal activities are one of the few forms of employment available to residents of immigrant neighborhoods. In contrast, with the decline of manufacturing and the rise of finance and specialized services, economic growth has become disproportionately concentrated in Central Business Districts and suburban office complexes.

Therefore, day labor is probably the most visible form of informal economic activity growing in low income communities and in the ethnic enclaves of the U.S. southwest. The day labor industry is characterized by predominantly young Latino males, usually ‘undocumented’, who congregate in open spaces, such as parking lots, streets corners, and store fronts, to solicit temporary daily work. Valenzuela et al. (2006) estimated that every day 117,600 workers are either looking for day labor or working as day laborers and that the largest concentration of day labor is in the U.S. west region

(42 %). Informal hiring sites operate in seemingly chaotic processes. Day labor sites can be categorized as connected, unconnected, and regulated sites (Valenzuela 2003a). Connected are those sites that are located near specific industries such as painting, gardening stores, moving, and home improvement stores. On the contrary, unconnected sites are not linked to a specific industry, but exist for other reasons. Both connected and unconnected sites often face complaints from local merchants, residents, and law enforcement forces. Regulated day labor sites are primarily a response to merchant and neighborhood organizations' complaints. Those sites are officially designated areas that resemble the informal sites but are regulated by the local authority and can be managed by the municipality, churches, or community-based organizations (Valenzuela 2000; Valenzuela 2003a; Valenzuela et al. 2006). Recently, Valenzuela et al. (2006) presented a portrait of day labor based on a nation-wide survey. The study found that the vast majority (79 %) of hiring sites are informal and include connected sites such as standing in front of businesses (24 %), home improvement stores (22 %), and unconnected sites such as gas stations (10 %) and busy streets (8 %). Most of the sites are near residential neighborhoods. The day labor workforce in the US is predominantly immigrant and Latino; 59 % were born in Mexico, 28 % in Central America. Three-quarters (75 %) are undocumented immigrants.

Data and Methods

This study located and characterized informal day labor hiring sites in Greater Phoenix using a combination of archival research, key informant interviews, snowball referrals, and windshield surveys. Similar strategies have been used by other researchers inventorying and surveying day labor activities in the U.S. (Valenzuela el al 2006; Biernacki and Waldorf 1981; Van Meter 1990). Archival research included searching in several regional and local newspapers using the keywords "day labor", "day workers", or "casual workers". Online city documents, including citizen complaints and studies conducted by municipal agencies were also used as a source of information in this investigation. In addition, a number of day laborers in well-known hiring sites were asked to indicate other locations where they had looked for work or know that other people use to look for work. Finally, windshield surveys were conducted in parking lots and other open spaces near home improvement stores, moving companies, gardening nurseries, and painting stores when evidence signaled the presence of day labor hiring sites. Windshield surveys provided the information to classify hiring sites in terms of their connection to a formal business and the number of workers using each identified site.

As result of these activities, a total of 13 hiring sites were identified in Greater Phoenix during April 2006. The location of these sites was geocoded and mapped using road and boundary maps from Census (2000) TIGER/Line Data. This exercise allowed us to locate each hiring site within the corresponding census block groups, the spatial used in this study for the representation of the residential pattern in the urbanized area (UA) of the Phoenix-Mesa Metropolitan Statistical Area

(MSA).[1] The census designated UA was considered a better geography for this analysis because enclosed continuously densely populated areas and central places in the Phoenix-Mesa MSA (Greater Phoenix).

Data from the short-form (100 % count of population) and long-form (sample) of the 2000 Census were used to characterize neighborhoods and identify residential clusters of recent immigrants in Greater Phoenix. In this study, immigrants are defined as foreign-born persons who were living in Greater Phoenix at the moment of the census but moved to the area after 1995 (U.S. Census 2002). The census defines foreign-born residents as those persons living in the U.S. that were not citizens at birth. This includes persons who are naturalized, legal permanent residents, long-term visa holders (students and guest workers), and undocumented foreigners.

A combination of techniques was used to explore residential segregation and the spatial clustering of immigrants. Since this analysis is based on census data at the block group level, the primary approach to measure clustering of foreign-born residents are location quotients. Location quotients are a measure of relative specialization that is calculated as the ratio of the fraction of foreign-born residents in the block group to its fraction in the total population in the Greater Phoenix area. Once calculated, location quotients are easy to interpret because they can assume only three magnitudes that are really relevant. If the value is less than 1, the quotient will indicate that the proportion of foreign-born residents in the block group is lower than what you would expect under an absolute even distribution of this population in the area. In contrast, a value greater than 1 will mean overrepresentation of the foreign-born population, while the unity will indicate that the population composition of a particular block group aligns with that of the area.

Location quotients are relevant when the spatial pattern of a group of variables is of interest, but not when the objective is the analysis of statistical correlation. To measure to what extent block groups with similar characteristics are next to one another and form spatial clusters, we used Local Moran I (*Ii*), a local indicator of spatial association. Local Moran I for each block group may be defined as follows (Anselin 1995; Lee and Wong 2001):

$$I_{\mathrm{i}} = Z_i \sum_{j,j\neq}^{n} W_{ij} Z_j$$

where the observations Z_i and Z_j are the location quotients in deviations from the mean and the weight W_{ij} is in row-standardized form. High values of local Moran indicate a clustering of similar location quotients scores (high or low), while low values indicate a clustering of dissimilar scores. A pseudo significance level of 0.05 of the I_i was utilized to test the hypotheses of spatial clustering of block groups with high or low values, and therefore, to spot the formation of

[1] A census block group is comparable to a neighborhood that contains about 800-1400 residents with similar socioeconomic characteristics.

residential enclaves of foreign-born population in Greater Phoenix. Moran scatter-plot maps are used to depict the spatial pattern of immigration residential segregation and explore its connection with the location of day labor hiring sites.

Results

The Geography of Day Labor

Day labor activity is a conspicuous component of the urban landscape in Greater Phoenix as many informal workers congregate daily in open-areas to offer their labor to a variety of employers. In Greater Phoenix, 18-day labor hiring sites were detected in street corners, parking lots, churches, and some in ad hoc spaces. Of the 18 sites 5 were connected to home improvement stores, truck rentals, and the city of Phoenix disposal center. The rest were disconnected sites located along arterial roads or some kind of regulated spaces. Two regulated sites were established by local churches whose members were concerned with the safety of day laborers. The other regulated hiring site was the Macehualli Day Work Center, a place sponsored by the city of Phoenix in 2003 and ultimately managed by a group of community organizations concerned with the safety of workers and employers as well as supporting business owners and residents affected by the activity of day laborers on the street (Collom 2003). The distribution of the different types of day labor hiring sites is shown in Fig. 8.1.

Seven jurisdictions in the Greater Phoenix area contain informal day labor hiring sites (Fig. 8.1). These jurisdictions are Phoenix proper, Mesa, Chandler, Cave Creek, Queen Creek, Surprise, and Guadalupe. Among these only Phoenix, Chandler, and Cave Creek have some type of regulated day labor sites. The city of Phoenix also contains seven unregulated hiring sites. Mesa, which is the second largest city in the area, contains three unregulated hiring sites. Due to their proximity, some of the sites form day labor corridors extending for several miles where laborers can be observed changing locations based on demand and other conditions. Some corridors, like the ones in the Palomino neighborhood in Phoenix or Chandler, include regulated hiring sites next to unregulated sites functioning on parking lots or street corners. Another example is the Broadway corridor in the city of Mesa where three distinctive sites operate simultaneously.

Day labor sites are of varying dimensions as indicated in Table 8.1. Following Valenzuela et al. (2006), we classified as small sites those concentrating less than 25 laborers in average at any point during the day. Likewise, medium-sized sites concentrate between 26 and 50 workers, large sites about 51–100 and mega sites more than 100 day laborers. Only by consolidating individual sites into day labor corridors, as described above, is it possible to talk about mega-sites in Greater Phoenix. Otherwise, half of the sites identified were classified as large and only two as medium size. With the exception of Queen Creek, located at the southeast corner of Greater Phoenix, all cities contained at least one large hiring site.

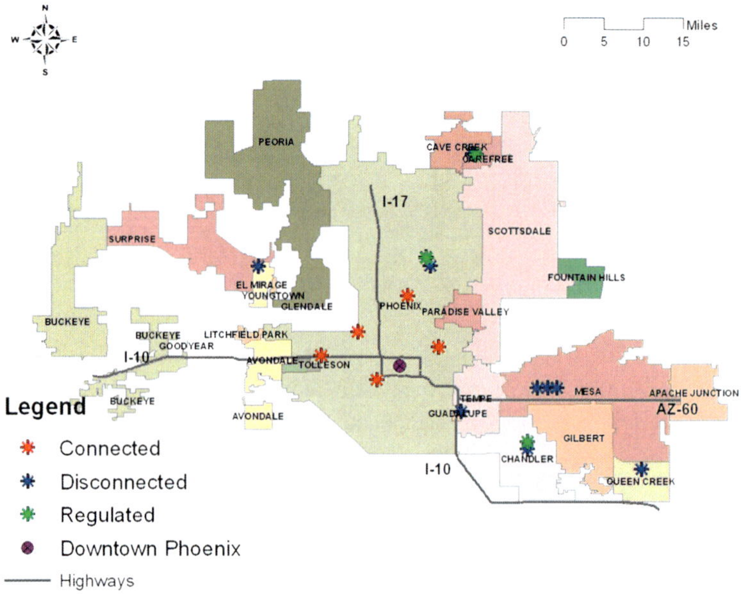

Fig. 8.1 Distribution and type of day labor hiring sites in Greater Phoenix

Table 8.1 Day labor hiring sites in Greater Phoenix

City	Location	Type	Size
Chandler	Downtown Chandler	Unregulated	Large
	Light and Life Free Methodist Church	Regulated	Medium
Guadalupe/Tempe	Guadalupe	Unregulated	Large
Mesa	Broadway Corridor (M)	Unregulated	Large
	Broadway Corridor (S)	Unregulated	Small
	Broadway Corridor (G)	Unregulated	Large
Phoenix	Phoenix Transfer Station	Unregulated	Small
	Home Depot at Thomas	Unregulated	Large
	Home Depot at Maryvale	Unregulated	Large
	Home Depot at West Phoenix	Unregulated	Large
	Palomino at Greenway Rd	Unregulated	Small
	Palomino at Bell Rd.	Unregulated	Med
	Macehualli Work Center	Regulated	Large
	U-Haul at Sunnyslope	Unregulated	Small
Cave Creek	Good Shepherd of the Hills Episcopal Church	Regulated	Small
	Cave Creek	Unregulated	Small
Surprise/El Mirage	Surprise/El Mirage	Unregulated	Large
Queen Creek	Queen Creek	Unregulated	Small

Source Fisher 2006

Interaction Between Hiring Sites and Neighborhoods

Figure 8.2a shows the distribution of block groups with higher or lower than average levels of foreign-born residents in Greater Phoenix. The map shows a metropolitan area with clear boundaries in terms of concentration of immigrant population. Cities in the north and east are predominantly non-immigrant while cities in the south and west present a significant number of residential areas with high concentration of immigrants (LQ $\geq$ 2). The largest grouping of darker blocks is mostly in the south and west sections of the city of Phoenix, but spills over south Glendale and Tolleson. Smaller groupings of immigrant population are formed in the cities of Mesa, Chandler, and Avondale. With the exception of scattered pockets of immigrant population in northern Phoenix, the rest of the metropolitan area presents below average concentrations of this demographic group. Cities like Scottsdale, Paradise Valley, Fountain Hills, Gilbert, and Surprise contain mostly block groups with location quotients under 0.75, which indicates that the immigrant population is underrepresented within their boundaries.

Figure 8.2b renders a more definitive picture of the level of segregation of the immigrant population. Again, we can observe in the south and west of Phoenix a very large residential cluster formed by block groups with population predominantly immigrant next to other blocks that are also predominantly immigrants (high–high). Another significant immigrant cluster is formed in the City of Mesa, and two smaller ones in Chandler and Avondale. While 14.2 % of the population in the entire metro area is foreign-born, the proportion of foreign-born in the block groups within these clusters averaged 33.8 %. Block groups with high concentration of immigrants that are next to block groups with little or non-immigrant population are shown in light red color and they averaged 17.4 % of foreign-born residents. Non-immigrant populations also form clusters in the north and east section of metropolitan area. These clusters are represented in blue block groups for which the proportion of foreign-born residents averaged 6.6 %. Block groups with little or non-immigrant population next

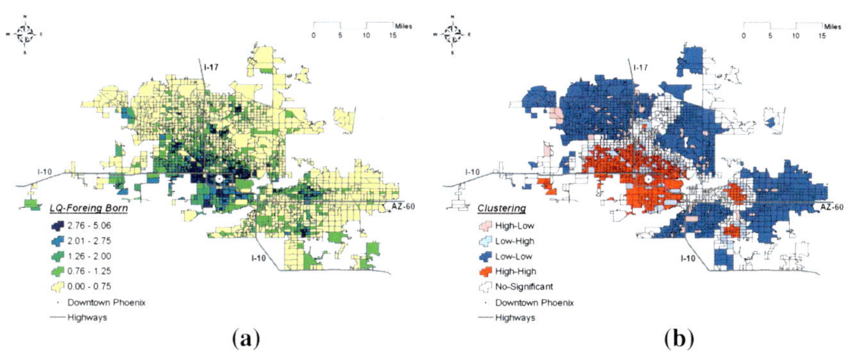

Fig. 8.2 Residential segregation **a** and clustering, **b** of foreign-born population in the Phoenix Metropolitan Area

to block groups with predominantly foreign-born population are shown in purple and their average proportion of immigrant residents is 11.8 %. A strip of block groups of mixed ethnic composition, represented in white color, acts a buffer zone between the immigrant and non-immigrant clusters in the south and north of the metropolitan area.

Overall clusters of adjacent block groups with significant immigrant populations are denser than the city average and denser than the non-immigrant clusters. Predominantly immigrants block groups have an average density of 40.5 residents per hectare, while the Greater Phoenix overall density is 13.9 persons per hectare.

The clustering of block groups of similar concentrations of Hispanic and foreign-born populations is confirmed by the relatively high global Moran's I coefficients (0.580 and 0.414, respectively). Positive multivariate spatial correlation of the Hispanic and foreign-born residents location quotients points also to a substantial overlaps between Hispanic and foreign-born residential areas (Global $I = 0.465$). Therefore, maps and statistics show a stark pattern of spatial segregation along ethnic and migratory status in Greater Phoenix, as well as a strong spatial correlation between Hispanic and foreign-born residential areas.

Figure 8.3 maps location of hiring sites in relation to the clustering of the immigrant population. The first and most salient characteristic of day labor hiring sites in Greater Phoenix is their location within or near neighborhoods with a high concentration of new immigrants. Four hiring sites are located within the limits of the large immigrant cluster in south Phoenix, three in the clusters formed in the city of Mesa, and two more in the smallest cluster formed in the city of Chandler. Six other sites were located within or near neighborhoods dominated by immigrant population, but surrounded by neighborhood forming clusters of non-immigrant populations. The only exceptions to this rule are the sites located in Cave Creek and Queen Creek, two cities experiencing accelerated expansion mainly due to the construction of high-scale residential areas in northern Phoenix. In general, hiring sites located within neighborhoods with a high concentration of immigrants tend to be larger.

Table 8.2 presents an estimation of the concentration of Hispanic population within a 1-mile buffer area around the hiring sites. The estimation is based on location quotients comparing the ratio of Hispanics within the buffer against the ratio of Hispanics in the city where the site is located. The results show that almost all sites are surrounded by neighborhoods with a concentration of Hispanics that exceeds the share of this population in the city of reference. In Chandler, Surprise/El-Mirage, and Mesa the ratio is more than two times higher while in the city of Phoenix the sites around the Palomino community and Sunnyslope have lower ratio values than the city itself, simply because the city of Phoenix has a large Hispanic population in many other places citywide. Even the sites located in Cave Creek, which is considered an upscale Anglo community at the fringe of the metropolitan area, have a value of 1.5 times than the town ratio.

The same analysis was performed using several socioeconomic indicators, including income and home ownership. The analysis shows that the quotient of household income under $ 35,000 is higher around day labor hiring sites than in Greater Phoenix. Overall, more poor families live around day labor hiring sites.

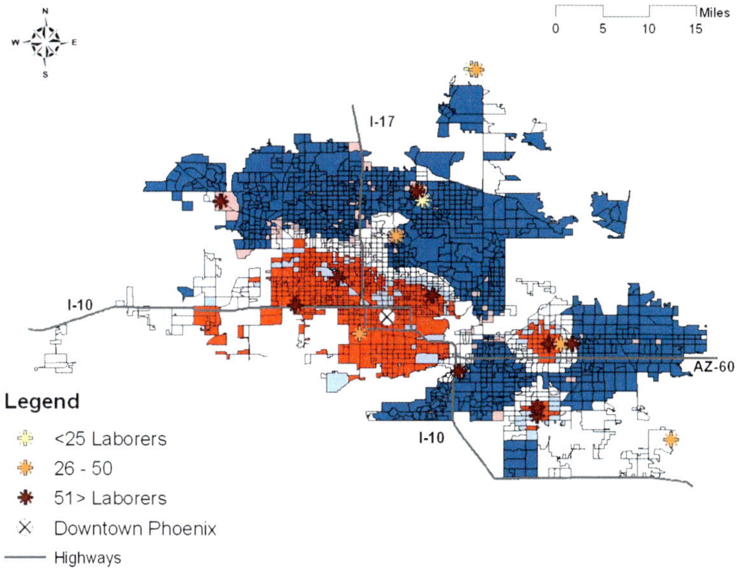

Fig. 8.3 Spatial association between hiring sites and immigrant neighborhoods

Table 8.2 Demographics of 1-mile buffer around day labor hiring sites

Site	Total population	Hispanic population	Concentration of Hispanics
Arizona Av. (Chandler)	24,241	14,074	2.77
Guadalupe/Tempe	17,109	5,972	1.77
Broadway Corridor (Mesa)	53,779	22,969	2.16
27th Av. Station (Phoenix)	14,993	9,422	1.84
HD on Thomas (Phoenix)	24,315	10,912	1.32
HD in Maryvale (Phoenix)	15,545	8,186	1.55
HD on McDowell&75 (Phoenix)	10,572	6,577	1.83
Palomino (Phoenix)	30,537	9,608	0.92
Sunnyslope (Phoenix)	18,509	6,237	0.99
Cave Creek	1,730	166	1.51
Surprise/El Mirage	10,199	7,012	2.16
Queen Creek	216	77	1.19
Total	221,745	101,212	

Source Own calculations based on 2000 census data

Typology of Hiring Sites

Recent research as shown that as day laborers try to connect to the life of their new city, they face language barriers, racial discrimination, unfamiliar labor markets and police harassment that can make integration a daunting experience. At the same time, the extent of their success as a mobile labor force depends on their ability to engage with the new urban economy landing a job and earning an income. Thus, these migrants must find an appropriate balance between guarding themselves from an unfriendly surrounding while simultaneously accessing their new city's economic opportunities.

The importance of this balance is highlighted in the literature by the use of terms like "encounter spaces" and "non-places", which refer to geographies within the city with the potential to facilitate the engagement of day laborers and employers in mutually beneficial, non-conflictive interactions (Crotty and Bosco 2008). In particular, the term non-place coined by Marc Augé to describe mainly architectural and technological spaces designed to be "passed through" or "consumed" rather than appropriated; it is also applied to urban spaces that are transient in character and are chiefly devoid of social and cultural meaning (Méndez and Rodríguez 2009). In spaces such as arterial streets, street corners, sidewalks, and parking lots individuals are generally "invisible" as these territories normally do not perform a role in identity-making as do schools, neighborhood parks, or community centers within residential areas. However, these spaces have the potential to turn into locations of conflict if the presence of day laborers is not tolerated anymore, as happen when anti-immigrant groups claim ownership of these spaces based on citizenship or race. It happens also when public or semi-public spaces become connected to residential neighborhoods where residents perceived the presence of workers as too close for comfort (Valenzuela 2003). Whether public or semipublic space is friendly or hostile, day laborers are strongly attracted to these locations as they provide the greater exposure to the demand side of the market they are part of. Yet, they will retreat to the protection of the Hispanic enclave as they perceive an unreasonable level of risk by gathering at these locations.

Based on this fundamental fact and the analysis above, we developed a typology of day labor hiring sites that seeks to illuminate the role that neighborhoods play in their distribution. The proposed typology identifies three basic types of hiring sites: embedded, detached, and exurban.

Embedded sites are generally located at the outer edge of residential neighborhoods where foreign-born or Hispanic origin residents are the dominant social group. They represented almost one in two hiring sites identified in Greater Phoenix and most of them are classifiable as large for the number of workers they tend to congregate. Their specific location is along major arterial roads, in some cases in the parking lots of home improvement stores, which gives workers access to potential employers while staying in close proximity to their neighborhood. These sites are probably the safest location for immigrant workers that entered the U.S. unauthorized because while there, laborers can mix easier with their surroundings and face the lowest minority-to-majority tension in the city. Paraphrasing Cardenas (1989), embedded sites are at encounter spaces where the "imagined community" of the dominant majority finds acceptable a visible presence of minority groups.

Detached sites are located in areas that can be characterized as non-place spaces because the dominance of minority or majority populations is not obvious. In consequence, hiring sites are not surrounded by racialized territories where individual and collective imaginaries and identities are reproduced. In these sites laborers get the highest exposure to potential employers but also to the risks resulting from being away from the ethnic enclave. We identified five of this type of hiring sites, four in northern Phoenix and one in East Mesa, which are areas within Greater Phoenix characterized by their predominantly Anglo population. Two of the sites are large and the remaining three medium or small.

Finally, exurban sites are at the outer fringe of the metropolitan area surrounded by new low-density residential developments interspersed by active farms. The sprawling growth experienced by Greater Phoenix in recent years created areas that are in transition from rural to urban and where day laborers can find plenty of job opportunities in construction, landscaping, and even farming. Two exurban sites were identified in Cave Creek (north) and one in Queen Creek (south). These sites ranged in size from small to medium and are at the most distant locations from the ethnic enclaves.

Discussion

The study discovered 18-day labor hiring sites in seven cities around the Phoenix metropolitan area. Although the sites are spread all over Greater Phoenix, they tend to be located in major roads in close proximity to residential areas of predominantly poor Mexican and other Central American immigrants. Therefore, the location of day labor hiring sites is driven by ethnicity and proximity more than by connection to a specific industry. A typology based on location in the metropolitan area was offered. The hiring sites are identified as embedded, exposed, and exurban type.

The relationship between ethnicity, immigration, and informality is well established in the literature (Castells and Portes 1989; Portes 1995; Sassen 1989; Sassen 1995; Williams and Windebank 1998). The idea that "informal activities thrive within well developed enclaves" (Portes 1995, p. 31) seems to find strong support in the case of day labor in Greater Phoenix, though only from the supply side of the equation. The demand side of the day labor market is clearly not coming from the ethnic enclave. The employers come from all over the metropolitan area, and in Phoenix they are by large, almost 60 %, private homeowners (Fisher 2006). The demand side, i.e., employers, is part of an exchange of labor for wages without the control of the government regulatory system. Therefore, employers are also part of the informal activity.

The location of a day labor hiring site can not be explained by only by the analysis of the moment of exchange, that is the completion of transaction whereby a worker is offered a job and also accepts it. It can also be explained by the journey to work as "immigrants have a different sensitivity to job location than natives with analogous characteristics" (Sassen 1995, p. 113). Day labor hiring sites are located in close proximity to the 'ethnic enclave' because the relative high cost of travel in the face of the uncertainty of finding a job in a particular location on a specific day. The sensitivity starts from the will of immigrants to make a large travel for migration, and continues by their will to make a long distance travel within the metro area (Sassen 1995).

The day labor hiring site is a good illustration of the relationship between a formal and informal economy. The constitution of the transaction moment in the day labor activity happens in a day labor hiring site. The hiring site functions as a broker, a place for transaction between laborers and employers. It offers the employer and worker a place for the 'moment of exchange'. Therefore, the hiring site is an informal employment establishment for day labor. It is unregulated yet legal. The hiring site is not a place where formal and informal meet. Both sides of the transaction are on the same side. However, it is a meeting place between the marginal and the mainstream.

Conclusions

The theme of informal day labor provides an extraordinary window to explore the intersection between globalization, borders and migration along with the complex processes that shape the way local communities react to the growing presence of immigrant workers in city neighborhoods. The association of day labor with unauthorized immigration in the collective mind, in addition to the proliferation of hiring sites, has increasingly generated mobilization against their presence in the streets of Greater Phoenix, as well as actions defending their right to inhabit the city.

As shown above, day labor depends on access to public space, the streets, sidewalks, vacant lots and other 'interstitial territories" within the city, even when they have become increasingly contested spaces as the activism of local anti-immigrant groups intensifies and their effort are echoed by state and local policies and regulations formalizing their exclusionary demands. According to Versanyi (2008), in recent years there has been a proliferation of grassroots policies that try to deal with the presence of undocumented residents in U.S. cities by regulating and policing public space via local land-use and zoning regulations, laws that criminalize loitering, and the enforcement of trespassing regulations and traffic ordinances. On the other hand, Carpio and colleagues (2011) show that although anti-immigrant activism is widespread, pro-immigrant activism is also expanding its efforts to protect basic rights of day laborers and migrants in general. These opposing perspectives collide in a political arena where local governance turns into a test of strength to close or keep open spaces that are vital for the immigrant community, while the right to be in the city and benefit from the city is negotiated wielding moral versus legal arguments.

While divergent, these perspectives of day labor are not disconnected from each other, rather they are energized by the same underlying forces. Firstly, globalization has dramatically enhanced the free flow of goods and capital across borders, but has failed to facilitate the international movement of labor, forcing irregular migration and engendering informal labor markets in cities around the world. International migration of all kind, but particularly undocumented migration, is a response to the employment opportunities created by economic expansion of cities in developed countries and the effect of the restructuring of global labor division bring about by new market dynamics, technologies and institutions. Cities like Phoenix have many advantages for new immigrants from Mexico and Central America, providing the best opportunities for access to better living conditions and social networks due to its proximity to the border and the presence of one of the largest Hispanic community in the United States. Because of their vulnerable legal situation, undocumented workers are highly dependent on family and kinship networks for shelter and navigation of the labor market. As shown above, their connection with Hispanic neighborhoods is not only social but also physical as distance and access to the neighborhood correlates simultaneously with mobility costs and refuge. Secondly, immigrants contribute to the metropolitan growth machine fueled by globalization by providing low-cost flexible labor in the construction and hospitality industries, but also in personal and home care activities which are essential for the reproduction of the workforce in the formal economy. Such connection between the informal and the formal, the undocumented and documented, is at the origin of what Sassen (2003) refers to as the "informal social contract" that links undocumented immigrant workers with the city where they live and work. Therefore, the increasing concentration of immigrant workers, including day laborers, in Greater Phoenix is both a cause and consequence of its growth and reflects the role this city is playing in the new global economy. Finally, as suggested by Sassen (2003), the practice of citizenship in a globalized world has to do with the "production of presence", this is with a constant struggle of the powerless against their exclusion from streets, sidewalks, plazas, and ultimately, against the commodification and regulation of public space. Therefore, what we are witnessing in Greater Phoenix is the accommodation of the city polity to a new social landscape where traditional modes of inclusion, participation, and appropriation of space are relentlessly contested.

References

Anselin L (1995). Local Indicators of Spatial Association-LISA. Geogr Anal. 27(2):93–115

Biernacki P and Waldorf D (1981) Snowball sampling: problem and techniques of chain referral sampling. Socio Meth Res 10(2):141–163

Bohley S (1990) The Informal economy of San Antonio's "Westside", Tomás Rivera Center, pp 55

Carpio G, Irazabal C, Pulido L (2011) Right to the suburb? Rethingking Lefebre and immigrant activist. J Urban Aff 33(2):185–208

Castells M, Portes A (1989) World underneath: the origins, dynamics, and effects of the informal economy. In: Portes A, Castells M, Benton LA (eds) The informal economy: studies in advanced and less developed countries. The John Hopkins University Press, London

Census US (2000) Characteristics of the population, population and Housing Census. http://www.census.gov/

Census US (2002) American community survey. http://www.census.gov/acs/

Census US (2007) American community survey. http://www.census.gov/acs/

Census US (2011) American community survey. http://www.census.gov/acs/

Collom L (2003) Day laborer center opens in Phoenix. Arizona Repub, 2

Crotty S, Boscoa F (2008) Racial geographies and the challenges of day labor formalization: a case study from San Diego County. J Cult Geogr 25(3):223–244
Fisher J (2006) Street and work center day labor hiring sites in Phoenix Metro Area. School of Planning, Arizona State University, Tempe
GPEC (2007) Regional Profile, Greater Phoenix Economic Council, Phoenix, AZ
Lee J, Wong D (2001) Statistical analysis with ArcView GIS. Wiley, New York
MAG (2005) Regional report, a resource for policy makers in the Maricopa region. Maricopa Association of Governments, AZ
Mayors (2004) The U.S. Conference. U.S. metro economies: global insight
Méndez E, Rodriguez I (2009) Imaginaries and migration. J Southwest 51(4):477–490
Portes A (1995) Economic sociology and the sociology of immigration: a concepyual overview. In: Portes A (ed) The economic sociology of immigration. Russell Saga Foundation, New York
Sassen S (1989) New York city's informal economy. In: Portes A, Castells M, Benton LA (eds) The informal economy: studies in advanced and less developed countries. The Johns Hopkins University Press, London
Sassen S (1991) The global city. Princeton: Princeton University Press, London
Sassen S (2003) The repositioning of citizenship: Emergent subjects and spaces for politics. The New Centennial Rev 3(2):42--66
Sassen S (1995) Immigration and the local labor market. In: Portes A (ed) The economic sociology of immigration. Russell Saga Foundation, New York
Sassen S (2000) Informalization: imported through immigration or a feature of advances economies. WorkingUSA 3(6):6–26
Valenzuela A (2000) Controlling day labor: government, community and worker responses. In: California Policy Option 2001. Mitchell D J B, Nomura P (ed) Los Angeles: UCLA anderson business forecast and school of public policy and social research
Valenzuela A (2003) Day labor work. Annu Rev Sociol 29(1):307–333
Van Meter KM (1990) Methodological and design issues: techniques for assessing the representatives of snowball samples. NIDA Res Monogr Series. Mono 98:31–43
Valenzuela A, Nikolas T, Edwin M, Ana Luz G (2006) On the corner: day labor in the United State. Center for the study of Urban Poverty, UCLA, Los Angeles
Williams CC, Windebank J (1998) Informal employment in the advanced economies. Routledge, London

Chapter 9
Mexico Renews its Relationship with its Expatriate Community in the U.S.: Comparing the Post-revolutionary Era with the Technocratic Free Trade Period

Jaime R. Aguila and Erik Lee

The contemporary immigration debate is polarizing, but certainly not an unprecedented controversy, especially concerning the status of Mexican citizens residing in the United States. For over a century Mexican labor has held a paradoxical position within U.S. politics because of its seminal contribution to the economy and yet controversial place within society. At the center of its contentious presence is the tremendous amount of mis- and dis-information about immigration in general, including the role of the Mexican Government within the overall phenomenon of immigration. At a basic level, we argue that since the mid nineteenth century, Mexican officials have sought to build a formal relationship with its emigrant community within the United States, but various transnational factors have hindered such efforts. But this is not to say that some level of success has not been achieved. In the twenty-first century, the Mexican Government acts both to protect its citizens (in a broad sense) within the United States, while also encouraging them to maintain their Mexican identity and remain loyal to the Mexican state.

Comparing and contrasting different historical stages of the Mexican emigration process demonstrate the methods the home government has used to fulfill its responsibility for the social welfare of its people regardless of their geographical location. Within this context it also reveals the barriers that both government and citizens encounter in fulfilling these public objectives. Specifically, comparing the immediate post-revolutionary period, 1920–1940 with the current era of *libre comercio*, which began in 1988 with the election of Carlos Salinas de Gortari, the chief architect of the North American Free Trade Agreement (NAFTA), will improve comprehension of contemporary conditions and highlight the role of the

J. R. Aguila (✉) · E. Lee
School of Letters and Sciences, Polytechnic Campus, 411 North Central Avenue,
Suite 363, 85004-0696, Mailcode 0320, Phoenix, Arizona, USA
e-mail: elaguila@asu.edu

L. Magaña and E. Lee (eds.), *Latino Politics and Arizona's Immigration Law SB 1070*,
Immigrants and Minorities, Politics and Policy, DOI: 10.1007/978-1-4614-0296-1_9,

Mexican consul. These two eras are pivotal milestones marking significant shifts in Mexican politics and the Mexican state's formal relationship with its expatriate community in the United States.

In the twenty-first century, the Mexican Government has aggressively sought to solidify its connection with its expatriate community in the United States. The primacy of this objective has resulted from many historical legacies that have intensified in recent years, especially the increased size of the expatriate population and Mexican public opinion that no longer views emigrants as *vende patrias*, or traitors to the nation. The complexity of such a notion is demonstrated by an October 22, 1901 editorial in the Mexico City daily, *El País* lamenting the poor economic conditions that force Mexicans to abandon their native land for Texas where they will find work, but suffer humiliation. In the present, what were once commonly held beliefs no longer prevail in Mexico as most citizens have relatives in the United States and as a result of remittances the nation receives concrete benefits from the migration process.

One of the principal ways in which Mexico—or any other country, for that matter—interacts with its expatriate community is through its consulates, whose role is distinct from that of the embassy, which takes a leading and direct role in formal diplomatic relations. Former Director General of Consular Protection and Services within the Secretaría de Relaciones Exteriores, Edgardo Flores Rivas, described the international role of the consul as theoretically a commercial agent, a tourist promoter, a supplier of government documents, and to defend specific interests of his compatriots. Although the Consular Relations Section of the Vienna Convention cites the role of protection as a primary duty for the consul, its role as commercial promoter is of prime importance. However, for the specific case of the *Mexican* consul in the United States, his duty is first and foremost to provide consular protection.[1] Secondary duties include fostering trade between Mexico and the community under the Mexican consulates' jurisdiction and maintaining relations with American authorities in order to meet the previous two responsibilities through the use of diplomatic pressure and specific interventions. They also issue passports, provide proof of Mexican citizenship through naturalization certificates, assist in the acquisition of Mexican citizenship, and register Mexican nationals residing in the United States through the issuance of consular identification cards (*matrículas consulares*).

Historical Background

This relationship between Mexican expatriate communities and the Mexican nation-state dates back to the events related to the 1846–1848 Mexican–American War, which transformed the northern Mexican population into a community of

[1] Edgardo Flores Rivas (1987) La Institución Consular Conforme a la Práctica Mexicana, found in Instituto Matías Romero de Estudios Diplomáticos El Servicio Exterior Mexicano (Secretaría de Relaciones Exteriores, Mexico City), p 61.

expatriates even though they themselves had not physically moved. Mexican officials were concerned with their compatriots in the contested territories as early as September 5, 1847. According to one Mexican official:

> Yet, notwithstanding all this, they have been the truest Mexicans, and most faithful patriots forgetting their private grievances, they at this time remember only that they are, and wish to, belong to the Mexican family, exposing themselves to be sacrificed to the vengeance of their invaders, against whom they have raised... Before the nationality of the rest of the republic shall be lost to them, we will all perish together.[2]

Mexican officials had many motives for reuniting their displaced compatriots with their homeland. President Manuel de la Peña y Peña in a message to Congress described the territorial losses agreed upon by the Treaty of Guadalupe Hidalgo as dishonorable and lamented their compatriot's distress. "...I suffer the deepest regrets for the separation of those Mexicans in Alta California and New Mexico from the Union". He also claimed that, "...if it would have been possible, the ceded territories would have been enlarged in order to ensure the freedom of that Mexican population."[3] In addition to reviving its damaged patriotic sentiment, there was one significant pragmatic motive for recovering their compatriots. Populating the northern frontier was a policy objective that predated the existence of the Mexican Republic, which had necessitated the original contract between Moses Austin and the Spanish Government, and then later following independence between his son, Stephen Austin, and the New Mexican nation. Even after 1848, the desolate northern region continued to be susceptible to Indian raids and continued U.S. territorial encroachment, which continually threatened the government's tenuous dominion. From this point forward, Mexican officials pursued various colonization efforts aimed at attracting immigrants from Europe and repatriating their compatriots from the United States.

Nonetheless, by 1848 the region was engulfed by the land-hungry United States. According to Article VIII of the Treaty of Guadalupe Hidalgo signed by U.S. and Mexican representatives on February 2, 1848, Mexicans residing in the ceded territories could have maintained their Mexican citizenship, should have been free to continue where they resided, and their property was supposed to be inviolably respected.[4] Despite such guarantees, the United States failed to uphold many of the treaty's provisions, and an unstable Mexican nation was incapable of

---

[2] Letter from J.R. Pacheco to Mexican Commissioners Jose Joaquín de Herrera, Bernardo Couto, Ignacio Mora y Villareal, and Miguel Atristain, September 5, 1847 found in U.S. Treaties, etc. 1845–1849, The Treaty between the United States and Mexico: In Proceedings of the Senate thereon, and Message of the President and Documents Communicated therewith (Washington, DC: United States. 30th Congress, 1st session, 1847–1848), pp 342–343.

[3] El Señor de la Peña y Peña, al abrir las sesiones del Congreso en Querétaro, en 7 de Mayo de 1848, found in Archivo Histórico Diplomático Mexicano, *Un siglo de relaciones internacionales de México (A través de los mensajes presidenciales)* Editorial Porrua, S.A., Mexico City 1970, p 72.

[4] Article VIII of the Treaty of Guadalupe Hidalgo, signed February 2, 1848 found in Richard Griswold del Castillo, The Treaty of Guadalupe Hidalgo: A Legacy of Conflict. Norman: University of Oklahoma Press, 1990), pp 189–190.

demanding their assurances. The U.S. Government's failure to honor property rights and Mexican–Americans' inability to achieve full citizenship are two of the most notable lapses and enduring legacies of this period.[5]

Mexican authorities commissioned various agents in the ceded territories to implement repatriation projects for their compatriots wishing to become reintegrated into the homeland. Although there are no conclusive statistics for the size of this population, estimates claim around 118,000 Mexican nationals resided in what was to become the American Southwest (Martinez 1975). However, even at this early juncture, the conditions under which this community resided demonstrated their contradictory existence within the United States. Their presence was seen as absolutely necessary in some areas. For example, in New Mexico, officials were reluctant to allow Mexican workers to leave for fear of labor shortages. Local officials there forced Mexicans to apply for U.S. citizenship so that they could stay and work in the United States. On the other hand, Mexicans were reviled in Northern California. Westward migration attracted by the Gold Rush caused state officials to pass legislation such as the 1851 Foreign Miner's Tax forcing all foreigners out of the territory (Pitt 1970). Many migrated to Los Angeles where they continued to find employment and held on to some political influence (Galeana 1999).

Furthermore, the U.S. federal government was unconcerned about Mexican immigration and local labor demands, while Mexican officials encouraged their compatriot's migration home within the newly defined political boundary, primarily to populate the recently defined, but still barren northern regions. These issues in varying degrees would continue to plague Mexican emigrants and both governments throughout the course of the next century.

Mexican Governmental efforts at aiding their compatriots were cumbersome, lacked adequate resources and planning, and encountered barriers placed before them by U.S. employers who feared labor shortages. The protection granted by the envoys of the Ministry of Foreign Relations (SRE) began with the arrival of their representatives, commissioned to repatriate anyone who wished to return to their country of origin (Angela Moyano Pahissa 1989). A large number of the 80,000 inhabitants of New Mexico attempted to return, but failed because of inadequate funds (Moisés González Navarro 1977). At the conclusion of the war about 3,000 Mexicans migrated home refusing to reside under U.S. hegemony. [6] The Mexican Government continued to discuss repatriation plans with Mexicans in Los Angeles

[5] Remedios Gómez Arnau, México y la protección de sus nacionales en Estados Unidos (Mexico City: Universidad Nacional Autónoma de México, 1990), 130–131; Iris H.W. Engstrand, "The Impact of the U.S.-Mexican War on the Spanish Southwest," 23–24 found in Iris H.W. Engstrand et all, eds., Culture y Cultura: Consequences of the U.S.-Mexican War, 1846–1848 (Los Angeles: Autry Museum of Western Heritage, 1998); Oscar J. Martinez, Border Boom Town: Ciudad Juárez since 1848 (Austin: University of Texas Press, 1978), pp 11–15.

[6] Martinez, On the size of the Chicano population, p 51.

as late as the 1860s, but unfortunately they proved fruitless.[7] This first repatriation effort foreshadowed future government sponsored projects that were always hindered by inadequate funds and ad hoc planning.

During the 1876–1910 dictatorship of Porfirio Díaz, Mexicans working in the United States remained a significant policy concern for the Porfirian officials. Consuls were directed to look after the well being of their compatriots in order to minimize international incidents along the border that might hinder the growing and significant economic relationship between the two nations.[8] In the northern region and particularly along the border, under population and labor shortages remained. Officials encouraged *braceros*[9] to take advantage of Mexico's 1883 Public Land act, which sought repatriates along with European and Asian immigrants for promoting economic development in northern rural areas to defend Mexico from US filibusters, marauders, and also to minimize contraband trading. Policy-makers believed that their returning countrymen would cost less to attract and would be more likely to colonize those regions. They were offered 100 free hectares of land, a 10 year release from military service, and tax exemptions. 31,658 repatriates took advantage of the program, with the majority coming from New Mexico and south Texas (Moisés González Navarro 1994).

The 1907 worldwide recession interrupted the United States' growing demand for Mexican workers and the economic interdependency between the two nations more broadly. In addition, it foreshadowed similar calamities in 1921, 1929, and 2010. Consular officials were forced to implement an ad hoc repatriation program as a result of the global recession. Recently arrived immigrants were the first to be fired and were pressured to repatriate just months after they were recruited to work in various U.S. industries. Local officials and consular personnel aided the destitute, but the overwhelming response from southwestern communities was for their exodus. By January 25, 1908, 2,700 Mexicans were repatriated from Los Angeles to El Paso. At this point, the program came to end because the consulates had run out of funds and railroad companies ceased offering discounted or free transportation.[10] Nonetheless, a month later Los Angeles consul Antonio Lozano publicly thanked the Southern Pacific and Santa Fe railroads for their assistance in helping repatriate so many of his compatriots to El Paso.[11] Within Mexico, the Governor of Chihuahua had supplied the bulk of financial support, providing approximately 8,000 pesos for transportation from Ciudad Juárez into the interior.[12] Unfortunately, the repatriates, the return home meant competing for work with thousands of their

---

[7] Juan Gómez-Quiñones (1973) Piedras contral la luna, México en Aztlán y Aztlán en México: Chicano-Mexican Relations and the Mexican Consulates, 1900–1920. In: James Wilkie, Michael Meyer and Edna Monzón de Wilkie (eds) Contemporary Mexico: Papers of the IV International Congress of Mexican History. University of California, Berkeley, p 498.

[8] Mexico is the United States' third most significant trading partner, behind Canada and China. Mexico is also the top trading partner of over 20 U.S. states and is a G-20 economy.

[9] *Bracero* literally means someone who works with his arms or in other words a manual laborer.

[10] The *El Paso Times, January 21, 2008* and *The Los Angeles Times* January 26, 1908, Friedrich Katz (1998) *The Life and Times of Pancho Villa*. Stanford University Press, Stanford, p 49.

[11] The Los Angeles Times February 26, 1908

[12] The El Paso Times January 27, 1908.

unemployed countrymen.[13] After 1910, Mexicans returned to the United States in greater numbers due to labor demands induced by the U.S. economy's recovery, the 1910–1920 Mexican Revolution, and World War I induced labor shortages.

Over 100 years later and despite a much higher number of Mexicans working in the United States and closer economic ties, officials from both nations are still relying on similar ad hoc policies. There are multiple reasons for this perpetual state of circularity. For one, the history of Mexican emigration and the Mexican Government's official role within this process remains a peripheral historical topic, despite the tremendous controversy over this political issue. Federal officials in Mexico City and Washington D.C. have contrasting and often naïve interpretations of the border's realities and the marginality of the Mexican emigrant community. As demonstrated by the events induced by the Panic of 1907, Mexican officials were forced into developing a federally organized repatriation drive. Over the course of this process, U.S. federal involvement was non-existent as local labor demands dictated the physical status of Mexicans.

The 1910–1920 Mexican Revolution had created unprecedented challenges for officials because it not only increased the size of the emigrant community, but also expanded its geographical scope. By the end of the Revolution, *California*, rather than Texas, was the dominant receiving area with 86,638 Mexicans.[14] Emigrants had also settled in the Midwest in great numbers, especially in Kansas City, Missouri and Chicago, Illinois. In 1900, there were only 71 Mexicans in Kansas City, but by 1920, there were 8,429 (Moisés González Navarro 1977). The size of the expatriate population is magnified even more when the human loss caused by the Revolution is taken into account. Mexico's population dropped from 15,160,377 in 1910 to 14,334,780 in 1921. Consequently, the over 800,000 Mexicans in the United State in 1920 equaled 5.5 % of the total Mexican populace (Cardoso 1897). By 1930, over two million Mexicans, well over one-tenth of its population, representing every class and political persuasion, resided in the United States.[15] In addition, undocumented emigration during the 1901–1920 period probably exceeded 200,000. As many as 75 % of the Mexicans in the United States were estimated to have entered illegally and were uncounted during the 1910–1930 period.[16]

---

[13] Ibid., February 1, 1908.

[14] Report on Mexican Emigrants in the United States, Minister of the Interior to Minister of Foreign Relations, March 15, 1922, Archivo Histórico de la Secretaría de Relaciones Exteriores (hereafter cited as AHSRE) 36-16-318.

[15] Francisco Alba, The Mexican Demographic Situation, in Frank D. Bean, Jurgen Schmandt and Sidney Weintraub, eds., Mexican and Central American Population and U.S. Immigration Policy (Austin: Center for Mexican American Studies, 1989), 9; Secretaría de Relaciones Exteriores, La immigración y protección de Mexicanos en el extranjero (Mexico City: Ministry of Foreign Relations, 1928), 33 and Secretaría de Relaciones Exteriores, Memorias, 1925–1926, 151 found in John R. Mexican Emigration to the United States, 1910–1930. Doctoral Dissertation, University of California, 1957, p 136.

[16] Louis Bloch, Facts About Mexican Immigration Before and Since the Quota Restriction Laws, Journal of the American Statistical Association 24 (1929): 51 and Jay S. Stowell, The Dangers of Unrestricted Mexican Immigration, Current History (1938): p. 763.

Today, the expansion of the Mexican-born population within the United States and its geographic scope provides two significant examples for Mexican labor's seminal role within the evolution of the United States since the 1920s. As of 2008, the Mexican population stood at 106,682,518. Today, Mexico is a much more urban society than it was a century ago with over 70 % of the population living in an urban environment and one out of every ten Mexicans living in the United States. In 2008, there were 11.6 million foreign-born Mexicans residing in the United States. Maybe more significant are the locations that emigrants are seeking in the twenty-first century. Since 1992, large segments of immigrants have been avoiding states with large foreign-born populations such as California and New York, instead preferring new settlement states such as North Carolina and Iowa.[17] Consequently, one reason for the upswing in immigration-related controversies is that many contemporary receiving areas are simply not accustomed to immigrants.[18]

1920s and 1930s

Only after the 1910–1920 Mexican Revolution—at the beginning of a period of unparalleled political stability in Latin America—did the relationship between the Mexican Government and Mexican citizens abroad become consistent and formalized. The political stability that evolved during the administrations of Alvaro Obregón, 1920–1924 and Plutarco Elías Calles, 1924–1928 included reaching into the United States through consulates and consular-led mutual aid organizations known as *Comisiones Honorificas Mexicanas* and *Brigadas de La Cruz Azul*. These networks were precursors to current projects and provided social welfare services and legal advice to facilitate life for Mexican expatriates in the United States. They also pursued nationalistic projects that encouraged Mexican citizens to maintain their ties to the homeland, particularly financial ties through remittances. If not for the overwhelming impact of the Great Depression, these organizations might have continued into the present.[19]

Notwithstanding *México de afuera*'s size, Mexican policy-makers had many reasons for improving relations with their compatriots that the Revolution had

[17] Instituto Nacional de Estadística y Geografía, Anuario estadístico de los Estados Unidos Mexicanos 2008 (Mexico City: Instituto Nacional de Estadística y Geografía, 2009), 71; Jeffrey S. Passel and D'Vera Cohn, Mexican Immigrants: How many come? How many leave? (Washington, DC: The Pew Hispanic Center, 2009), i; Jeffrey S. Passel and Roberto Suro, "Rise, Peak, and Decline: Trends in U.S. Immigration, 1992–2004, (Washington, DC: The Pew Hispanic Center, 2005), p iv.

[18] Immigration Raids Draw Protest from Labor Officials, The New York Times, January 26, 2007.

[19] Convención de Comisiones Honoríficas y Brigadas de la Cruz Azul Mexicana. (II), August 13, 1923, 6-13-70 Archivo Histórico de la Secretaría de Relaciones Exteriores (hereafter cited as AHSRE).

forced out of Mexico. Although Obregón committed unprecedented resources for aiding this community, he nonetheless continued along a path begun by his predecessor, Venustiano Carranza whose 1916 solidification of the presidency allowed him to help his countrymen in the United States. Carranza's ardent nationalism compelled his administration to take the first steps toward including the social welfare of their compatriots abroad into consideration (Douglas Richmond 1910).[20] However, such objectives were not merely patriotic commitments but also self-serving since many members of *México de afuera* were considered enemies of the state. For example, in 1919 the New York consuls proposed a plan to encourage Mexican workers in the United States to affiliate themselves with U.S. working class organizations that may lead to new allies for the Mexican state.[21] Such endeavors and public propaganda on behalf of braceros caused subsequent administrations to include assisting them as an essential element of their foreign policy.

This responsibility was a vital objective of the Obregón administration, intricately related to his plans for obtaining U.S. diplomatic recognition. Obregón as a *Norteño* from Sonora understood the economic and political significance of his compatriots abroad because he had been personally very concerned with the social welfare of his countrymen and had observed first hand some of the abuses they had suffered.[22]

One obvious reason for nourishing *México de afuera*'s support was because the United States border region was a time-honored and battle-tested region from which to mount a rebellion against a government in Mexico City. Rebellious groups ranged from radical socialists and anarchists who were former followers of Ricardo Flores Magón to conservative movements wishing to return Mexico to a pre-Revolutionary political structure (Dirk Raat and Brescia 2010). Consequently, Obregón and his successor Plutarco Elías Calles were not only bound to demonstrate their concern for Mexico's emigrants, but it was also in their best interest. The significance of this topic is further underscored by the fact that Obregón did not obtain formal recognition from the United States until 1923, the same year that Adolfo de la Huerta broke with Obregón and rebelled. De la Huerta's agents campaigned throughout the Southwest in search of funds and

[20] For a more thorough description of President Carranza's emigration policy see Ibid., 269–288 and Cardoso, Mexican Emigration to the United States, pp 44–70.

[21] New York Consul to Salvador Diego Fernández Ofical Mayor de la SRE Encargado del Despacho, September 9, 1919. AHSRE, 17-18-138.

[22] Linda Hall, Alvaro Obregón and Mexican Migrant Labor to the United States, 1920–1924, found in Ricardo Sanchez, Eric Van Young, and Gisela Von Wobeser, eds., La ciudad, el campo, y la frontera en la historia de México (Mexico City: Universidad Nacional Autonoma de México, 1991), 760: Other books by Hall on Obregón include Alvaro Obregón: power and revolution in Mexico, 1911–1920 (College Station: Texas A&M University Press, 1981 and Oil, banks, and politics: the United States and postrevolutionary Mexico, 1917–1924 (Austin: University of Texas Press, 1995).

support from *México de afuera*.[23] Another potential threat appeared in 1922 when various consulates throughout the United States and in Guatemala tracked the activities of Felix Díaz, the nephew of Porfirio Díaz. Díaz was particularly attractive to U.S. oilmen such as Edward Laurence Doheny, who feared that Obregón would nationalize Mexico's oil fields under Article 27 of the 1917 Constitution.[24] Ultimately, the Mexican Supreme Court ruled that the doctrine of "positive acts" protected most foreign owned oil fields obtained prior to 1917 from the threat of nationalization.[25]

As early as 1920, Obregón began addressing the needs of his compatriots abroad. As a consequence of the post-World War I recession, he ordered all departments and officials with responsibilities associated with external and internal migration matters to propose new and more efficient methods for helping *México de afuera*, regulating the emigration process, and also for benefiting the post-revolutionary state. One of his initial measures included enlarging the SRE's budget and increasing the size of the consular corps. In July 1921, the Department of Labor was moved to the Ministry of Industry and Commerce and given a threefold directive: to investigate migration cases, discourage emigration, and assist emigrants who were the victims of discriminatory treatment abroad. These reforms also empowered *cónsul comisionados* (inspectors), within the Labor Department to assess consular activity and labor conditions in Mexico and the United States (Arturo Rosales and Chicano! 1996).

On October 23, 1921, Obregón declared that conditions for *braceros* in the United States had stabilized enough to end the emergency repatriation drive. His administration had spent over 1,750,000 pesos spent on food and railway passages for over 50,000 repatriates. By the end of 1921 over 106,242 emigrants returned to Mexico and a year later, 50,171 more followed. Similar circumstances would repeat themselves during the Great Depression, however, in a much larger and harsher context (Aguila 2007). Foreign Ministry officials realized that repatriation drives were at best short-term solutions and instead a much more proactive plan had to be developed in order to address the demands of Mexicans living and working within the United States.

In January 1921, Obregón had sent Los Angeles consul Eduardo Ruiz to inspect labor conditions throughout the Southwest and develop a strategy for assisting their compatriots. He encountered frequent examples of employers failing to honor labor contracts, merchants over charging for basic necessities, and ethnic discrimination. In addition, local law enforcement usually aware of such episodes generally

[23] A definitive study of México de afuera's role in the 1923–1924 de la Huerta revolt does not exist. However based on Aguila's research particularly at the AHSRE in Mexico City, Obregón's support from Mexicans in the U.S. contributed to this rebellion's defeat. See AHSRE 44-24-1 (I).

[24] Various Consular Dispatches from the New York Consul to the SRE concerning Felix Díaz rebel activity in New York City, Emigrados Politicos: Actividades Rebeldes, 1922, AHSRE 21-5-7.

[25] Raat, Mexico and the United States, 155.

refused to protect the *braceros'* rights. Ruiz also found that the emigrants were unable to protect themselves because most were illiterate, lacked minimal English proficiency, and were unfamiliar with immigration laws and/or American customs. However, few of them pursued U.S. citizenship, believing their tenure abroad to be temporary and that the only source of protection was their Mexican citizenship.[26]

After seeing firsthand the deplorable conditions of his countrymen and the inability of consular personnel to aid them, Ruiz determined that the consulates needed a more effective structure for addressing immigrant hardships that included the backing of local Mexican communities. The *Comisiones* emerged as consular-led mutual aid organizations that Ruíz believed would be the most effective use of the consul corps's limited resources. Officials envisioned these groups as a formal means of interaction between emigrants and the consulates, and as a tool for promoting Mexican nationalism within *México de afuera*.[27]

The formation process of the *Comisiones* required the commitment of private citizens committed to helping their own communities. One such figure was Jesús Franco who was a loyal, literate Mexican middle-class expatriate who wanted to improve his countrymen's living conditions in the United States and strengthen their loyalties to the Mexican state. Franco was one of the most vocal supporters of Ruiz's plan for sponsoring a mutual aid network as a means to prevent future hardships such as those created by the 1920–1921 recession. As a journalist, he had conducted various investigative trips throughout the Southwest on behalf of the Mexican Government assessing the living conditions of his compatriots. In April 1922, he presented the findings of his most recent trip through Oklahoma at the inaugural *Comisiones* meeting. For helping initiate the *Comisiones* and his investigative trips on behalf of the Mexican Government, he was named an official functionary of the Foreign Ministry.[28]

On April 9, 1921 in San Antonio, Texas consuls from throughout the state met so that Ruiz and Luis Montes de Oca could present their plan. Both men had substantial influence outside of their current consular posts and used it to promote the *Comisiones*. According to Fernando Alanis, The correspondence between President Obregón and Ruiz during this period showed a familiar relationship that was bolstered by a mutual sympathy for aiding their compatriots in the United States.

[26] Report of Edurado Ruíz on the investigative trip made on behalf of President Alvaro Obregón, February 1, 1921 Archivo General de la Nación-Ramo Obregón-Calles, 429-P-2; Cardoso, La repatriación de braceros, 579 and Hall, Alvaro Obregón and Mexican Migrant Labor, pp 761–763.

[27] Jesús Franco attended both the initial conference that created the Comisiones Honoríficas Mexicanas in San Antonio, Texas on April 9, 1921 and the first Convention of the Comisiones Honoríficas Mexicanas in Laredo Texas, May 5-7, 1922. At the May 1922 Convention Franco was the Secretary General. Jesús Franco, *El alma de la raza:. Narraciones históricas de episodios y la vida de los Mexicanos residentes in los Estados Unidos del Norte América: la repatriación. La vida y origen de las Comisiones Honoríficas Mexicanas y la Cruz Azul Mexicana* (El Paso, Texas: Compañia Editoria "La Patria", date?), 7.

[28] Franco (1922) El Alma, 7 and Programa Oficial de la convención de Comisiones Honoríficas Mexicanas y Brigadas de la Cruz Azul Mexicana, (May 5–7, 1922), AHSRE, 7-2-15, p 35.

Montes de Oca had already completed consular-general assignments in the United States and Europe and would later serve as Minister of the Treasury on three different occasions from 1927–1932. Therefore, both men brought with them great stature and confidence that their plans would be well-received and respected.[29]

Over the next 10 years, *Comisiones* and *Brigadas* were established predominately in the Southwest and especially in Texas. However, as late as 1930 well into the Great Depression, there were Comisiones established in communities such as Detroit, Michigan. Enrique Ruíz, the Consul General in New York City instructed his colleague in Detroit to provide extensive support for this new *Comisión* because of the growing population of Mexican sugar beet pickers.[30] Unfortunately, by 1932 most of these organizations in the Midwest were disbanded as a direct result of the repatriation campaigns. On May 28, 1932, Ruíz reported that only two *Comisiones* remaining in Illinois were in Fairmont City and East St. Louis.[31] To a large degree, the *Comisiones* were victims of their own success as they were instrumental in helping many of the compatriots repatriate.

The first half of the 1930s experienced the highest levels of return migration with approximately 350,000 Mexicans returning.[32] The process of repatriation was paid for by various sources that included local charities, donations from private citizens, and fundraisers such as sponsored dances. The Mexican consul was frequently called upon to act as the local coordinator, while continuing to fulfill its other duties on behalf of its compatriots. Some of the most requested types of assistance included securing a *bracero's* wages after he was fired or compelling employers to honor their labor contracts (Abraham Hoffman 1974). In March 1932, Consuelo Ruíz P. de Ramírez needed assistance so that she and her six children could return to Mexico. Her husband had brought the entire family to Texas fleeing the violence of the Revolution. Unfortunately in 1927 he, one of her sons, and her brother were killed in a car crash, leaving her destitute. On May 2, the Foreign Ministry agreed to provide the funding on behalf of the entire family and instructed the San Antonio consulate and the Department of Migration to organize their return.

Unfortunately, the level of direct involvement that was required to aid Consuelo Ruíz P. de Ramírez could not be provided for the entire Mexican

[29] Fernando Saúl Alanis (1921) La Labor Consular Mexicana En Estados Undios: El Caso de Eduardo Ruiz (1921), unpublished manuscript, 5. The final version was published as La Labor Consular Mexicana En Estados Undios: El Caso de Eduardo Ruiz (1921), Secuencia: revista de historia y ciencias sociales, 52 (202).

[30] New York Consul General, Enrique D. Ruíz. to Consul in Detroit, Michigan, September 2, 1930, AHSRE V-99-51.

[31] New York Consul General Enrique D. Ruíz 7-5-1932 to: SRE, May 28, 1932, AHSRE, IV–339–21.

[32] Fernando Saúl Alanís Enciso (2007) ¿Cuántos fueron? La repatriación de mexicanos en los Estados Unidos durante la Gran Depresión: Una interpretación cuantitativa 1930–1934, Aztlán: A Journal of Chicano Studies 32.2 (2007), 65–91, and Que se queden allá. El gobierno de México y la repatriación de mexicanos de Estados Unidos, 1934–1940 (México: El Colegio de la Frontera Norte, 2007).

diaspora. And once the Great Depression was over, the U.S. economy again demanded a near limitless supply of Mexican labor. Clearly, the post-revolutionary governments in Mexico understood the strategic nature of the Mexican expatriate community in the United States. Bureaucratic restructuring, larger budgets and increased consular activity reaching out to this this ever-larger community was linked to an even more strategic objective for enhancing a fragile relationship with the United States, whose support was needed by the nascent post-revolutionary Mexican state. However, as was the case in the nineteenth century and again in the 1920s, Mexican officials at the end of the twentieth century would again have to reinvent another system for protecting its compatriots in the United States. In the 1980s, Mexico experienced a number of large economic shocks that fed growing political unrest and calls for reform. Once again the government's relationship with its expatriate community would be reinterpreted as the country sought an improved relationship with the United States based on expanded binational trade.

The Technocratic Era and Mexico's Renewed Interest in Mexicans Abroad

By the 1980s the Mexican population in the United States had expanded significantly, continuing to illustrate its historical roots from the pre WWII era. In 1980 the Mexican immigrant community in theU.S. stood at 2.2 million and then doubled in 1990 when it reached 4.3 million. In 1990, the 9.2 million Mexican immigrants represented 30% of the total immigration to the United States. In 2008 the Mexican-origin population (Mexican and U.S. born) surpassed 30 million and included 18 million U.S. citizens. The same year 2.5 million Mexican became naturalized U.S. citizens (Francisco Alba 2010). Within Mexico, the 1980s represented a transitional period for the Mexican economy and political system, which by the end of the century opened the economy to world trade and ended the one party system in place since 1929.

The fragile and volatile Mexican economy remains the primary elemental cause of Mexican emigration to the United States. It simply cannot provide sufficient employment for its growing population. Vicente Fox described the contemporary relationship between the economy and emigration:

> In reality the economy has not grown in 25 years. We continue with the same per capita income that we had since then. Like we say here: the blanket has been shrinking, the the population continues to grow and today it does not cover everyone. What we need to do is grow the economy. This is an enormous challenge (Jorge Ramos 2001).

Mexico's form of import substitution industrialization sputtered to an end during the 1970s and 1980s as its economy experienced a number of significant shocks. Indeed, an increasing number of countries around the world were questioning long-held tenets of economic nationalism and the protective tariffs that were the foundation of many national economies, and key cadres within the Mexican federal government followed these global developments closely. Policy-makers increasingly believed that the only method of developing sustained economic growth was to following the global trend toward free trade. Such a strategy was the surest path for rapid economic development because it would take advantage of the economic globalization process and help Mexico more effectively compete for financial capital from throughout the world. Policies such as the 1985 Entendimiento Bilateral en Materia de Subsidios y Derechos Compensatorios reduced U.S. protectionist measures toward Mexican products (Carlos Salinas de Gortari 2000).

A new profile of federal official in the Mexican Government increasingly favored opening its economy to foreign investment for Mexico to be able to compete against emerging economies around the world. The 1988 Global Agreement on Trade and Tariffs coincided with the presidential election of the technocrat Carlos Salinas de Gortari.[33] The technocratic leadership was generally from Mexico City, lacked both electoral and political party experience, attended private universities, and obtained postgraduate degrees within the United States. Their professional training usually came from very narrow range of federal bureaucratic offices such as treasury, the Bank of Mexico, and programming and budgeting (Camp 2010). Its background was a stark difference from the traditional party leadership made up of union leaders, lawyers, and popular sector professionals.

The period of 1970s and 1980s has been described as an era of "no policy politics" when Mexican officials purposely chose to react to conditions in the United States and had no expectations for developing a centralized emigration policy. By the late 1980s, this passive approach was another example of the PRI's failings and civic society growing impatient with its leadership.

> The 1988 elections highlighted the growing estrangement between the official Partido Revolucionario Institucional (Institutional Revolutionary Party, PRI), which had monopolized the government for 70 years, and its citizens abroad. The elections of 1988 and the government's credibility were questioned by broad sectors of the diaspora community. At the same time, Mexicans at home viewed their migrant compatriots as traitors for boycotting Independence Day festivals in Los Angeles and other places, as signs of protest (Jorge Duran 2010).

The acceleration and expansion of the relationships with its diaspora was *undoubtedly* driven by two outcomes from the presence of Mexicans working in the United States: the growing historical and economic size of emigrant remittances and the more recent rise of hometown associations (HTAs). The anthropologist Manuel Gamio was the first scholar to measure the quantity of emigrant remittances determining that from 1919 to 1927 Mexican workers sent over five million dollars per year home to their families (Manuel Gamio 1971). According

---

[33] See Miguel Angel Centeno's Democracy within Reason: Technocratic Revolution in Mexico for a comprehensive discussion of the rise of technocratic governance in Mexico.

to the Banco de Mexico in the twenty-first century their amount has grown significantly; from $6.6 billion in 2000 to 26.1 billion in 2007.[34]

> In 1985, several Zacatecan hometown organizations in and around Los Angeles area formed the *Federación de Clubes Zacatecanos Unidos*, which empowered Zacatecanos in the United States to work with local and state leaders in Zacatecas on infrastructure and service-delivery projects, cultural exchanges, and political mobilization projects (Laglagaron 2010). By 1998 over 500 HTAs had registered with Mexican consulates throughout the United States. According to Robert Leiken, most HTAs and similar organizations work independent of the consulates due to suspicion and distrust of the Mexican government. Nonetheless, the Mexican government has pursued policies to harness their potential (Robert Leiken 2000).

The Carlos Salinas de Gortari administration, 1988–1994 introduced a more complex set of objectives to gain more effective relations with its diaspora—the vast majority of which lived in the United States—to compliment and hopefully bolster its new free trade agenda. To this end, in 1990 Salinas de Gortari strengthened and expanded consular offices in the United States by creating the *Programa de las Comunidades Mexicanas en el Exterior* (PCME) within the Foreign Ministry. The Directorate General of Mexican Communities Abroad and the PCME focused on improving the images of Mexican emigrants within the nation state of Mexico directly challenging the damaging and unfair historical interpretation that they were disloyal citizens. The PCME defined the Mexican nation as a transnational community whose cultural identity is not limited by geographic borders, but includes the inherent role of the emigration process, which drives a pluralistic and dynamic reality. Consequently, this program sought "to preserve the organic unity of its nationals within and beyond its physical limits, as well as consolidate the relationship between its citizens and the cultural institutions that embody the Mexican national will (Figueroa-Aramoni 1999)". Such initiatives sought to help Mexican emigrants take advantage of the social, economic, and civil rights entitlements that their citizenship offered such as the right to carry a Mexican passport. PCME prioritized adult and K-12 education, sports, health, culture, business, and tourism remained core features of Mexican public policy. During the Salinas de Gortari administration, there were forty consulates operating within the United States: these included the largest consulate in Los Angeles, California, and consulates farther away from the Mexican/U.S. border such as those in Detroit and Philadelphia (Carlos González Gutiérrez 1997).

The revival of the governments' relation with its citizens abroad went hand-in-hand with a transformed trade relationship with the United States. One of the major initiatives of the Salinas de Gortari administration was the negotiation of the NAFTA, which was signed by Salinas de Gortari and his U.S. and Canadian counterparts, George H.W. Bush and Brian Mulroney, in 1992. When it took effect on January 1, 1994, NAFTA ended Mexico's closed economic system that had focused on promoting domestic industrial development and diversification of the

[34] Alba, "Mexico: A Crucial Crossroads".

Mexican economy to specifically prevent over dependence on U.S. investments and markets. NAFTA signaled a major reversal of 60 years of nationalistic economic policy. Salinas de Gortari himself expressed enthusiasm that NAFTA would make Mexico a first-world country and implied that the agreement would reduce the need for Mexicans to migrate to the United States. In addition, his administration aggressively sought to gain the confidence and support of its people residing in the United States (Rafael Alarcón 2006).

The new agenda sought to facilitate the migrants' own economic development projects within their own local communities. As stated earlier, accumulating financial resources for improvements in their hometowns was a well established process, especially with the support of local church leaders and local public officials. In 1992 this program became the *Programa Dos Por Uno*, by which the Zacatecas and federal governments each committed themselves to match every dollar contributed by the migrant organization on jointly agreed-upon projects. By 1999, the program morphed into 'three for one', with municipal governments also matching funds. This expansion was bolstered with special offices for migrant affairs in locations throughout Mexico.[35]

The Ernesto Zedillo Administration, 1994–2000 bolstered this relationship by launching the *Nación Mexicana* initiative within the 1995–2000 Mexican National Development Plan. He promised more legal protections for emigrants and sought to eliminate discrimination against emigrants and their families. In 1997 a dual citizenship program allowed Mexicans who had become naturalized U.S. citizens maintain their Mexican citizenship, although the U.S. Government does not recognize this dual status. Congress amended the 1917 Constitution stating that voluntary acquisition of another nationality no longer caused an automatic loss of Mexican nationality. Dual citizenship also set the foundation for emigrants to take part in Mexican elections; on June 28, 2005 Congress overwhelming approved absentee voting rights for emigrants.

Vicente Fox, who had campaigned in the United States, championed emigrants as national heroes and prioritized their concerns during his 2000–2006 administration. He established the Presidential Office for Mexicans Abroad (OPME) promoting Mexican business relationships and Mexican investments. OPME by directly working with many Mexican–American community organizations bypassed the consular system and conducted its work largely through the personal contacts of the OPME's leadership. In 2003, he merged the PCME and OPME into a single office, creating the Institute for Mexicans Abroad (IME), a decentralized agency of the Foreign Ministry.

The IME carries out the functions of the Presidential Office for Mexican Communities Abroad and the Mexican Communities Abroad Program and has an Advisory Board made up of 152 members representing the Mexican and

[35] David Ayón, Mexican policy & Emigré communities in the U.S., work presented at the conference for Mexican Migrant Civic and Political Participation, Woodrow Wilson Center, Nov 4–5, 10–11

Table 9.1 Evolution of Mexican Government programs for citizens abroad

Administration	Period	Agency/innovations	Principal activities
Post-revolutionary period			
Alvaro Obregón	1920–1924	Comisiones Honorificas Mexicanas and Brigadas de La Cruz Azul	Social welfare and financial services, legal advice
Plutarco Elias Calles	1924–1928		
Technocratic period/democratic transition			
Carlos Salinas	1988–1994	Programa de las Comunidades Mexicanas en el exterior (PCME)	Enhancement of Mexican migrants' image in Mexico; adult and K-12 education, sports, health, culture, business, and tourism
Ernesto Zedillo	1994–2000	Nación Mexicana; dual citizenship;	Enhanced legal rights for Mexicans living abroad
Vicente fox	2000–2006	Presidential office for Mexicans abroad (OPME). PCME and OPME merged into Instituto para Mexicanos en el exterior (IME) in 2003; absentee voting (congress). National council for Mexican communities abroad	Advisory board

Mexican–American community in the United States. It promotes strategies, creates programs, and receives proposals and recommendations from the communities, their members, their organizations, and advisory agencies that improve the living standards of the Mexican communities abroad and that follow the guidelines established by the National Council for the Mexican Communities Abroad. Its objectives include improving the treatment of emigrants; encouraging and promoting communication amongst emigrant communities; coordinating collaboration between Mexico's diplomatic offices with the emigrant communities; and improving the social development of the Mexican communities abroad.

A summary of these policies is found in Table 9.1.

Conclusion

IME's policies and practices underscore a shift in Mexico's approach to its migrants, from relatively limited engagement to the creation of an institution that cultivates a formal and active relationship with its diaspora. Since the 1990s, consular offices have become important service delivery sites and coordinating entities for immigrant integration. This development coincides with the expansion of the number of Mexican consular offices in the United States since the 1980s. A total of 19 Consulate Generals and 31 Consulates now operate in the United States; the most recent Mexican consulate to be opened was in Anchorage, Alaska.

Such programs demonstrate that the Mexican Government views its relationship and responsibilities toward its compatriots abroad within a transnational paradigm rather than a traditional model defined by the nation-state's physical borders. The traditional model limited the scope of the government's activities to consular protection activities such as issuing consular identifications and promoting their acceptance as valid identification at US banks, police departments, and other local government agencies. These new strategies are not limited by such traditional notions of consular protection, but instead put in place a broad institutional structure that provide various civic, health, education, and financial services to its emigrants who overwhelmingly live in the United States (some estimates claim 95 %). What is important to note here is that such services seek to integrate its migrants in a receiving country, which has traditionally been the work of receiving-country's institutions, and not the sending-country's government.

Nonetheless, U.S. public opinion and many U.S. policy-makers continue to ignore the fact that Mexican immigration to the United States is a consequence of the North American economy. According to George W. Bush,

> The people come from Mexico to the United States to work. Family values do not stop at the border. Fathers and mothers love their children the same in Mexico as in the United States. And if you have a hungry child and you look for work and it only pays you fifty cents to one dollar in the interior of Mexico or you can obtain fifty dollars in the interior of the United States, you are going to come for those fifty dollars if you are a loving parent (Jorge Ramos 2001).

Bush's analysis seems to be lost within the very polarized nature of the contemporary immigration debate. This effect adds one more barrier for Mexican consuls who must operate under very politically charged and at times xenophobic circumstances in order fulfill their elemental mission of protecting their compatriots.

A number of key challenges face the Government of Mexico as attempts to provide services to its citizens abroad at the broadest level, the U.S. federal government works on a large number of issues involving Mexico and Mexican citizens through an immensely complex maze of federal agencies, including the new U.S. Department of Homeland Security, the Department of State, and the Department of Justice, among many others. Heightened staffing and security infrastructure along the southwestern border both prior to and following the September 11, 2001 terrorist attacks have driven up prices and profits for migrant smuggling and trafficking groups (Operation Gatekeeper and Hold-the-Line in San Diego and El Paso, respectively, are prime examples). The newly reformulated Mérida Initiative seeks to improve security cooperation between the two countries does not directly address migration but nonetheless impacts migration in a number of ways.

In addition, the defeat of comprehensive immigration reform in the U.S. Congress in 2007 was a major setback and dashed Mexico's hopes for a large-scale regularization of the millions of undocumented emigrants from Mexico. The rise of local anti-immigrant measures such as Arizona's Senate Bill 1070 in the absence of real immigration reform at the federal level presents a daunting challenge for consular personnel and their efforts in Arizona and other states because of heightened uncertainty and anxiety within the Mexican-origin community. And last but certainly not least, despite recently improved binational collaboration on a number of issues, the two countries' global interests diverge significantly and their publics and policy-makers have great difficulty understanding each other's history, culture, institutions, and public policy challenges.

As demonstrated above, the Mexican-origin community in the United States is not offering its universal support for Mexican foreign policy nor is it a potential fifth column as some conservative fringe movements would have the U.S. public believe. The engagement of the Mexican Government with the expatriate community in the United States is not an easy one. Despite the recent political developments in Mexico that favor greater democracy at all levels of government, Mexicans in the United States are often weary of gestures from their government due to a long history of corruption and ad hoc policy implementation. [36] Yet paradoxically, its new policies seek to enhance the integration of Mexicans in the United States. Furthermore, its transnational nature forces the Mexican-origin community in the United States to identify themselves within a seemingly paradoxical nationalistic context as it seeks to maintain its ethnic and historical heritage while showing appreciation for the opportunities provided by the United States. Many critics of the presence of Mexicans fail to understand the complexity of the Mexican emigrants' status. This status is often misinterpreted by conservative pundits, who see the

[36] For example, only a bit more than 32,000 Mexican expatriates voted in the 2006 presidential election, a disappointing turnout.

waving of a Mexican flag during pro-immigrant demonstrations as a call to arms rather than as a community desperate to create a safe and law-abiding place alongside all the other immigrant communities who arrived before them. These paradoxes will continue to present challenges to the Mexican Government as it seeks increased and meaningful engagement with its diaspora.

References

Martinez OJ (1975) On the size of the Chicano population: new estimates (1850–1900). Aztlan 6(1):56

Pitt Leonard (1970) The decline of the Californios: a social history of the Spanish-speaking Californians 1846–1890. University of California Press, Berkeley, pp 60–64

Galeana P (ed) (1999) Nuestra Frontera Norte. Archivo General de la Nación, Mexico City, p 10

Angela Moyano Pahissa (1989) Protección consular a mexicanos en los Estados Unidos, 1849–1900 Archivo Historico Diplomático Mexicano, Mexico City, p 17

Moisés González Navarro (1977) Anatomía del poder en México, 1848–1853 El Colegio de México, Mexico City, p 7

Moisés González Navarro (1994) Los extranjeros en México y los mexicanos en el extranjero, 1821–1970, vol. II. El Colegio de México, Mexico City, p 125

Moisés González Navarro (1977) Anatomía del poder en México, 1848–1853 El Colegio de México, Mexico City, p 7

Cardoso, "La repatriación de braceros," 579 and idem., Mexican Emigration to the United States, 1897–1931 (Tucson: University of Arizona Press, 1980), 38, pp. 51–54

Douglas Richmond, Mexican Immigration and Border Strategy During the Revolution, 1910–1920, New Mexico Historical Review 57 1982 3:270–272

Dirk Raat W, Michael M. Brescia (2010) Mexico and the United States: Ambivalent Vistas. University of Georgia Press, Athens, p 134

F. Arturo Rosales, Chicano! (1996) The history of the Mexican American civil rights movement. Arte Público Press, Houston, p. 79

Jaime R. Aguila (2007) Mexican/U.S. Immigration policy prior to the great depression, diplomatic history 31, 2:217

Abraham Hoffman (1974) Unwanted Mexicans in the great depression: repatriation pressures, 1929–1939. University of Arizona Press, Tucson, pp 168–169

Francisco Alba (2010) Mexico: A Crucial Crossroads, Country Studies: The Migration Policy Institute. http://www.migrationinformation.org/Profiles/display.cfm?ID=772. Accessed 7 Dec 2010

Jorge Ramos (2001) Vicente Fox: el cambio con botas, found in Jorge Ramos Avalos, A la caza del león. Editorial Grijalbo, S.A. de C.V., Mexico City, p 87

Carlos Salinas de Gortari (2000) México: Un paso difícil a la modernidad. Plaza & Janés Editores, S.A., Barcelona, pp 43–44

Roderic I. Camp (2010) The time of the technocrats and deconstruction of the revolution, found in William H. Beezley and Michael C. Meyer, eds., The Oxford History of Mexico. Oxford University Press, Oxford, pp 577–578

Jorge Duran (2010) From traitors to heroes: 100 years of Mexican migration policies, the migration policy institute. http://www.migrationinformation.org/Feature/display.cfm?ID=203. Accessed 8 Dec 2010

Manuel Gamio (1971) Mexican immigration to the United states: a study of human migration and adjustment. Dover Publications, New York City, p 30

Laglagaron Laureen (2010) Protection through integration: the Mexican government's efforts to aid migrants in the United States Washington, DC. The Migration Policy Institute, Washington, pp 8–9

Robert Leiken (2000) The melting border: Mexico and Mexican communities in the United States, center for equal opportunity, Washington, p 6. https:www.ceousa.org/pdfs/MELTBORDER.pdf

Figueroa-Aramoni Rodulfo (1999) A nation beyond its borders: the program for Mexican communities abroad. J Am Hist 86(2):537

Carlos González Gutiérrez (1997) Decentralized diplomacy: the role of the consular offices in Mexico's relations with its Diaspora, found in Rodolfo O. de la Garza and Jesús Velasco, eds., Bridging the Border: Transforming Mexico-U.S. Relations. Rowman and Littlefield Publishers, INC., Lanham, p 49

Rafael Alarcón (2006) Hacia la construcción de una política de emigración en México, found in Carlos González Gutiérrez, ed., Relaciones Estado-diáspora: aproximaciones desde curato continents vol. 1. Secretaría de Relaciones Exteriores, Mexico City, p 159

Jorge Ramos (2001) En el tren con George W. Bush, la primera entrvista: el gobernador, found in Jorge Ramos Avalos, A la caza del león (Editorial Grijalbo, S.A. de C.V), pp 146–147

Author Biography

Jaime R. Aguila's work focuses on Mexican emigration policy and the relationship between the Mexican state and its relationship with its expatriate population in the United States. He is near completion of his manuscript, "Forjando 'México de afuera': Mexico-Mexican American relations, 1876–1940". He has published his work in Diplomatic History and The Journal of American Ethnic History. He is a former farmworker and the son of former illegal immigrants from Mexico.

Eileen Diaz McConnell is in the School of Transborder Studies at ASU. She is a sociologist and social demographer with research interests in the experiences of Latinos in non-traditional areas of the United States, racial/ethnic and nativity disparities in homeownership and housing wealth accumulation, and media representations of racial/ethnic statistics. Her work is published in academic journals and as book chapters and reports. Dr. McConnell teaches courses in Latina/o Demography, Latina/o Migration, and Research Methods in the School of Transborder Studies.

Robert A. Donnelly, earned his Bachelor's Degree in History and Journalism from University of Georgia and his M.A. in Latin American Studies from the University of California, San Diego. Mr. Donnelly is the former Coordinator of the Justice in Mexico Project at the University of San Diego's Trans-Border Institute. As Coordinator, Donnelly organized a nine-part working group meeting series that examined criminal justice reforms at the state level in Mexico, wrote and edited a monthly news synthesis on rule-of-law-related developments in Mexico, coordinated project publications, and assisted with the planning of a five-part speaker series on legal ethics. He currently serves as Program Associate at the Mexico Institute within the Woodrow Wilson International Center for Scholars.

Rodolfo Espino is an Associate professor in the School of Politics and Global Studies at Arizona State University. He received his B.A. from Luther College and his M.A. and Ph.D. from the University of Wisconsin-Madison. Espino's primary research and teaching interests are in the fields of minority politics, Congress,

L. Magaña and E. Lee (eds.), *Latino Politics and Arizona's Immigration Law SB 1070*,
Immigrants and Minorities, Politics and Policy, DOI: 10.1007/978-1-4614-0296-1,

political behavior, and political methodology. His current research projects include examining political behavior in response to Latinos, the consistency of support for Latino interests in Congress, the ideological dimensions of the Arizona territorial legislature, and the influence of boardinghouse networks in the early U.S. Congresses.

Jacob Fisher is a planner and architect practicing in Israel, where he designs commercial, industrial and public buildings. He obtained a Master's degree in Urban Planning from Arizona State University in 2008 and worked as an assistant planner for the City of Chandler, AZ between 2009 and 2010.

Erin Brooke Godfrey received her Ph.D. in Developmental and Community Psychology from the Graduate School of Arts and Sciences at New York University in 2010 and is now an Assistant Professor of Applied Psychology at New York University's Steinhardt School of Culture, Education, and Human Development. Her research explores how individuals interact with, understand, and are influenced by the social and political systems in which they are embedded, focusing in particular on families and youth from disadvantaged and immigrant backgrounds. Her work has appeared in a variety of peer-reviewed journals, including *Child Development*, *New Directions in Child and Adolescent Development,* and *Journal of the American Planning Association* as well as edited books such as *Making it Work: Low-wage employment, family life and child development.*

Francisco Lara-Valencia is an Assistant Professor of the School of Transborder Studies and Southwest Borderland Scholar at ASU. He is also a faculty affiliated to the School of Geographical Sciences and Urban Planning and the North American Center for Transborder Studies (NACTS) in ASU. He received his Ph.D. in Urban Planning from The University of Michigan at Ann Arbor and did graduate and undergraduate work in Mexico. He has lectured in Mexico and the United States where he has taught courses on urban land use planning, urban economics, environmental planning, and research methods for planners. Francisco's major areas of inquiry include socio-environmental vulnerability, urban health, regional development, binational planning, and the role of community networks on sustainable development. His policy research focuses on issues of equity and efficiency of policy making and planning along the US-Mexico border.

Erik Lee serves as Associate Director at the North American Center for Transborder Studies. From 2006 to 2007, Mr. Lee was program officer for the Merage Foundation for the American Dream, a foundation based in Newport Beach, California. He was assistant director at the Center for U.S.-Mexican Studies at the University of California, San Diego from 2002 to 2006. Before that, Lee served as assistant managing director at the Southwest Consortium for Environmental Research and Policy at San Diego State University. He has consulted for philanthropic and educational organizations and has also served as a resource for a large number of local, national and international media outlets.

Lisa Magaña is an Associate Professor in the Department of Transborder Studies at Arizona State University. She has published in the area of immigration and Latino public policy issues, such as in the *Harvard Hispanic Policy Journal*, the *Journal of Policy Studies and* the *Journal of Social Psychology. She is the author of* the books, *Straddling the Border* (University of Texas Press) and *The Politics of Diversity (University of Arizona Press).* She is completing *From A to Z, Latino Immigration and Politics in Arizona.* Dr. Magaña has been a research associate at the Tomas Rivera Policy Institute and visiting Lecturer and Assistant Professor at Pitzer College, UCLA and Williams College. She received her doctorate from the Center for Politics and Economics at Claremont Graduate University.

Meghan McDowell, M.S. is a doctoral student in Justice and Social Inquiry at Arizona State University. Her research interests include immigration, race, space, and inequality. Her most recent publication was in *Social Justice* (2010) entitled, "Keeping Migrants in Their Place: Technologies of Control and Racialized Public Space in Arizona".

Cecilia Menjívar is Professor of Sociology in the School of Social and Family Dynamics at Arizona State University. Her interests focus on the social aspects of immigration, including social networks, religious participation, and gender and intergenerational relations, and is particularly interested in the effects of immigration laws on these social processes. Her research has appeared in various journals and she is the author of *Fragmented Ties: Salvadoran Immigrant Networks in America* (University of California Press), *Enduring Violence: Ladina Women's Lives in Guatemala* (University of California Press), editor of *Through the Eyes of Women: Gender, Social Networks, Family and Structural Change in Latin America and the Caribbean* (De Sitter), and co-editor of *When States Kill: Latin America, the US, and Techologies of Terror* (University of Texas Press), and *Latinos/as in the United States: Changing the Face of América* (Springer).

Doris Marie Provine is a Professor of Justice Studies at Arizona State University. A lawyer and political scientist, she writes on legal policy and its impact. Her most recent book is *Unequal Under Law: Race and the War on Drugs* (2007 Chicago). Currently she is principal investigator for a NSF-funded study of local policing of federal immigration law.

Professor Plascencia is a social anthropologist with a long-term involvement with issues related to Mexican migrants and migration. His research interests encompass the Mexico-United States boundary area, migrant contract labor programs, citizenship and nationalism, agricultural workers, and Latino communities in the United States. Prior to joining ASU, he was Project Coordinator/Research Associate for the Public Policy Institute in the Government Department, and Lecturer for the Center for Mexican American Studies, at The University of Texas at Austin. He has held the position of Policy and Budget Analyst at the Texas Governor's Office, and Associate Director of the Texas Office of The Tomás

Rivera Policy Institute. His work has appeared in International Migration Review, Urban Anthropology, Social Science Quarterly, and other journals. His forthcoming book *Disenchanting Citizenship: Mexican Migrants and the Boundaries of Belonging*, will be published by Rutgers University Press.

Carlos Eduardo Santos is Assistant Research Professor at Arizona State University's School of Social and Family Dynamics. He earned a Ph.D. degree in Developmental Psychology from New York University, and a Master's degree in education from Harvard University. His primary substantive interest lies in understanding the intersections of personal and social identities during adolescence, with emphases on dynamic processes and mental health. His research has appeared in various volumes, including *Latina and Latino Children's Mental Health*, and peer reviewed journals, including *Global Public Health*.

Index

L. Magaña and E. Lee (eds.), *Latino Politics and Arizona's Immigration Law SB 1070*,
Immigrants and Minorities, Politics and Policy, DOI: 10.1007/978-1-4614-0296-1,

Printed by Publishers' Graphics LLC